Routledge Library Editions

THE WITCH FIGURE

ANTHROPOLOGY AND ETHNOGRAPHY

Routledge Library Editions
Anthropology and Ethnography

WITCHCRAFT, FOLKLORE AND MYTHOLOGY
In 6 Volumes

I	Japanese Rainmaking	*Bownas*
II	Witchcraft Confessions and Accusations	*Douglas*
III	The Life-Giving Myth	*Hocart*
IV	The Structural Study of Myth and Totemism	*Leach*
V	Witchcraft and Sorcery in East Africa	*Middleton & Winter*
VI	The Witch Figure	*Newall*

THE WITCH FIGURE

Folklore Essays by a Group of
Scholars in England Honouring
the 75th Birthday of
Katharine M Briggs

EDITED BY VENETIA NEWALL

LONDON AND NEW YORK

First published in 1973

Reprinted in 2004 by
Routledge
2 Park Square, Milton Park, Abingdon, Oxon, OX14 4RN
711 Third Avenue, New York, NY 10017

Transferred to Digital Printing 2009

Routledge is an imprint of the Taylor & Francis Group

First issued in paperback 2013

© Contributors their Respective Contributions

All rights reserved. No part of this book may be reprinted or reproduced or utilized in any form or by any electronic, mechanical, or other means, now known or hereafter invented, including photocopying and recording, or in any information storage or retrieval system, without permission in writing from the publishers.

The publishers have made every effort to contact authors/copyright holders of the works reprinted in *Routledge Library Editions – Anthropology and Ethnography*. This has not been possible in every case, however, and we would welcome correspondence from those individuals/companies we have been unable to trace.

These reprints are taken from original copies of each book. In many cases the condition of these originals is not perfect. The publisher has gone to great lengths to ensure the quality of these reprints, but wishes to point out that certain characteristics of the original copies will, of necessity, be apparent in reprints thereof.

British Library Cataloguing in Publication Data
A CIP catalogue record for this book is available from the British Library

The Witch Figure
ISBN 978-0-415-32556-1 (set)
ISBN 978-0-415-33074-9 (hbk)
ISBN 978-0-415-86933-1 (pbk)

Miniset: Witchcraft, Folklore and Mythology

Series: Routledge Library Editions – Anthropology and Ethnography

Katharine M. Briggs

THE WITCH FIGURE

Folklore essays by a group of scholars in England honouring the 75th birthday of Katharine M. Briggs

Edited by
Venetia Newall

Routledge & Kegan Paul
London and Boston

*First published in 1973
by Routledge & Kegan Paul Ltd
Broadway House, 68–74 Carter Lane,
London EC4V 5EL and
9 Park Street,
Boston, Mass. 02108, U.S.A.
Printed in Great Britain by
W & J Mackay Limited, Chatham*

© *in their respective contributions
Venetia Newall, Ruth Michaelis-Jena,
Carmen Blacker, H. R. Ellis Davidson,
Margaret Dean-Smith, L. V. Grinsell,
Christina Hole, Geoffrey Parrinder,
Anne Ross, Jacqueline Simpson,
Beatrice White, John Widdowson*

*No part of this book may be reproduced in
any form without permission from the
publisher, except for the quotation of brief
passages in criticism*

ISBN 0 7100 7696 7

Library of Congress Catalog Card No. 73-83077

To
Katharine M. Briggs
in recognition of the great debt owed
to her by English folklore

Contents

		page
	Editor's Preface	ix
	Katharine M. Briggs: An Appreciation *Ruth Michaelis-Jena*	xi
1	Animal Witchcraft in Japan *Carmen Blacker*	1
2	Hostile Magic in the Icelandic Sagas *H. R. Ellis Davidson*	20
3	The Ominous Wood *Margaret Dean-Smith*	42
4	Witchcraft at some Prehistoric Sites *L. V. Grinsell*	72
5	Some Instances of Image-Magic in Great Britain *Christina Hole*	80
6	The Jew as a Witch Figure *Venetia Newall*	95
7	The Witch as Victim *Geoffrey Parrinder*	125

Contents

8 The Divine Hag of the Pagan Celts 139
  Anne Ross

9 Olaf Tryggvason versus the Powers of Darkness 165
  Jacqueline Simpson

10 Cain's Kin 188
  Beatrice White

11 The Witch as a Frightening and Threatening Figure 200
  John Widdowson

Publications by Katharine M. Briggs 221

The Contributors 224

Index 227

Editor's Preface

As I write, it is almost exactly four years since the first Anglo-American Folklore Conference at Ditchley Park in Oxfordshire, an occasion initiated by Katharine Briggs and Professor Richard M. Dorson to establish new guide lines for the future of English folklore. Professor Dorson's book *The British Folklorists* appeared at the same time and in it he paid special tribute to Katharine Briggs as a herald of the new era in folklore studies beginning in this country.

At the Ditchley Conference, which it was my privilege to help organise, there were scholars not only from the United States and England, but also from the other countries of the British Isles in which folklore studies have achieved a status well in advance of that in England. The situation has already improved during the few years since the Conference—Katharine Briggs herself has received the degree Doctor of Letters from Oxford University in recognition of her own work—yet vigorous efforts are still needed to press ahead along the lines which Katharine Briggs has done so much to establish. Dr Briggs herself shares this view. For this reason, and not because of any parochialism, the essays contributed to this volume are confined to scholars resident in England.

As her many friends and admirers know, Katharine Briggs herself could never be described as parochial. Her special ties with Scotland—her training of Scottish children during the war years is well known—are acknowledged by a contribution from Anne Ross and the appreciation by Ruth Michaelis-Jena, and the span of these papers is as wide as Katharine Briggs's own links throughout the world.

Editor's Preface

The Witch Figure is a collection of folklore essays by a group of scholars in England honouring the seventy-fifth birthday of Katharine Briggs. The theme, the witch figure as a malevolent intermediary in folk belief—and here the term witch figure is used in its broadest sense—was carefully chosen to reflect the aspect of Dr Briggs's own scholarship exemplified in her own distinguished study of witchcraft, *Pale Hecate's Team*. John Widdowson writes in his essay: 'Witch figures of various types, whatever their sex or function, share characteristics which mark them out as not only abnormal but also frightening.' The scholars who have contributed to this volume, and for whose co-operation I am deeply grateful, bring the complementary disciplines of archaeology, comparative religion, sociology and literature to augment folklore in exploring and throwing fresh light upon this theme.

It has been a great pleasure for me to edit these essays, paying tribute to Katharine Briggs. She was President of the Folklore Society from 1967 to 1970, during my first three years as Honorary Secretary, and was a constant source of strength and encouragement, as she has been to so many folklorists starting out on their careers. She read the manuscript of my first book and her thoughtful comments were not only invaluable but of direct help in gaining publication. Since first I knew her, I have come to regard her as among my dearest friends.

The University of London Venetia Newall
March 1973

# Katharine M. Briggs
M.A., D.Phil., D.Litt., F.I.A.L.
An Appreciation

Ruth Michaelis-Jena

I first came across Katharine Briggs's name when a good few years ago I chanced upon one of her historical novels, and was struck by the author's sense of realism in background and the inherent truth even in romantic description. I admired her knowledge of country lore, her sincerity of approach combined with careful research and a powerful imagination. I kept looking for more, enjoyed other novels and some pleasing short plays. The plays, too, showed clearly an understanding of history, and sympathy with tradition. I did not then know that Katharine Briggs had for years been connected with play production, mime and folk dancing, had indeed run her own company, and toured with it.

Her book, *The Personnel of Fairyland*, appeared in 1953, and reading it, I experienced a warm fellow feeling for someone who was drawing attention to 'the robust tradition of folklore' in opposition to the prevailing trend for the whimsical, for prettifying the fairies, letting them hover over the flowers at the bottom of the garden, or raise their magic wand in the Christmas pantomime. In 1963 I discovered Katharine Briggs's contribution to the *Brüder Grimm Gedenken*, 'The influence of the brothers Grimm in England'. In it she referred to my own translations from the German *Märchen* which came into being from the very desire to give young and old alike genuine traditional tales, different from the deliberately fanciful.

About that time I was checking material in the folklore archives of Dublin and Kassel, and in both places colleagues and friends insisted that I must meet a like-minded person: Katharine Briggs.

And eventually we did meet.

Not long after I was privileged to be a guest at the Barn House, her Cotswold home. There, in her book-lined study, in the garden, with her beloved cats, she revealed her true self: a kind and eager human being who carried her scholarship lightly. I marvelled at her tireless working energy as I saw her busy at her desk till well into the small hours. At Burford I heard of her Scottish childhood spent mostly in the beauty and quietness of Perthshire. I heard, too, of her love for acting and miming, and above all I listened to her telling a tale. Here was the born story-teller who holds an audience spellbound, and wins it over into believing every word of a tale to be true, and the characters to be real.

It appears to me that it is this deep understanding of and respect for oral tradition which led Katharine Briggs to her chosen field of study, and that it is the key to all her achievements.

In 1959 she published *The Anatomy of Puck*, an examination of the fairy beliefs among Shakespeare's contemporaries and successors. To the specialist and to the common reader it opens a wide view on that Secret Commonwealth which even in this matter-of-fact age motivates, if subconsciously, many of our actions. *Pale Hecate's Team* (1962) deals with the darker side of beliefs: witchcraft and sorcery, and their grim trail through the thought and emotions of earlier centuries. Both books were the outcome of Katharine Briggs's extensive research into sixteenth- and seventeenth-century sources of folk tradition.

The Fairies in Tradition and Literature came out in 1967, as a sequel to *The Anatomy of Puck*. Here fairy beliefs are traced up to our own day, with accounts of witnesses to fairy appearances, and the literary use of these beliefs.

In 1965 Katharine Briggs edited with her friend, Ruth Tongue (with whom she also collaborated on a volume of *Somerset Folklore*) *Folktales of England* in the series *Folktales of the World* under the general editorship of Professor Richard M. Dorson. She had then started the mammoth work which will be regarded as her most distinguished contribution to folklore studies. The investigation into the folk narrative in these islands and beyond has taken a great step forward with the publication (1970–71) of her four-volume *Dictionary of British Folk-tales in the English Language*. The first two volumes—narratives—and the second two—legends—will, with their wealth of material, introductions, notes and bibliographies, be indispensable tools to folklorists the world over. But beyond

Katharine M. Briggs: An Appreciation

that the books are, in Peter Opie's words, 'a British Pentamerone in which story after story can be savoured simply for the pleasure of a good tale well told . . .'. The *Dictionary* owes this particular quality to the warm humanity of Katharine Briggs's scholarship.

This very quality made her an outstanding and well-loved President of the Folklore Society where, during her term of office, she delivered three important addresses: 'The transmission of folk-tales in Britain', 'Heywood's Hierarchie of the Blessed Angells' and 'The fairies and the realms of the dead'.

She is a sought-after lecturer at home and abroad, gathering disciples wherever she goes. A volume of English folktales edited by her was recently published in Germany. She has many friends among the young; and she herself, though her research is into the past, is eternally young and forward-looking. In a contribution to a volume of essays on Charlotte Yonge, Katharine Briggs praised two cardinal virtues of many of the present-day generation: truth and kindness. And it might well be said that these are her own outstanding virtues. In the same essay she described Charlotte Yonge's world as a world 'overshadowed by higher truths and in touch with greater realities than we are introduced to even by the gigantic sweep of modern Science'.

This same world might well be equated to the world Katharine is concerned with, and to which she has introduced so many so successfully.

I

Animal Witchcraft in Japan

Carmen Blacker

In certain rural districts in Japan a surprising number of ailments and afflictions are still laid at the door of evil spiritual powers. The cure for these conditions does not lie within the province of medicine. No *materia medica*, whether western or Chinese, no hospital treatment, no doctors can possibly reach the root of the trouble. For this lies, not in bacteria, nor in physiological imbalances, but in demoniacal possession. Certain malignant spiritual entities are believed to enter into the human body, take up their abode there, and by their consequent possession to cause a displacement of the normal bodily functions so great sometimes as to affect the entire personality.

The symptoms of malign possession naturally tend to differ in different parts of the country, both according to what is laid down in local tradition, and to the nature and virulence of the entity. In certain villages along the coast of the Japan Sea, for example, it was customary until not long ago to attribute almost every misfortune, every sickness, every ache and pain, to the work of demoniacal foxes, sinisterly controlled by certain families. In other districts the symptoms are fewer and more distinctive. A woman exorcist on the outskirts of Kyoto told me that in her experience the usual symptoms of fox possession were a torrent of nonsensical talk, voices speaking in one's ear, the face elongated to resemble a pointed snout, a huge and indiscriminate appetite and nocturnal feelings of suffocation. Elsewhere the morbid symptoms sometimes reach the lengths of total dissociation of character. The patient's personality is apparently entirely displaced by that of the fox, who speaks through her mouth in a dry, cracked voice, often in language of a coarse obscenity which horrifies the poor woman when she returns to her normal state of mind.[1]

The entities believed to perpetrate these malignant possessions fall broadly into two categories. First, and in some districts most numerous, are discontented ghosts. A ghost expects to receive from its descendants certain obsequies which in due course will enable it to find rest and peace. Those who find these offerings neglected will in their anger and misery turn and curse their progeny in the manner described.

It is the other category of demoniacal possessors, however, which concerns us now. These are the witch animals; those creatures believed to be capable of assuming a discarnate and invisible form, and in such guise of penetrating inside the human body.

Yanagita Kunio, the great authority on Japanese ethnology and folklore, distinguished two broad categories of witch animal: the snake and the four-legged variety usually known as a fox or a dog. The snake, known as *tōbyō*, *tombogami* or simply *hebigami*, covers a relatively small area, being found only in the island of Shikoku and the Chūgoku district of the main island. The distribution of the four-legged creature is far wider. As a fox, it is found all along the Japan Sea coast, in both the Kantō and the Kansai districts, and over most of Kyūshū. As a dog, *inugami*, it is found in much the same areas as the snake, that is to say Shikoku and the Chūgoku district. Under the name of *izuna*, it abounds over much of the Tōhoku district, Aomori and Iwate prefectures. And again, under the peculiar name of *gedō*, it appears in the old province of Bingo in Hiroshima prefecture.

Even here our problems do not end, for the fox itself, *kitsune*, falls into a baffling number of sub-species. In Izumo, for example, it is known as *ninko*, man fox. In southern Kyūshū it is known as *yako*, field fox. In the Kantō regions it is called *osaki*, and in Shizuoka, Nagano and Yamanashi it sports the name of *kuda*, pipe fox.[2]

Surely, it will be objected, these various names must indicate different species of animal. Apparently not so. When asked to describe what the creature actually looks like, they will tell you in all these districts, regardless of what name they give it, that it is long and thin, with reddish-brown fur, short legs and sharp claws. Clearly we have the same creature appearing under a variety of names, none of which, incidentally, seems particularly appropriate.

The creature described does not in the least resemble a fox or a dog, but rather a small weasel or large shrew. Nor indeed does the name 'snake' seem very appropriate to the animal described. Yanagita's informants in Bitchū told him that it was short and fat, resembling a squat earthworm or small bonito.[3] Indeed, this peculiar separation of name from thing is one of the odd features of the belief.

The first question which comes to mind is, why should these creatures wish to enter the body of a human being, causing him pain and distress? Of what possible benefit could it be to a fox or a snake to take up its abode in so alien a species?

Two clearly distinct answers present themselves.

First, the creature may enter the body of the sufferer through its own volition. Its motive may be *urami*, malice. It possesses its victim in revenge for some slight: killing one of its cubs, for example, or startling it out of an afternoon nap are reasons frequently alleged. Another motive may be greed or desire: the creature wants something which it cannot obtain in its ordinary shape. It may want a meal of red rice or fried bean curd, delicacies irresistible to foxes, but which they are unlikely to come across in their usual form. Or it may want a little shrine set up to it and worship paid to it every day, and can only make this wish known through a human mouth. I have spent several mornings listening to the exorcisms of possessed patients in Buddhist temples of the Nichiren sect, and have been astonished at the way in which time and again the same motives are alleged by one possessing creature after another.

What concerns us here, however, is not so much the incidence of voluntary possession as the cases in which the animal attacks its victim because it is compelled to do so by certain baleful persons known as fox employers, *kitsune-tsukai*, or fox owners, *kitsune-mochi*.

These people are believed to have fox familiars at their beck and call. They feed them every day, and in return for their commons the foxes are compelled to exercise their supernatural powers in the service of their masters. They thus correspond with what in the west is known as either a witch or a sorcerer.[4]

These sinister figures fall at once into two distinct groups. First we find the solitary sorcerer, the single lone figure who 'employs' a fox or a dog in order to gain power or wealth, or in order to harm those whom he dislikes. As we shall see, he often turns out to be a degenerate priest or exorcist. Second and more commonly met with today are families who are believed to be the hereditary owners of foxes, and to transmit this evil power from generation to generation in the female line.

These two kinds of witch figure are not found together in the same district. In the regions where the belief in hereditary fox owning families is still strong, the solitary witch is not to be discovered. His territory lies chiefly in the north-eastern districts of the main island, where the fear of fox owning families so far as we know has never existed. We must therefore give these two types of witch separate treatment.

The solitary 'employer of foxes', *kitsune-tsukai*, is a figure which invites immediate comparison with our own witches and their cat or toad familiars. In the Japan of today however he is rarely met with, though stories of such people were reported as late as the 1920s. Here is an example recorded in the journal *Minzoku to Rekishi* of 1922 by a Buddhist priest of the Suwa district.

A woman came to him, he writes, complaining that every night she was assailed by deathly feelings of suffocation and waves of inexplicable bodily heat. Suspecting a case of possession, the priest sat her down in front of his household shrine and caused her to recite several powerful prayers. At once her babbling speech and the convulsive shaking of her clasped hands proclaimed her to be unmistakably in the power of a fox. The priest at once began the *mondō* or dialogue which is one of the standard methods of exorcism.

'Who are you?' he asked, 'and why are you molesting this woman?'

'I have nothing against her myself,' replied the fox, 'but I am compelled by a certain person to torment her and if possible to kill her.'

'Who is this person?' demanded the priest.

'He is an ascetic,' replied the fox. 'Another woman paid him three yen to send me on this errand. I am sorry about it, but I have to obey orders if I say I am to receive my daily food.'

The possessed woman, it soon transpired, was the mistress of a certain man whose legal wife had naturally become jealous. She had paid the ascetic to use his power over the fox to have the woman killed.

'How did you fall into the power of this man?' the priest then asked.

'I used to live under a rock on the mountainside,' the fox answered.

'One day the ascetic found me and offered me some delicious fried bean curd if I would go on errands for him. I refused; I wanted nothing to do with the man. But, alas, one of my cubs ate the bean curd. From that day I found myself in his power, forced to obey his commands in return for my daily food.'

The priest, after threatening the fox with a portrait of the Emperor Meiji which reduced it to an abject state of shame and terror, eventually cajoled it into leaving the woman's body by promises of a place in the retinue of the deity Inari. The fox professed itself delighted with the arrangement, promising thereafter to protect the poor woman rather than molest her.[5]

This story, recorded, of course, as circumstantially true, is instructive in many ways. The description of how the ascetic first acquired power over the fox, finding it in its lair, tempting it with food, is the standard account which has been repeated over and over again for several centuries. Compare it, for example, with what in the works of the Tokugawa period is called the *Izuna-hō* or Izuna rite, the magical means whereby power may be gained over fox familiars. The late seventeenth-century work *Honchō Shokkan* contains a much quoted account. Magicians have recently appeared in Japan, it runs, who employ foxes by means of the Izuna rite. For this rite you must first find a pregnant vixen in her lair. You feed her and tame her, taking particular care of her at the time when her cubs are born. When the cubs are grown up, the vixen will bring one of them to you and ask you to give it a name. Once you have done this you will find that you only have to call the young fox by name for it to come to you in invisible form. Then you can ask it any questions you like, on any matter however secret, and always it will be able to find out the answer for you. Other people cannot see the fox in its invisible form, so when you show them that you know of these hidden things they will all think that you possess divine power.[6]

This peculiar rite, described in almost identical terms in several other Tokugawa works, seems to be a degraded vestige of something which in early medieval times was a true religious rite of heretical but not very evil character. The Izuna rite, as de Visser has shown us, was at this period another name for the Dagini or Daten rite, much performed by warriors, noblemen or priests anxious for power or wealth. It was by dint of performing the Dagini rite, the *Gempei Seisuiki* tells us, that Taira Kiyomori rose from obscurity to be virtual dictator of the land. It was by causing a priest to perform the Dagini rite for fourteen days that the Kampaku Fujiwara Tadazane gained his heart's desire. It was through performing the Dagini rite for thirty-seven days that the Zen priest Myōkitsu-jisha gained everything he ever wished for. Throughout medieval literature references are legion to the successful performance of this rite by perfectly respectable people.[7]

But always the Dagini rite, although it appears to have been a ritual of the pattern usually found in esoteric Buddhism, was in some way associated with a fox. The figure of Dagini might appear as a fox; or the *shirushi*, or sign as to whether the rite had proved efficacious, was given by a fox. The seventeenth-century account of the *Izuna-hō* is clearly a degraded version of this medieval ritual.[8]

In modern times this solitary sorcerer seems to have been usually a debased religious figure: a *yamabushi* or mountain ascetic, a *kitōshi* or exorcist who has allowed the desire for money to corrupt him. In the manner described by our Suwa priest he may employ the fox, in return for a fee, to prosecute other people's hatreds and grudges. Or he may on the face of it be a respectable exorcist, making an honest living by *curing* people of fox, snake or ghost possession, as well as by finding lost things and giving advice on marriages and business transactions. But underneath it is he all the time who has set the fox to molest its victim, in order that he should be paid, all unwittingly, to remove the nuisance.

Since the war, however, little seems to have been heard of such evil men. Far more common are the cases in which the foxes or snakes are commanded by the people known as *tsukimono-suji*, hereditary witch families.

In a few districts of rural Japan, most notoriously along the coast of the Japan Sea, certain families are still subject to a peculiar form of ostracism. It is alleged that for generations they have kept foxes, snakes or dogs in their houses, and that, thanks to the malign powers of these creatures, they have not only become extremely rich, but also are able to revenge themselves on those whom they dislike by setting the creatures to possess them. The stigma of fox owning is regarded first as a kind of contagion; you can 'catch' the contamination, for example, by living in a house occupied by a former fox owner, or by buying his land after he has gone bankrupt.[9] But it is also a hereditary pollution, transmitted, it is interesting to note, largely in the female line.

Animal Witchcraft in Japan

If you wish to avoid the stigma therefore, you must eschew all business dealings with fox owning families. You must not visit their houses, you must not borrow money from them or buy land from them. You must avoid giving them offence. But above all you must see that neither you nor your kith and kin marry any of their girls. To receive into your family a bride who is even remotely associated with the fox owning stigma is to risk acquiring the stigma in full measure yourself. In some places it was believed that the foxes, even to the number of seventy-five, accompanied the girl when she went to her bridegroom's house. Henceforth that house, and all the ramifications and sub-branches of the family, would be contaminated. Thus it used to be said that when a marriage was arranged in these districts the first question to be asked about the bride's family, even before making sure that it was free from tuberculosis, insanity and shortsight, was whether or not the slightest suspicion of fox owning attached to it. If such was found to be the case, negotiations were broken off at once.

The creatures, whether foxes, dogs, or snakes, are believed to be kept in the houses of their masters and to receive daily rations of food. In return for their board and lodging they hold themselves ready to obey the behests of their master, using their powers of invisibility and possession to molest those whom he happens to dislike. Not only will they inflict on their victims all the approved symptoms of possession—pain, hysteria, madness—but they will also quietly remove the valuables of their victims to the houses of their masters. Hence the fox or snake owners are believed to be one and all extremely rich. In the case of the fox and the dog, the number kept in their master's house varies considerably. Sometimes ten, I was told, sometimes twenty, sometimes as many as a hundred have been counted. But a common number is seventy-five, though the reasons for preferring it are far from clear.

In the case of the snake, only one at a time seems to be the rule, and that is kept in a pot in the kitchen, fed on the same food as the family gets, with a tot of saké occasionally thrown in. If a snake owner in Sanuki happens to quarrel with anyone, Yanagita informs us, he is believed to say to the snake, 'All these years I have been feeding you, so it is time you did me a good turn in exchange. Go at once to so-and-so's house and make things as unpleasant for him as you can.' The snake then sallies forth and possesses one or more members of the marked family. In this part of Shikoku the principal symptom of snake possession is a sudden and unbearable pain in the joints, similar to acute rheumatism.[10]

A couple of centuries ago these unfortunate families were subjected to a fairly ruthless persecution. Banishment from the fief and extirpation of the family line within the fief were not uncommon measures during the feudal period. Motoori Norinaga mentions a case in 1747 in which the daimyo of the Hirose fief ordered the extirpation of a family accused of fox owning.[11] Their house was burnt and their entire family banished from the fief. Only rarely, however, were the unhappy victims condemned to death, and never, so far as I can discover, death by burning.

During the past century, however, it is rare to hear of violence of any kind directed against the accused. Cold and implacable ostracism is rather the rule.

As a result of surveys done in the early 1950s Professor Ishizuka has designated four districts in Japan where he considers the fox owning superstition to persist particularly obstinately, and where in consequence the families branded as 'black' are especially numerous. The first two are in Shimane prefecture, where the prevalent animal is the fox. They are the district of Izumo and the island of Oki. In the last two, a district in southern Oita prefecture in Kyūshū and another in Kōchi, Shikoku, the stigma was not for fox but for dog owning. Both these last districts showed peculiarities of distribution. Out of eleven *buraku* or villages investigated in the Kyūshū area, three proved to consist entirely of dog owning families. But next door to one of them was a village with no dog owning families at all. Again, out of ten *buraku* investigated in the Shikoku district, one was composed entirely, save for a single household, of dog owning families. Yet next door was a village with no dog owning families at all. The obvious inference was, of course, that the ostracised families had sensibly congregated in their own villages and intermarried among themselves, with their own schools and social groups.[12]

Let us look at one or two examples of the misery perpetrated by these obstinate beliefs. As late as the 1950s several cases were reported in the newspapers whereby *jinken*, human rights, were claimed to have been infringed by the belief in hereditary fox owners. In 1952 the Shimane edition of the Mainichi Shimbun reported that a young couple had committed a double suicide because the young man's parents had forbidden him to marry the girl on the grounds that the fox owning stigma attached to her family.[13]

In 1951 a case of malicious slander came before the Bureau of Justice in Matsue. A month-old baby in a family called Mita suddenly fell ill and died. The child's father declared that its death had been caused by demoniacal dogs, sent to bite it from the dog owning family of one Abe. The rumour spread, with the result that Abe was soon ostracised by the neighbourhood. His daughter's engagement was broken off; all the workmen in his building company left so that the business came to grief. Investigation proved that the Abe family had recently come into money, was unpopular in the district, and had quarrelled with Mita over a plot of land. When Mita's baby died, an exorcist called Myōkō told him that the cause of death was a demoniacal dog from the Abe household.[14]

Which brings us to the problem: how did these unfortunate families originally receive so extraordinary a stigma? Outwardly they are the same as anyone else; what has earned them their reputation for evil witchcraft?

As the Mita-Abe story illustrates in all too melancholy a way, many have fallen into this unhappy state of social ostracism through little more than untested slander, an accusation made by an exorcist in a state of trance, perhaps, or even by the patient herself. In 1922 a case was reported from Bungo province of a girl who rushed out one night and fell unconscious outside a house belonging to a man named Genjū. Her parents pursued her, and on no other evidence concluded that she was possessed by a dog sent by Genjū. Reviling Genjū in the strongest terms, they beat the girl violently on the back for a quarter of an hour, after which she recovered. After this incident Genjū and his family suffered great misery from slander and ostracism. His sister, who had been happily and prosperously married, was divorced on account of the scandal. At length, in desperation, he brought an action for libel against the girl's parents, and was awarded suitable damages.[15]

To our question, what have these families done to be thus singled out as witches, the answer one is likely to receive in the district is a simple one: because they do in fact keep foxes in their houses. In the winter of 1963 I visited a temple called Taikyūji, not far from Tottori, which since the Meiji period had been a renowned centre for the exorcism of fox possessed patients. The priest was an elderly man who had served in the Russo-Japanese war, and he was certainly well educated. But he had been the incumbent of the temple for twenty years and had exorcised a great many fox possessed people. It is easy to tell, he told me, who are the fox owning families, because you can see the foxes sitting on the eaves of their roofs. Time and again during his evening stroll he had seen them playing outside the houses of the marked families, or sitting in a row on the eaves, shading their eyes with their paws. Often they would rush up to him, snarling and snapping at his robe. Nor was he the only one who could see them. Everyone in the village could do so.

Again, a Mr Ikuta, a schoolmaster in Tottori whom I met in 1963, told me that he had spent a great deal of time lecturing in various villages in the area, exhorting them to abandon the evil superstition of fox owning. But he had made little headway. After his lecture he was usually challenged by one of the villagers: how could an outsider know anything whatever of the matter? The whole village knew which families were the fox owning ones because they could see the foxes outside the houses.

Detached investigation has however yielded one or two more likely solutions to our problem. Mr Hayami Yasutaka in his interesting book published in 1953, *Tsukimono-mochi Meishin no Rekishiteki Kōsatsu*, describes how he himself was brought up in a family with the reputation for fox owning in a village near Matsue. Having suffered mockery and inconveniences of various kinds during his childhood, he eventually, after the war, carried out a number of investigations in the Izumo district which formed the nucleus of a thesis on the fox owning superstition. His principal conclusions were as follows.

(1) That as late as 1952 10 per cent of the families in the Izumo district bore the stigma of fox owning.

(2) That the belief arose during the middle Tokugawa period, at the end of the seventeenth and beginning of the eighteenth centuries, at a time when the money economy was beginning to penetrate into the countryside, bringing in its train a new class of *nouveaux riches* landlords.

(3) That the fox owning families originated in these *nouveaux riches* landlords, through accusations of fox owning first brought through the jealous slander of the older inhabitants of the village, ousted and impoverished by the newcomers.

(4) And that the superstition was inflamed and exacerbated by

Animal Witchcraft in Japan

Shingon priests, *yamabushi*, exorcists and suchlike people who would be likely to make money from the discovery of such witchcraft and the exorcism of its effects.[16]

These conclusions agree by and large with those of Ishizuka's surveys of the fox owning districts. His investigations pointed to the fox owning families being the *nouveaux riches* of about a century ago. They were neither the oldest families, that is to say the descendants of the founders of the village, nor the most recent settlers. They were the middle layer. Ishizuka too attributes the origin of the accusations of witchcraft to the jealousy of the impoverished older settlers.[17]

These explanations, however, account for no more than the grounds for hostility; they in no way explain its nature. They do not tell us why so extraordinary an accusation should be levelled against the intruders. You may hate and dislike someone, and a new, hardfisted, intruding landlord is an understandable object of dislike. But you will not necessarily accuse him of having acquired his wealth and power through the medium of witch animals. There must have existed in the district, deeply rooted in its beliefs, some prior conviction that fox witchcraft was possible and dangerous. We must therefore try to look even further back to see in what possible context this fear originated.

Several Japanese ethnologists, including the great Yanagita Kunio, have attributed its origin at least in part to the *ku* magic of China. Let us look into this.

The practice of *ku* magic is apparently of great antiquity. The character *ku* appears on the oracle bones (1500 BC) and gives its name to one of the hexagrams of the *I Ching*. But what exactly the word meant does not become really clear before the sixth century AD. Here, in a work called *Tsao shih chu-ping yüan-hou tsung-lun* we find the first clear description of how the *ku* magic is performed and the poisoned manufactured.

You take a pot and put inside it a variety of venomous creatures, snakes, toads, lizards, centipedes. You then let them devour each other until only one is left. This survivor is the *ku*. 'It can change its appearance and bewitch people,' the work continues, 'and when put into food and drink it causes disease and disaster.'[18]

This *ku* creature, be it snake, toad, centipede or caterpillar, can be used by its master both for enriching himself and for killing his enemies, very much as we have seen the fox or snake to do in

Japan. But its mode of activity seems altogether different. It does not possess its victim so much as poison him. The *ku* creature is introduced into the food and drink of the sorcerer's enemies, causing death in a variety of horrible ways. Sometimes they simply die in terrible pain spitting blood. Sometimes the fish and meat they have just eaten come alive again in the stomach, and they not only die but their spirit becomes a slave in the house of the sorcerer. The fourth-century work *Sou shên chi* has a story of a monk who went to dinner with a family who made *ku*. All the other guests died spitting blood, but the monk took the precaution of reciting a spell before beginning his meal, and saw two black centipedes a foot long crawl away from the dish. He ate his dinner and survived unharmed.[19]

A favourite form of *ku* creature from the Sung period onwards is the *ch'in tsan* or golden caterpillar. But here the procedure is rather different. You do not invite your enemies to dinner and put the golden caterpillar in their food. You leave it on the roadside wrapped up in a parcel with pieces of gold and old flowered satin. A stranger will then pick up these rich and glittering things, to find himself cursed with the caterpillar. In a manner not clearly explained the caterpillar will slowly kill its victim, at the same time removing all his valuables to the house of the sorcerer, who suddenly becomes extremely rich.

At the same time, once you have such a caterpillar at your command, it is extremely difficult to get rid of it. You cannot burn it or drown it or hack it to pieces with a sword. The only sure defence indeed, both against its attacks and against the risks of ownership, seems to be moral virtue. Several Sung works tell stories to illustrate how scholars were protected by their moral virtue against *ku* magic. They pick up mysterious parcels on the roadside, only to be persistently haunted by frogs, snakes or caterpillars which cannot be killed. Eventually, to the dismay of their families, they eat the creature. But they do not die, as everyone expects. They live happily ever after, both rich and free from *ku* haunting.

The *Yi chien san chih*, for example, tells of a brave scholar in the district of Ch'ang-chou, so brave in fact that there was really nothing that he was afraid of. One day he was walking with some friends when he saw on the ground a parcel wrapped in silk. The friends were too afraid even to look at it, but the scholar laughed

Animal Witchcraft in Japan

and said, 'I am a poor man, so why shouldn't I take it?' He opened the parcel then and there, to find inside several rolls of silk, three pieces of silver and a *ku* frog. Saying to the frog, 'I don't care what you do; it is the silk and the silver that I want', he took the things home. His family were horrified and wept bitterly, expecting a calamity to fall upon them at any moment. But the scholar told them not to worry; it was his business, not theirs.

That night he found two frogs in his bed, as big as year-old babies. He killed them both and ate them. His family were even more terrified, but he simply said he was lucky to get such good meat. He then got drunk, went to bed, and had an excellent night's sleep.

The next night he found ten frogs in his bed, though they were smaller than the previous ones. These also he cooked and ate. The next night there were thirty. Every night thereafter the frogs in his bed became more and more numerous, though always they got smaller in size. At last the whole house was full of frogs and it was impossible to eat them all. Yet his courage never failed, and he hired a man to bury them outside the village. Finally, after a month, the thing stopped. The scholar laughed and said, 'If this is all that the *ku* calamity is, it does not amount to much.' Nothing more happened and everyone was filled with admiration for his bravery.[20]

Now on the face of it there seems to be little in common between these Chinese practices and the hereditary animal witchcraft found in Japan. Let us review the facts.

First, the *ku* creature is nearly always cited as a reptile, insect or batrachian. It is a creature, in short, of the scaly variety indicated by the radical classifier 142. The pot, after all, is a receptacle suitable only for such creatures. The only exception to this rule that I can discover is the story in the *Sou shên chi*, a fourth-century collection of supernatural tales, which describes a man called Chao Shou who had a dog *ku*, and how guests to his house were attacked by large yellow dogs.[21] And in any case this description points more to a case of hydrophobia than one of *ku*.

Second, there is no mention of the *ku* creature having powers of possession. It seems either to be administered as a poison in food, or to haunt its victim, as did the frogs in the scholar's bed. This is very different from the activity of the Japanese *tsukimono*, which enters into the minds as well as the bodies of its victims.

Third, I can find only one mention of the *ku* animal being the hereditary property of a family. This is in the *Sui shu ti li chih*, the geographical section of the Sui dynasty history, where it is written that *ku* is handed down from generation to generation in a family, and is given to a daughter as a dowry when she marries.[22] But for the rest, there is no indication that possession of a *ku* creature or the ability to manufacture *ku* is something which runs in certain families, least of all that it is handed down in the female line.

On the other hand several curious similarities do occur between the *ku* magic and the Japanese belief in snake witchcraft. In the first place, as Yanagita Kunio assures us, the snake is believed to be kept in a pot in the owner's kitchen. To possess one is by no means an unmixed blessing and many families are anxious to get rid of theirs. The only way in which this can be accomplished without bringing misfortune on oneself, is to get a total stranger to kill it unwittingly.

A man once came to a certain village in Sanuki province on a building job. He lodged in a house in the village and every day went to work on the building site. One day he came back to find all the family out. He saw a kettle of water boiling on the stove, and thought that a cup of tea would be nice after his day's work. On the floor he saw a jar with a lid, and thinking that it contained tea he took the lid off. Inside he saw a snake coiled up like a lamprey. He poured some of the boiling water on it and replaced the lid. When the family returned he told them what he had done, and one and all rejoiced at their deliverance by a stranger from the curse which had plagued them for so long.[23]

But for its ending, this story is remarkably similar to one in the *Sou shên chi*. A family called Liao had manufactured *ku* for a long time, and had become very rich thereby. One of the sons married, but the bride was not told about the *ku*. One day everyone went out, leaving the bride alone in the house. She noticed a large pot, and on lifting the lid, saw inside a big snake. She poured boiling water into the pot and killed the snake. When the family returned and heard what she had done they were all terrified. And soon after, sure enough, they all died of plague.[24]

Stories so similar must certainly have a common origin. The origin of the Chinese story, as also of the story of the yellow dog *ku*, is the fourth-century work *Sou shên chi*. This book we know to have found its way to Japan at least by the Tokugawa period, and its stories in a curious manner to have become absorbed in the oral tradition of Japan. Is it not more likely that the parallels are due to the dissemination of this book and others like it in Japan, rather than to a common origin between the magical practices themselves? In any case knowledge of *ku* magic imported through books is surely not enough to account for this widespread and tenacious belief in hereditary animal witchcraft.

Another suggested explanation is that the belief in fox witchcraft is a degraded survival of a former household or village deity in animal form.

There is abundant evidence that both the fox and the snake used to be, and in some places still are, regarded as benevolent protective deities of a family or village group. It is perhaps perilous to use the word totem in view of the work of Lévi-Strauss, who tells us that the term no longer has any real meaning. Nevertheless, it still seems to me to be a useful one by which to designate an animal which lives in a special and mutually beneficial relationship with a particular family, an animal which, in return for food and the spiritual nourishment imparted by worship, will exercise tutelary protection over the family and reserve for them the benefits of its powers of clairvoyance and healing.

Examples still survive today of foxes enshrined in private houses, usually under the nomenclature of Inari and his messenger, which in return for the usual offerings and recitations will give useful supernatural information. In return for such 'worship', he will pronounce on the whereabouts of lost things and missing persons, on the prospects for the rice harvest or the fishing catches, on the cause of sickness or the advisability of marriage. Such information used often to be delivered in the form of a *takusen* or oracular utterance through a medium. So also is the snake found, usually conflated with the deity Ryūgū, invoked as a benevolent family or village oracle in return for worship offered at a special little shrine.

Even in the districts along the coast of the Japan Sea where the fox owning belief is still strong, there still survive indications of the fox as a benevolent protector. Ishizuka found several interesting cases of families with the fox owning reputation, but who were not hated or feared because they were so assiduous in their daily worship at the animal's shrine. In other words, we are back with the familiar Japanese belief that a spiritual being, whether numen, ghost or animal, will remain benevolent so long as it is treated right. Once neglect the nourishing rituals and the being will change its nature completely, becoming a source of curses rather than blessings.[25]

But how did these originally benevolent and useful divinities become degraded into witch animals? The answer can only be conjecture. But perhaps we see here yet another example of the familiar psychology of the witch fear. It comes as an explanation of otherwise incomprehensible strokes of fate. Why should my baby die? Why should my back ache? Why should my wife go mad? And again, why should *they* suddenly become rich and successful? The origin lies in the overwhelming necessity for finding an explanation of disaster, disparity, sickness, which will lay the blame on someone else and exonerate me. They surely could not have become so rich by their wits alone; they must have had help of some kind, non-human help. The fox they used to worship at once springs to mind, and accounts also very conveniently for the pains in my back and the sudden death of my baby.

Though the totem theory accounts fairly satisfactorily for the hereditary character of Japanese witch animals, it does not explain why the great majority of them should be passed down in the female line.[26] The present hereditary family system known as *ie* is an overwhelmingly masculine institution; the bride is received and absorbed, but brings virtually nothing from her own family which will affect or modify her husband's. To look back to some distant period of antiquity when power may have been transmitted in the female line would be carrying speculation too far. This aspect of the problem still awaits solution.

A final problem is the hallucinatory one. The priest of Taikyūji was quite certain that he had seen the foxes outside the houses of the condemned families, not once but many times. He is only typical of large numbers of people in the district whose proof that foxes are kept in those houses is that they have actually seen them there. It would be easy, of course, to dismiss the whole problem as one of collective wishful vision. They see the creatures, as one rationally minded Japanese told me, because they wish to see them, much as those involved in African witch cults will swear that they have seen the witches with their phosphorescent teeth flying on their malign errands. But I cannot refrain from drawing at least a tentative comparison with those families in this country which appear to possess a spectral attendant animal. These creatures usually appear as birds or dogs, though radiant boys are not

Animal Witchcraft in Japan

unknown, but as a rule they do not manifest themselves unless a member of the family is about to die. The black dog of the Herefordshire Baskervilles and the birds of the Bishop of Salisbury are merely two among many instances of animal apparitions seen at such critical junctures.[27] If we are not inclined to dismiss these at once as 'mere' hallucinations, we may at least accept them as food for further speculation about survivals of former, closer relationships between a family and an overshadowing animal.

It thus seems reasonable to conclude that the practices we have discussed under the name of Japanese animal witchcraft are probably, in both their principal forms, survivals of former cult practices not in themselves evil. The Izuna or Dagini rite was a *gehō* or heretical ritual, but not necessarily an evil one. Nor was the worship of the fox or snake as a household guardian; the creatures were possessed of useful supernatural powers and, like a friendly watchdog or efficient mouser, would behave in general benevolently if kindly treated. That they should have evolved into uncanny, often atrocious, instruments of evil is due to a shift in emphasis. The same set of symbols, which originally benefited one family, is now seen as primarily harmful to others. Their gain has become my loss.

Notes

1 Dr E. Baelz, who was Professor of Medicine in the University of Tokyo during the 1890s, and had many opportunities for personal observation of cases of fox possession in the hospital under his charge, has left several particularly interesting descriptions. His 'Über Besessenheit', in *Verhandlung der Gesellschaft deutscher Naturforscher und Aerzte*, Leipzig, 1907, was kindly procured for me by Dr Peter Baelz of Jesus College, Cambridge. Extracts in English may be found in Oesterreich's *Possession, Demoniacal and Other*, pp. 224-8, and in B. H. Chamberlain's *Things Japanese*, p. 131.
2 Yanagita Kunio, 'Hebigami Inugami no Tagui', *Teihon Yanagita Kunio Shū*, vol. 9, p. 261. The distribution of witch animals over the Japanese islands may be found clearly set out, with illuminating maps, in Ishizuka Takatoshi's *Nihon no Tsukimono*, 1959, pp. 20-74.
3 Yanagita, op. cit., p. 261.
4 The distinction drawn by Sir E. E. Evans-Pritchard in his *Witchcraft, Oracles and Magic among the Azande* may be useful here: a witch is someone who possesses innately harmful powers, such as overlooking, evil eyeing. A sorcerer has to perform a ritual of some kind in order to achieve his ends.
5 Yazu Shusei, 'Kitsunegami oyobi kitsunetsuki jikkendan', *Minzoku to Rekishi*, vol. 8, no. 1, August 1922, pp. 218-22.

6 Quoted in Ishizuka, op. cit., p. 192. Further information about the relation of the Izuna rite and foxes is given in Tsubosaka Yutaka, 'Izuna-hō', *Minzoku to Rekishi*, vol. 8, no. 1, pp. 187–90.
7 'The fox and badger in Japanese folklore', *Transactions of the Asiatic Society of Japan*, vol. 36, 1908–9, pp. 105–29. The Taira Kiyomori story is in *Gempei Seisuiki*, Nihon Bungaku Taikei edition, vol. 15, pp. 36–8. The story of Fujiwara Tadazane, otherwise known as Chisokuin-dono, is in *Kokonchomonjū*, same edition, vol. 10, p. 495. The priest Myōkitsu-jisha appears in the *Taiheiki*, same edition, vol. 18, pp. 105–12.
8 The Dakini figure in Indian or Tibetan iconography bears no relation to a fox. In Tibetan Buddhism the *dakini* usually appear in the form of beautiful women, who bestow secret knowledge on the neophyte and render him aid in certain kinds of meditation. Elsewhere the *dakini* may appear as a group of three red demons, as illustrated in Mochizuki's *Bukkyō Daijiten*.
9 Miura Shuyu writes that in the Okayama district there still persists the belief that to live in the house of a former fox owner will infect your own family with the stigma. The same suspicion attaches to the rice fields of former fox owners. In the Izumo district few people will not hesitate to buy such land, however cheap the price. *San-in Minzoku*, no. 3, quoted by Ishizuka, op. cit., pp. 131–2.
10 Yanagita, op. cit., p. 262. An abundance of information on cases of fox, dog and snake possession, albeit collected with a view to disproving it on rational grounds, may be found in Inoue Enryō's *Yōkaigaku Kōgi*, vol. 4, pp. 215–45.
11 Motoori Norinaga, 'Senshakō', *Motoori Norinaga Zenshū*, vol. 12, p. 172. Quoted in Ishizuka, op. cit., p. 124.
12 Ishizuka, op. cit., pp. 86–116.
13 Hayami Yasutaka, *Tsukimono-mochi Meishin no Rekishiteki Kōsatsu*, 1953, p. 46.
14 Miyake Hitoshi, 'Shugendō no Tsukimono-otoshi', in *Yoneyama Keizō Sensei Kanreki Kinen Rombunshū*, p. 292.
15 'Bungo no Inugami-sawagi Jitsuwa', *Minzoku to Rekishi*, vol. 8, no. 1, pp. 302–3.
16 Hayami, op. cit., pp. 28–30.
17 Ishizuka, op. cit., pp. 168–9.
18 Quoted in H. Y. Feng and J. K. Shryock, 'The black magic in China known as Ku', *Journal of the American Oriental Society*, vol. 55, no. 1, 1935, p. 8. A full account of the dynastic feuds, in which numerous members of the Imperial family were murdered, which the alleged practice of *ku* provoked in the early Han period, may be found in Michael Loewe, 'The case of witchcraft in 91 B.C.', *Asia Major*, vol. 15, part 2.
19 Feng and Shryock, op. cit., p. 8.
20 Ibid., p. 27.
21 Ibid., p. 7.
22 *Sui-shu* 31, (*chih* 26); 14a, b (*Po-na* ed.); Feng and Shryock, op. cit., p. 13.
23 Yanagita, op. cit., p. 262.
24 Feng and Shryock, op. cit., p. 7.
25 Ishizuka, op. cit., pp. 230–44.

26 Ishizuka writes that in some districts, notably Shimane and Oita, the *tsukimono* is prepared to accompany a bridegroom as well as a bride. Elsewhere the creature only goes with a girl. *Gedō* are said to multiply at the birth of a girl, but not of a boy. Ishizuka, op. cit., p. 272.
27 I owe these examples to Theo Brown's chapter on family ghosts in her unpublished manuscript on the Black Dog. Also Edith Olivier, *Four Victorian Ladies of Wiltshire*, pp. 33–4, for Miss Annie Moberley's vision of the Bishop of Salisbury's birds. Further examples of such visions of animals may be found in Professor Henry Sidgwick's 'Report on the census of hallucinations', *Proceedings of the Society for Psychical Research*, vol. 10, 1894.

2

Hostile Magic in the Icelandic Sagas

H. R. Ellis Davidson

In 1935 the Swedish scholar Dag Strömbäck published his study of certain magic practices in Old Norse literature which come under the Icelandic term *seiðr*.[1] He showed how these bear a striking resemblance to shamanistic practices among the Lapps in pre-Christian times, and how the essential characteristic of *seiðr* is the falling of the practitioner into a state of trance in which he or she is able to foresee the future, discover hidden things and influence the minds of others. Descriptions of this kind of magic in the sagas vary considerably in date and reliability; some are clearly late additions to the story, but others seem based on a genuine interest in and considerable knowledge of Scandinavian magic practices. Strömbäck came to the conclusion that when the sagas were composed from the thirteenth century onwards there was not a great deal known about *seiðr*, but that sufficient information was scattered through the sources to build up a general picture.[2]

It is important for our understanding of pagan religion in Scandinavia to know that witchcraft as represented in the sagas is akin in many respects to the shamanism of the Lapps and other peoples of north-eastern Europe and Siberia. I propose here to follow up Strömbäck's survey by a brief investigation of the assumptions regarding hostile witchcraft to be found in the sagas. These were composed before the witchcraft trials and systematic persecution of those accused of magic practices, while memories of pagan customs still survived, so that the picture of witchcraft which they give is useful for comparative purposes and may throw light on the basis of later beliefs. There is no difficulty in finding examples of hostile witchcraft in the Icelandic sagas, as it plays a large part; sometimes it has a direct bearing on the plot, accounting for major events, strange behaviour of the characters, or the downfall of the hero.

One of the powers of the witch was the ability to conceal a person from his pursuers, a means by which criminals might be protected from justice. An entertaining story of this kind of magic is given in *Eyrbyggja Saga* (XX). A woman called Katla, skilled in magic, wished to save her son Odd from a band of men determined to kill him because he had cut off a woman's hand during a fight. As the men approached the house, Katla told Odd to sit beside her without moving, while she sat on the dais spinning yarn. Arnkell and his men searched the house but saw nothing beside Katla but a distaff. They returned a second time, to find Katla in the porch; she was combing Odd's hair, but it seemed to them that she was grooming her goat. The third time Odd was lying in a heap of ashes, and they thought that it was Katla's boar sleeping there. Each time they left the house they realised that a trick had been played on them, or 'a goatskin waved round our heads', as Arnkell put it, so that Katla could not try the same deception twice. Finally Geirrid, another woman skilled in witchcraft and a bitter enemy of Katla, offered to come with them. When Katla saw her blue cloak from the window she declared that now *sjónhverfing* (deceiving of the sight) would no longer be sufficient. She hid Odd inside the hollow dais, but Geirrid unhesitatingly slipped a sealskin bag over Katla's head and told the men to open the dais and take Odd out. He was hanged on the neighbouring headland and Katla stoned to death.

In *Harðar Saga* (XXVI) a less unpleasant character, Skroppa, hid herself and her two foster-daughters from the outlaw Hord, making them appear first as chests of ashwood and then as a sow and two piglets running in the yard. Hord, of whom it was said that no *sjónhverfing* could affect his eyes (XI), threw a stone at the sow and Skroppa was seen lying dead on the spot. Similarly the wizard Askman in *Gull-Thóris Saga* (X) was brought down by a blazing firebrand as he escaped from his house in the shape of a boar. Although less explicit, the tale of Sveinung's concealing of Gunnar in *Fljotsdæla Saga* (XIX) seems to be basically of the same type. Sveinung was known to possess special powers; he hid Gunnar first in a load of turf, then in a dark stable, and finally under a ship, the pursuers realising in each case that they had been tricked after they had left the house. On their last visit they were terrified by Sveinung's appearance, for he was by turn pale and darkly flushed and his hair seemed to stand on end; they thought he was in a terrible rage and would work evil magic on them if they found Gunnar.[3]

A parallel to stories of this type is found in shamanistic lore from Siberia, and a striking example is furnished by a myth of the Chukchis about the attempt of Moon to carry off the daughter of a reindeer breeder.[4] She was warned by a great bull in the herd, who promised to protect her:

> He dug in the snow with his hoof. 'Sit down here.' She sat, he banked up the snow, cast a spell, and it turned into a hillock. The moon came, looked for the girl, walked round, but could not find her. The top of her head was visible to be sure, but it looked like a hillock.

Moon went away, declaring he would return. The reindeer pulled the girl's sledge swiftly back to her house:

> 'Well, what shall I turn you into, quickly, before he gets here? Perhaps a stone block?' 'He will know it.' 'Well, a hammer?' 'He will know it.' 'Well, a hair in the bed curtain?' 'He will know it, he will know it.' 'You know what, I shall turn you into a lamp.' 'Good, good.'

Moon examined everything in the house, but did not touch the lamp because it would be dangerous for two fires to come together and he himself was a fire. As he was leaving, the girl called to him from the window, and he came back to search for her again, but without success. This happened a second time, and gradually Moon began to shrivel and become weak (a reference to the moon's waning), so the girl bound him. As the price of his freedom he promised to create the seasons of the year for the people of the Chukchis and not to leave the upper sky.

A different term for the magic of concealment is found in a story in *Fóstbrœðra Saga* (X), where a woman called Grima hid her servant by seating him on a bench and moving her hands over his head: this is called 'placing the *huliðshjálmr* (helmet of hiding or invisibility) over him, so that he could not be seen'. In the same saga another Grima living in Greenland hid Thormod by seating him on a chair with the figure of Thor carved on it and warning him not to move, while her husband put rubbish on the fire and filled the

Hostile Magic in the Icelandic Sagas

house with smoke.[5] When the smoke-hole was opened and the air cleared, the chair was visible but Thormod was not seen by the searchers. The same term is used on other occasions in the sagas when an attacking party is rendered invisible by magic.[6] Similarly the wizard Svan in *Njáls Saga* (XII) called up darkness on men pursuing a murderer by taking a goatskin and wrapping it round his own head, with the words: 'Let there be mist, let there be phantoms and confounding to all those seeking you.' The witch Thorbiorg in *Harðar Saga* (XXV) is said to have wrapped her hood round her head to cause darkness, while Isgerd in *Reykdæla Saga* (XIV) thrust a skin rug (*fótaskinn*) over a servant's head to cause mist and darkness. When however Eyvind tried a spell of this kind against Olaf Tryggvason, the Christian king was able to reverse the spell, so that:[7]

> the dark mist that Eyvind had raised by his magic came upon him and his men, and they became like blind men and saw no better with their eyes than with the backs of their heads, so that they all walked round in circles.

A more interesting example of rival witchcraft, so that the supernatural sight of the witch is defeated by the raising of darkness not in the real world but on the spirit journey undertaken in trance, is found in the *Fornaldarsǫgur* in the first chapter of *Hrólfs Saga kraka*. Here a man with special powers is able to raise a thick mist round the island where two boys are concealed, so that the king's wizards are unable to perceive them by means of their magic arts.

In the story of Thorir Hund's expedition to plunder the sacred place of the Biarmians, the inhabitants of the land across the Baltic around the northern Dvina,[8] Thorir concealed his party from pursuing natives by taking something 'resembling ashes' from a sack, sprinkling it over their tracks and throwing it above their heads, according to Snorri's account.[9] Thorir was well acquainted with Biarmian customs, and the tradition that he was using Lapp magic is early, since it is referred to in the poem *Erfidrápa*.[10] Saxo Grammaticus in the twelfth century tells how the Lapps escaped from their enemies by throwing first three pebbles behind them, which appeared to those pursuing to be hills, and later a heap of snow, which seemed to be a mighty river.[11]

As represented in the sagas, *sjónhverfing* appears to be a delusion caused by the witch on the minds of others so that they cannot see things as they really are, while placing the *huliðshjálmr* on them causes darkness and mist so that those at whom the spell is aimed are lost and bewildered. The reference of Arnkell, however, to 'waving a goatskin round our heads' when he cannot see Odd (p. 21 above) links these two kinds of magic together. The gods themselves were familiar with *sjónhverfing*, and so were the giants; the most famous account of its use is in the story of the visit of the god Thor to the realm of Utgarðar-Loki, as told by Snorri in the *Prose Edda*. Saxo describes it as one of the powers of both gods and giants in the first book of his Danish history:[12]

> ... extreme skill in deluding the eyesight, knowing how to obscure their own faces and those of others with divers semblances, and to darken the true aspect of things with beguiling shapes.

and he declared that certain of their human descendants inherited something of this skill. The spells, however, had no effect on those who were themselves skilled in magic, like Geirrid and Hord (p. 21 above). Such a man apparently was Steinrod the Strong, who in a little story in *Landnámabók*[13] is said to have taken a malevolent witch called Geirhild by surprise; she had taken the form of a goatskin full of water, and he belaboured her with an iron rod till her ribs were sore. The verse quoted, however, gives no clear indication of what kind of magic was involved. It is perhaps significant that in the story of the wizards in *Hrólfs Saga* this kind of magic is taken out of the familiar world; it is used by one wizard against others on the supernatural journey, and it is possible that Steinrod and Geirhild met in this fashion.

The witch's power to bewilder the mind is related to another kind of magic, illustrated by the encounter between Thordis, the wise woman from Spákonufell, and Gudmund the Mighty, as recounted in *Vatnsdæla Saga* (XLIV). Thordis, a woman of some repute, was asked to arbitrate in a lawsuit, but Gudmund refused to accept her ruling. She sent the defendant Thorkell to him, wearing her own black hood, which apparently rendered him invisible, and carrying a special staff called *Hognuðr* (Tamer), with which he had to touch Gudmund on the left cheek. When Gudmund arose to speak in the court, his memory failed him completely, and he could not continue the case; he did not recover until Thorkell touched his right cheek with the staff, and he was unable to understand what had happened.

Hostile Magic in the Icelandic Sagas

Another example of hostile magic affecting the mind is shown in *Egils Saga* (LX), where Egil, wrecked on the Yorkshire coast, inexplicably made his way to the court of Eirik Bloodaxe at York, although he knew that Eirik's queen Gunnhild was longing to take his life. The saga represents this as due to the spells of Gunnhild, drawing Egil to York against his will;[14] it is also implied that she was responsible for the swallow which distracted Egil by its twittering when he was working on the poem which was to save his life, until his loyal friend Arnbiorn drove the bird away.

Hostile witchcraft was particularly effective in battle. In *Vatnsdæla Saga* (XXVI) the old witch Ljot tried to save her son, Big Hrolleif, from being killed by the sons of Ingimund because he had caused their father's death. She began a magic ceremony to protect him, and here the saga-teller seems unable to understand what the shepherd saw inside her house when he was admitted after a long wait.[15] However the part played by Ljot when the brothers attack Hrolleif is quite explicit:

> Hogni exclaimed: 'What the devil is coming towards us? I can't make out what it is.' 'Here comes the old crone Ljot', said Thorstein, 'and a queer sight she has made of herself.' She had drawn her clothes over her head and was walking backwards, her head bent down between her legs, and the look in her eyes was not good to see as she darted troll-like glances at them.

However Jokull cut off Hroleif's head before she could intervene, and she declared they were lucky men indeed, for she would have made the land turn over, causing them to run mad with panic, had they not caught sight of her in time. Here the magic is associated with Ljot's glance, and this is emphasised in other tales; for this reason it was usual to put a skin bag over the witch's head before killing him or her, as was done to Katla (p. 21 above) and again to Stigandi in *Laxdæla Saga* (XXXVIII). In Stigandi's case there was a tear in the bag and the wizard's baleful gaze fell upon the hillside where the grass was green, and immediately 'it was as if a whirlwind had blown up; the earth turned over, so that grass never grew there again'. In the story of the finding of Queen Gunnhild, who as a girl went to learn magic from two wizards in Finnmark, Snorri attributes a similar power to them: when they were angry the earth turned over at their glance, and any living thing on which their gaze fell dropped dead.[16] The upside-down gaze of Ljot seems, by sympathetic magic, to have the power to reverse normality, blighting the earth and driving men mad. The peculiar expression 'make the land turn over' may have originated from the fact that the Icelanders often witnessed flows of lava which turned green land into rock in an instant, as though it had indeed been blighted and turned upside down by some supernatural power.

The witch's glance could also blunt weapons. In *Gull-Thóris Saga* (XVII) there is a fight between two groups of neighbours, each with a woman skilled in magic giving support. Kerling walked into the house of the enemy through locked doors, but her rival, Thurid, caused her to be driven out by a boar. When fighting started, Thurid's party found they were unable to wound their opponents, so Thurid went to look for Kerling. She found her in a field behind the house with her clothes up her back and her head down, so that she could see the sky through her legs. Thurid forthwith attacked her, and they fought until both lay unconscious; meanwhile the blunted weapons became effective again. In the same way a man called Thorgrim blunted the weapons of Ingimund's sons in a fight described in *Vatnsdæla Saga* (XXIX), and when Jokull found that his famous sword, Ættartangi, would not cut, he and Thorstein went to look for the wizard. They found him down by the river and we are told that he 'stared' (*koglaði*) at them from where he lay,[17] but Jokull rushed at him with his sword and gave him a humiliating wound from behind as he dived into the river. After that there was no more trouble from Ættartangi, and the implication is that it was Thorgrim's glance which was affecting the weapons.

The berserks also were held to have the power to blunt weapons by their gaze, and this is often presented in a very literal fashion, as when in *Gunnlaugs Saga* (VII) Gunnlaug showed one of two swords to the man he was about to fight and then used the second one which had not been exposed to the gaze of his opponent and therefore blunted. That there is a link between the blunting of weapons and the magic which affects the mind in battle however is indicated by the description of Odin's powers in *Ynglinga Saga* (7): he could cause his foes in battle, it is said, to become blind or deaf or panic-stricken and their weapons to pierce no more than wands, while against his own followers neither fire nor iron could prevail. An episode in one of the *Fornaldarsǫgur*[18] where a witch called Lara hovers over the head of her lover in battle in the form of a swan, chanting spells with such powerful magic arts that the enemy could not defend themselves, suggests a memory of the valkyrie tradition, when the supernatural spirits of battle hovered in the air to carry out the decrees of Odin. Another strange episode which might be a concrete representation of some form of valkyrie tradition is found in *Ljósvetninga Saga* (XI), where Gudmund the Mighty asked a witch called Thorhild to find out whether he and his sons would escape vengeance. She met him on the seashore, dressed as a man, with a helmet on her head and an axe in her hand, and she 'acted rather violently', wading out into the sea and striking at the waves with her weapon. She was able to assure Gudmund that no harm would come to him, but when there was a crash and the sea became stained with blood, this meant that one of his sons would have a narrow escape. It seems probable that the desired information was attained by means of supernatural sight, and that this was an adventure of the spirit world rather than a ritual on the seashore; certainly her words to him afterwards, that she would not undertake such a task again as it had cost her much, suggests that this is the case.[19]

A more frequent method of anticipating the results of battle was by the touching of the bodies of those who would take part. In *Heiðarvíga Saga* (XXIII) the old Kjannok touched her fosterson Bardi in this way and gave him a stone necklace to wear which later saved him from a dangerous wound. In *Kormáks Saga* (I) another old fostermother was said to touch men before battle, and when she did this to Ogmund she declared that there were no dangerous wounds to be felt anywhere, while in *Reykdæla Saga* (V) the fostermother of Hroi 'found something on his foot, but elsewhere she thought that he would be alright', and Hroi subsequently received a spearwound on the instep. In these passages we are told very little about the fostermothers, and sometimes even the name is not given. It is interesting to compare such episodes with the story of the visit of the messengers of King Harald, Hauk and Vighard, to an old woman called Heid, whom the king calls his fostermother, and who lives in Biarmaland.[20] They took her two flitches of bacon and a barrel of butter as gifts from the king, and when they met the old woman they found she was very ugly, taller than a tall man, and dressed in a skin kirtle so that she appeared to be a kind of giantess. She was delighted with the gifts, took off Hauk's clothes and stroked him all over, declaring that he was strong and lucky; she then asked him to kiss her and gave him two stones to use when attacked by the enemy. His companion, however, was unwilling either to strip or to kiss this repulsive creature, and he was afterwards killed in an ambush, while Hauk, although wounded, was rescued and healed by Heid and then guided back by her to the trading station to join his countrymen.

With this we may compare a story about King Harald's poets, in Rafn's collection.[21] Here the old fostermother (unnamed) of Thorfinn knows beforehand when strangers are approaching, advises Thorfinn about his coming expedition, influences the drawing of lots so that he will become leader, gives him salves and bandages, and finally examines him for wounds: 'I think few are equal to you at eighteen years of age,' she concluded; 'There are plenty of cuts, but still you will come back, and now I want you to kiss me goodbye.' The kiss at parting appears to be a means of infusing something of the witch's power into her fosterson.

These fostermothers often give gifts to protect men in battle. The shirt which no weapon could pierce is a widespread motif, which, as Ploss has pointed out,[22] should be viewed as a piece of medieval science fiction rather than a fairy-tale episode. There were many experiments in rendering garments weapon-proof by use of melted horn, tar, asbestos and so on, in the ancient world, and these methods were familiar in Viking times because of systematic experiments in the Byzantine army. In the sagas Katla made a wound-proof shirt for her son Odd,[23] Ljot for her son Hrolleif, who is taunted about his *gørningstakkr* (witch's shirt),[24] and Esja for her fosterson Bui,[25] while in *Landnámabók* Hildigunna is said to have given one to her son Einar.[26]

The story of Heid of Biarmaland may offer a clue to the origin of the witch fostermothers in the Icelandic sagas. Heid stands midway between these and the considerable company of giantesses and valkyries in the *Fornaldarsǫgur*, Saxo and the Edda poems who act as supernatural fostermothers and brides of the human heroes, which I have discussed elsewhere.[27] Clearly the old Icelandic fostermothers are conventional rather than realistic figures; the normal practice was to foster a child at the home of a neighbour or friend in an ordinary family setting. There is, moreover, a very close parallel between the stories of the supernatural fostermothers and the spiritual marriages of shamans in such Siberian tribes as the Goldi, the Buryat and the Yakut.[28] These 'wives' may be represented as the daughters of a powerful male spirit, like some of the giantesses of Norse tradition; they help the shaman during his life, doing battle for him in animal form, and again like the giantesses and valkyries they can change their aspect, varying from that of a beautiful girl to a hideous hag or threatening monster. Like the Norse hero, the shaman is able to make a normal human marriage while retaining his spiritual bride. It therefore appears probable that the tales of fostermothers skilled in magic have been inspired by shamanistic traditions, the effects of which are more obvious in the *Fornaldarsǫgur*, which deal with the fantastic and the marvellous, than in the sagas of Icelanders, where the saga-tellers have transformed the supernatural women into old 'wise' women in a familiar home setting.

Significant in view of this are stories where the witch makes an attack in animal form. In *Gull-Thóris Saga* (p. 26 above) it is implied that the witch Thurid was responsible for the boar which defended the house, while in *Harðar Saga* (p. 21 above) Skroppa was similarly protected by a bull. In *Kormáks Saga* (XVIII) the witch Thordis appears as a walrus, still recognisable by her eyes, and when Kormak injures the beast, the injury affects Thordis herself. Comparison may be made with the story of the Lapp wizard who visited Iceland for the Danish king in the shape of a whale, and was threatened by the spirits of the land in various animal forms, as related by Snorri in *Heimskringla*.[29] Almqvist has shown that this is likely to be an early tradition, although Snorri may well have substituted symbols representing the chiefs of the four quarters of Iceland for the original animal spirits.[30] The cats of Thorolf Sledge in *Vatnsdæla Saga* (XXVIII) seem to have been seen as protective spirits of this kind, although there is nothing really abnormal about their behaviour. Two stories from the *Fornaldarsǫgur* may also be considered here. In *Friðþjófs Saga* (IV) two witches working magic from a platform were seen some distance away riding on a whale;[31] when the hero attacked them, the women on the platform fell and broke their backs. In *Hjálmþérs Saga ok Ǫlvés* (XX) the two heroes were escaping from a wicked king, Hunding, who was in pursuit of his daughter Hervor. He appeared in the shape of a huge walrus, whereupon their companion Hord, himself skilled in magic, lay down beneath a heap of clothes and forbade them to utter his name while the walrus was near, in case this caused his death. Then a sword-fish appeared from beneath the ship, and attacked the walrus, helped by a porpoise which emerged from under the ship of the princess Hervor, while the heroes tried to drive off the beast with weapons. The battle was not won, however, until two supernatural women, protectors of Hjalmder, arrived in the form of vultures, and all united against the walrus. Then Hjalmder found Hord awakening from his trance, and saw that his body was wet. Hord produced a sword and knife which his friends had lost in the sea-battle, and told them to go and help Hervor. They found her still unconscious and very weak, but when Hjalmder revived her with wine she soon recovered.

In another of the *Fornaldarsǫgur*, *Sturlaugs Saga Starfsama* (XII) a contest is described between a youth and a Lapp wizard:

> They set upon one another and fought fiercely, so swiftly that they could not be followed with the eye, but neither of them managed to wound the other. When men looked again, they had vanished, and in their place were two dogs, biting one another furiously; and when they least expected it, the dogs disappeared too, and they heard a noise going on in the air. They looked up and saw two eagles flying there, and each tore out the other's feathers with claws and beak so that blood fell on to the earth. The end was that one fell dead to the ground, but the other flew away and they did not know which one it was.

No such elaborate magic contest as this is found in the Icelandic sagas, but in *Landnámabók* there is a reference to a fight between two early settlers in southern Iceland, Dufthak and his neighbour Storolf. One evening after sunset a man with second-sight saw a great bear coming from Storolf's farm and a boar from that of Dufthak, and they fought furiously until the bear was victorious. In the morning the earth looked as if it had been turned over, and the men were tired out.[32]

Once more close parallels can be found from shamanistic legends. Czaplicka refers to a quarrel between a shaman of the Samoyed and one of the Yakut said to have continued for years, during which the scene of strife was transformed from the earth to the sky and then to the water and below it.[33] Lapp shamans were believed to fight in the form of reindeer, according to traditions collected by early missionaries;[34] Jens Kildal and other authors insist that the *noidi*, the Lapp shamans, used spirits which assumed the shapes of demoniacal reindeer living in the sacred mountains, and that if one of these was injured, the shaman associated with it would himself fall ill, and if it were killed he would die. The confusion in the saga stories between the witch in animal form and the animal guardian spirit is exactly paralleled in the shamanistic tales: Hultkrantz for instance observes that the boundary line between the 'free-soul' of the North American shaman and his guardian spirit 'often tends to be affected, the shaman being able to journey in the form of his guardian spirit'.[35]

We know that such stories were available to the Scandinavians in the thirteenth century, from a passage in the *Chronicon Norvegiae*.[36] This tells how some Norwegian merchants visiting a Lapp home saw their hostess fall to the ground, apparently dead. A shaman was summoned to find out the cause of this, and he used a sieve-shaped object on which a whale, a reindeer and sledge, and a boat were depicted—clearly a drum. The spirit of the shaman, here called *gand*, used these means of transport to journey over lakes and mountains, while the shaman himself drummed and danced in a state of ecstasy for a long while. Suddenly however his belly burst, and with a cry he fell dead. A second shaman was brought in, and he was more successful, so that at last the woman recovered consciousness, and told them that the spirit of the first shaman, travelling in the shape of a whale, had been pierced by an enemy concealed in a deep lake in the form of a pointed stick, and when the whale's body was ripped open this caused the shaman's death.

The word *gand* is of Germanic origin, and is found in the sagas. It was also used by the Lapps, and Niurenius stated that the attendant spirits of their shamans could use flies kept in a *gand*-box to injure men and cattle.[37] Another word, *tyre*, also of Germanic origin, was used among the Lapps for a kind of magic witchball, or, as in the Lapp term *noidendirri*, for a magic arrow. This is an idea found in many parts of the world (cf. elfshot) but it seems probable that the term *gand* was at one time closely associated with the guardian spirit in human or animal form. In *Fóstbræðra Saga* (XXIII) the witch Thordis was observed by her son to be very restless in her sleep, and she drew her breath painfully when she awoke; she told him 'I have ridden the *gand* far tonight, and now I have found out something which I did not know before'. Similarly her rival Grima discovered in her sleep what Thordis herself was planning. There are many other examples of this acquisition of knowledge while asleep or in a trance. In *Havarðar Saga* (XIX) Thorgrim, riding with an attacking party, found himself so sleepy that he could not sit on his horse; his companions let him lie with a cloak over his head, and saw that he was very restless; he awoke hot and bewildered, and told them they must go on and burn down the house if they could. However, a rival had also had a dream of their approach, and he brought about Thorgrim's death in the fight that followed. The idea of two witches 'dreaming' against one another is a conventional motif in the sagas, and it is interesting to see how it echoes the pattern of a conflict between rival shamans. The sleepiness which heralds the trance is mentioned several times in *Njáls Saga*,[38] and characteristic signs are yawning at the outset and the drawing of deep and painful breaths when recovering consciousness; there is often a warning against naming the name of the sleeper.[39] In *Njáls Saga* (CV) we have a description of the *gand*-riding: a man describes the coming of a black rider on a grey horse, holding a firebrand and travelling in a circle of fire; he hurls the firebrand towards the mountains and a great blaze is kindled. The comment of Hjalti on this is that he has seen the *gand-reið*, always a portent of disaster. The picture is like that of Surt setting fire to the world at Ragnarok, and it may be compared with other visions of giants or trolls presaging death,[40] which stand out from the more conventional dreams of wolves or bears which foretell an attack. The idea of a troop of witches riding on their staffs seems to have developed from this.[41]

There are occasional examples of the witch harming others by use of runes. In *Grettis Saga* (LXXVIII) the fall of the hero, after resisting many attacks during his sojourn as an outlaw on the island of Drangey, is attributed to the witchcraft of the old fostermother of his enemy Thorbiorn. At her request, Thorbiorn rowed her out to the island, lying under a heap of clothes, and she sat up and uttered a curse on Grettir, declaring that his luck was about to change. Deeply stirred by these ominous words, Grettir flung a stone at her and broke her leg. When the limb had healed, she went down to the seashore and cut runes on a tree washed up by the tide, reddening them in her blood; then she had it pushed out to sea and it floated swiftly towards the island. Grettir suspected the tree and tried to get rid of it, but his thrall brought it home for firewood. When Grettir attempted to chop it, the axe glanced off the wood and wounded him in the leg. The limb festered and became gangrenous, until he was unable to stand, and consequently when his enemies attacked he and his brother were ultimately overcome and killed. Thorbiorn was accused of witchcraft and outlawed, according to the saga. Another example of physical illness caused by runes is in

Hostile Magic in the Icelandic Sagas

Egils Saga (LXXII). A young girl had become seriously ill because a piece of bone with runes on it was placed in her bed. The youth who carved the runes had wanted to win her love, but through ignorance of runic lore caused her sickness, which would have been fatal had not Egil destroyed the bone and cut fresh runes for her healing. On another occasion Egil used runes to detect poison in a horn of ale (XLIV). Such cases are in accordance with runic spells as described in certain of the Edda poems, but it may be noticed that in the sagas there is comparatively little about runes in the tales of witchcraft.

A particularly dreaded form of magic was that which prevented physical union between man and woman. Queen Gunnhild employed this against Hrut in *Njáls Saga* (VI) when he left her to return to Iceland and marry, and Unn's words to her father in the following chapter make it clear that intercourse between them had been prevented by her magic, although Hrut could have relations with other women. Possibly a similar spell prevented the marriage of Kormak to Steingerd, although it is not made clear in the saga exactly why they remained apart: Kormak declares that it was due to evil spirits (*Kormáks Saga* XXVI), and it is attributed to the malice of the witch Thorveig, whose sons Kormak killed. After Thorveig's death another witch, Thordis, tried to release him from the spell, but he interrupted a sacrificial rite before the three geese she had prepared were all killed, and so her efforts were useless (XXII).

The physical effects of a spoken spell are described with great vividness and humour in a story in *Flateyjarbók*[42] about the composing of a *nið* or lampoon against Jarl Hakon of Norway by the poet Thorleif. Almqvist[43] has analysed this in detail, showing that the story was known in the twelfth century and probably earlier. Thorleif took vengeance on the jarl after Hakon had burned his ship; he appeared in the guise of a beggar and asked leave to recite a poem in the jarl's honour. The first signs of the effect on the jarl took the form of a violent itch between his legs which nearly drove him frantic; he shouted to the reciter to change his poem, but Thorleif went on to recite lines which plunged the hall in darkness, whereupon all weapons clashed together, several men fell dead, and the jarl fainted. He recovered to find Thorleif gone, and he himself in a sorry state, for his beard had fallen off and all his hair on one side, never to grow again. Almqvist shows how this agrees with

Icelandic traditions about the power of a *nið* recited by certain gifted poets to 'bite', that is to have a direct physical effect on the victim; this idea is found as late as the nineteenth century. Such attacks were generally made against foreign rulers or authorities at home held to have acted unjustly. The loss of Hakon's beard and his embarassing itch is consistent with the Icelandic tradition that the poem charged the jarl with lack of virility.

This lampoon is an example of the *tongunið*, a poem composed for a particular occasion only; there is also the *trénið*, consisting of figures and runes carved on a pole, often obscene in character. Both were forbidden under heavy penalties in twelfth-century Icelandic law, and both were used to accuse the victim of *ergi* or dastardly conduct, which varied from treason, oathbreaking and violation of law to meanness and various sexual perversions. It appears to have been a *trénið* which Egil raised against Eirik Bloodaxe and his wife Gunnhild when they deprived him of an inheritance in Norway.[44] Just before he sailed, he raised a horse' head on a pole and set this up on an island, looking towards the land; he carved runes on the pole, claiming that the king had broken the decrees of the gods and that the landspirits should not rest until he and his queen, who had wrongly usurped her husband's power, were driven out of Norway. A similar example of a spell by a group of wizards is given in Saxo;[45] in this case the head fell and the curse recoiled on to the man holding the pole. Other examples of the *trénið* are found in the sagas,[46] and it is interesting to note that in one case, in *Vatnsdæla Saga* (XXXIV), the complete body of a mare killed for the purpose was set up on a pole on which a man's head had been carved. Here we have the usual *trénið* combined with a different custom, one familiar in the Viking Age and later among the peoples of the steppes in eastern Europe and Asia who practised shamanism and lived by horse-breeding;[47] a custom incidentally not to be found among the Scandinavian Lapps, who did not use horses.

The working of magic spells to cause immediate death is found in *Laxdæla Saga* (XXXVII), where Kotkell, his wife and two sons work *seiðr* from a platform after they have been hired to do hostile magic against Hrut. They sang powerful spells, and although Hrut had warned his household not to go outside, his young son Kari awoke, because the spell was aimed at him, and felt compelled to walk out in the direction of the singing; as he neared the platform he fell dead. Kotkell and his family were killed for this crime. Similarly in *Gísla Saga* (XVIII) the wizard Thorgrim was paid to put a curse on the slayer of Gisli's brother-in-law, and used a platform and equipment; in this case the effect of the spell was long delayed, but ultimately it resulted in Gisli being driven into outlawry and killed.

A particularly unpleasant type of witchcraft was the 'treading' to death of the victim by a hostile spirit, or by the witch herself in the form of a mare. This is first referred to in a poem on the death of Vanlandi, an early king of Sweden, and is extended by Snorri into a tale of a mare killing the king in his sleep, very close to modern folk beliefs about the nightmare.[48] In *Eyrbyggja Saga* (XVI) the witch Geirrid is accused of causing the death of her pupil Gunnlaug in this way: he was found after leaving her house at night lying covered in blood, with bruised shoulders and the flesh torn from his bones. He had ignored Geirrid's warning that *márliðendr* (those passing over the sea) were about, and later on Katla confessed that she was responsible for his injuries. In *Landnámabók* there is no reference to Katla and Odd, but Geirrid is said to have been accused of driving Gunnlaug mad by witchcraft.[49]

A familiar type of hostile magic was to raise bad weather against an enemy, and Icelandic witches were renowned for this, assisted no doubt by the fact that Icelandic weather is proverbially unreliable. In *Landnámabók*[50] Hakon Jarl called up a storm against Vebiorn and his brothers; Vebiorn had feared this and wished to do a counter-sacrifice before sailing, but was overruled. Kotkell and his family destroyed a ship by using their platform and uttering 'powerful and stubborn spells' (*Laxdæla Saga* XXXV). In *Gísla Saga* (XVIII) Audbiorg went round the house widdershins, sniffing the air like a dog in all directions, and brought down a great snowstorm on a neighbour's house, while the technique of Kjolver in *Víglundar Saga* (XII) was to go on to her roof and wave her hood towards the east. In *Eyrbyggja Saga* (XL) one of Biorn Asbrandsson's poems refers to 'witch-weather' which kept him in a cave while on his way to see Thurid; according to the saga this was a heavy snowstorm raised against him by Thorgrima Galdrakinn at the request of Thurid's husband.

Sometimes storms might be countered by spells. Grima in *Fóstbrœðra Saga* (X) went up on to high ground and recited 'an ancient song, learned in childhood', whereupon the unfavourable wind changed; in *Vatnsdæla Saga* (XLVII) a storm raised by Ulfhedin to prevent a duel was driven back by Bard:

> They asked him to call back the storm, since he was very skilled in magic. He told them to take hands and make a circle, then he walked widdershins round it three times and spoke Irish; he told them to reply 'yes' to this, and they did so. Then he waved a kerchief towards the mountains and the storm ceased.

Another example of a duel between wizards for control of nature is in *Landnámabók*:[51] Lodmund the Old, then blind, was told that his land was flooded, because his neighbour Thrasi was driving the water east to leave his own fields clear. Lodmund found that the water was fresh, not salt, and he then got his servant to lead him to a place where he could stick the point of his staff into the water, while he held the staff with both hands and bit the ring on it,[52] whereupon the waters began to recede. Finally the neighbours agreed that the water should run to the sea and form a barrier between them.

Earlier in his life Lodmund caused a landslide, putting a curse on the spot he had first settled when he heard that his high-seat pillars had drifted to land elsewhere and he knew he must move. When his ship was loaded, he lay down and forbade anyone to speak his name, and soon after this there was a crash and a landslide descended on the house. The witch Groa, in *Vatnsdæla Saga* (XXXVI) caused a landslide by walking widdershins round her house and waving a kerchief into which she had knotted gold, with the words 'Now let what is ready come.' This seems to have been intended to destroy Ingimund's sons, but they had been warned by a supernatural protector to stay at home, and the earth overwhelmed the witch's house and killed all inside. Another example of magic affecting the movements of the earth is the story of the wizard who tried to cause the death of Thangbrand the preacher of Christianity. He caused the earth to open beneath him, and Thangbrand's horse was lost, but he himself jumped clear.[53]

Obviously many of the types of magic instanced could be used for good as well as evil, and the accounts of the divination ceremony by means of *seiðr* may be classed as benevolent witchcraft, as may also the work of a seeress from northern Norway mentioned in *Landnámabók* who could attract fish into the sound.[54] There are a few references to healing, although this, so important in shamanistic

Hostile Magic in the Icelandic Sagas

practice, plays little part in the witchcraft stories.[55] The general assumption in the sagas, partly based on the demands of the plot and partly perhaps on observation of human nature, is that the powers of witches were in general put to hostile use. However, there is no condemnation of magic as such, and many using it were highly esteemed in the community; it was only condemned and punished when used to injure others or to protect those doing harm.

While the sagas contain magic of a kind familiar in later traditions of western witchcraft, raising of storms, physical effects on enemies, blunting of weapons, use of runes and so on, it is clear that a good deal of the material is of a different kind, which can be paralleled in shamanistic lore. Throughout the sagas there is much emphasis on the trance-like sleep of the witch, by which he gains information about distant places or future events, and in the course of which he may cause injury to others. There is no clear indication as to how this state was induced, and Strömbäck[56] was unable to find any firm evidence for the use of the drum, characteristic of Lapp shamanism as early as the thirteenth century (p. 31 above). It is perhaps significant however that Holtved in a study of Eskimo shamanism distinguishes between the use of the drum to induce the ecstatic state and what he calls 'a more passive and contemplative way of shamanising' by which the shaman received his visions 'sitting or lying in deep concentration at the back of the sleeping platform behind a curtain or covered with a skin'.[57] The use of a platform, though not a sleeping platform, which was something not found in an Icelandic house, and the covering of the witch's head with a cloak, hood or skin, is found frequently in the saga stories. It would seem that if shamanism forms the basis of these episodes, it is of Holtved's second type.

There is much emphasis also on the protective spirits of the witch, often in animal form. These might be summoned by the singing of spells, and the witch came into contact with them during the trance. They could be sent elsewhere to gain information, to do battle with the spirits of other witches, or to do harm to human victims. Such spirits were visible to those with second sight, especially before some great calamnity. The confusion between the spirit of the witch in animal form and her animal guardian spirit is characteristic of shamanistic stories also.

It may be noted that in general the witches worked as individuals.

Kotkell and his family are an exception, and the unusual case of the large band of wizards who opposed Harald Fairhair is outside the general picture of witchcraft in Iceland.[58] There is no trace of a coven or a company of witches meeting to feast together and plan mischief; references to the *gandreið* and to dangerous 'sea-travellers' appear in the context to refer to spirits known to the witch and not to human witches travelling through the air.[59] The witch's equipment is simple: a platform, a staff, a hood or cloak, a skin, rug, kerchief, and possibly a sealskin bag, while a small group of friends might help by uttering responses or singing spells.[60] There are two accounts of the learning of witchcraft from a teacher: Gunnhild learned it from two Lapp wizards and Gunnlaug from Geirrid (pp. 23, 35 above). In both cases it is implied that there was a sexual relationship between teacher and pupil, and there may be a connection here with the tradition of the 'spiritual wife' mentioned earlier.

The resemblance between the protective spirit acting as husband or wife to the shaman and the witch or giant fostermother in the sagas is of some importance. The stories of hostile witchcraft indeed confirm Strömbäck's conclusions regarding *seiðr* in that they imply an interest in and a knowledge of shamanistic practice. It appears that stories of shamanistic magic and of adventure in the spirit world have been translated, sometimes skilfully and sometimes clumsily, into a familiar Icelandic setting. In the *Fornaldarsǫgur*, where little attempt is made to be realistic, the stories are even closer to shamanistic material.

Where however I would differ from Strömbäck is in the assumption that the source of such lore must necessarily be sought among the Scandinavian Lapps. The word *Finnar* as used in the sagas could presumably be used of peoples further east in the Baltic regions and beyond, some of Finno-Ugric and others of Tatar origin. The Biarmians were famous workers of magic, and they, as Ross has shown, were a Finno-Ugric people, although akin to the Lapps in many ways. We know that in their penetration into Russia the Scandinavian merchants and settlers came into close contact with many Finno-Ugrian tribes and with the Bulgars of the Volga, who were a branch of the Tatars, all of whom practised shamanism. Two pieces of evidence which point in this direction are the lack of reference to the use of the drum by the witches, and the setting up of the body of a horse on a pole instead of a carved *tréníð* of the usual kind in one story in *Vatnsdæla* Saga (p. 34 above).

Hostile Magic in the Icelandic Sagas

These tales of magic can hardly be based on shamanistic practices within Iceland itself. But the Norsemen who travelled east must have often witnessed shamanistic ceremonies and heard stories of the exploits of shamans, both in real life and in the spirit world. These, like stories of journeys down the great Russian rivers,[61] seem to have found their way into a number of the *Fornaldarsǫgur*, and to have been introduced, suitably edited, into the sagas of Icelanders also. There they mingled with the traditions of magic based on more familiar Germanic practices, and the richness of the new material may account for the vigour and originality of the accounts of hostile witchcraft to be found in the Icelandic Sagas.

Notes

1. D. Strömbäck, *Sejd*, Lund, 1935.
2. Ibid., pp. 191 ff.
3. His brother Gunnstein, also said to be a 'shape-changer', later frightened them by similar manifestations of rage when he thought they had injured Sveinung.
4. A. F. Ansimov, 'Cosmological concepts of the peoples of the north', in *Studies in Siberian Shamanism* ed. H. N. Michael (Arctic Institute of North America, Translations from Russian Sources, 4), University of Toronto, 1963, pp. 216–17.
5. The same trick of rendering the room dark is used by Sveinung (p. 21 above) and Thorolf Sleggja (p. 29 above). The reason is not altogether clear in the sagas unless, as in the case of Sveinung, the story is rationalised but there are partial parallels in the darkening of the room and the use of steam as a preliminary to the shamanising ceremony (A. Hultkrantz, 'Spirit Lodge', in *Studies in Shamanism*, (ed. C. M. Edsman), Stockholm, 1967, pp. 40–1 and Strömbäck, op. cit., p. 116).
6. *Gull-Thóris Saga* XVII; *Fornmanna Sǫgur, Olaf. S. Trygg.* CXCVIII; *Fornaldar Sǫgur, Bosa S. ok Herrauðs* IX.
7. *Heimskringla, Olafs. S. Trygg.* 63; see Strömbäck, p. 46.
8. The problem of Biarmaland is discussed by A. S. C. Ross, *The Terfinnas and Beormas of Ohthere*, Leeds, 1941.
9. *Heimskringla, Olafs S. Helga* CXXXIII.
10. Strömbäck, op. cit., p. 201.
11. Saxo Grammaticus, V, 165; O. Elton, p. 204. (All references to Saxo are to the translation of the first nine books by Elton, Folk-Lore Society, London, 1894.) These are the people of Finnmark, next to Biarmaland.
12. Saxo Grammaticus, I, 20; Elton, pp. 24–5.
13. *Landndmabók* S. 225, pp. 257–8. (All references to *Landndmabók* are to the Íslenzk Fornrit edition, Reykjavik, 1968.)
14. G. Jones, *Egils Saga*, Syracuse University Press, 1960, pp. 11–13.
15. The saga mentions a newly kindled fire and some scarlet visible under

a heap of clothes, apparently Hrolleif in his ceremonial garments; *Landnámabók* refers to the clothes but not the fire.
16 *Heimskringla, Haralds S. Hárf.* XXXII.
17 A rare word *kogla* is used here (cf. M. E. *goggle*), which has the meaning 'stare', 'fix the eyes upon'.
18 *Hromundar S. Greipssonar* VII.
19 Cf. the words of the *spámaðr* in *Orkneyinga Saga* (XXXVI) and of the Lapp wizards after their 'journey' to Iceland in *Vatnsdæla Saga* (XII).
20 *Flateyjarbók, Haralds S. Hárf.* I, 468, p. 580.
21 *Fornmanna Sögur* (ed. Rafn, etc.), Copenhagen, 1827, III, pp. 72 ff.
22 E. Ploss, 'Siegfried-Sigurd der Drachenkämpfer', *Beihefte d. Bonner Jahrbücher*, 17, 1966, pp. 26 ff.
23 *Erybyggja Saga* XVIII.
24 *Vatnsdæla Saga* XIX.
25 *Gull-Thóris Saga* VI, X.
26 *Landnámabók* H. 63 pp. 107–9.
27 'Fostering by giants in Old Norse sagas', *Medium Ævum*, 10, 1941, pp. 70.
28 M. Eliade, *Shamanism; Archaic Techniques of Ecstasy*, London, 1964, pp. 71 ff, 421 ff.
29 *Heimskringla, Olafs S. Trygg.* XXXIII.
30 B. Almqvist, *Norrön Niddiktning*, Stockholm, 1965, pp. 222 ff.
31 For the probable age of this story, see Strömbäck, op. cit., pp. 90 ff.
32 *Landnámabók* S. 350, H. 309, pp. 355–6.
33 M. A. Czaplicka, *My Siberian Year*, London, 1916, p. 212.
34 R. Karsten, *The Religion of the Samek*, Leiden, 1955, pp. 76, 79.
35 A. Hultkrantz, op. cit., note 5
36 G. Munck, *Symbolae ad historiam antiquarum rerum norgegicarum*, Kristiania, 1850, pp. 4–5. Cf. Karsten, op. cit., p. 74.
37 N. Lid, 'Gand og Tyre', *Festskrift til Hjalmar Falk*, Oslo, 1927, pp. 331–50, and the same author's 'Folktro' in *Nordisk Kultur*, 11, pp. 34–9; cf. Karsten, op. cit., p. 87. The word *gand* is found in an early Runic inscription in the form *ungandiR*.
38 *Njáls Saga* XII, LXII, LXIX.
39 E.g. Svan in *Njáls Saga* XII; *Fostbræðra Saga* XXIII (p. 31 above); the seeress in *Hrólfs S. kraka* (p. 23 above); Heid (p. 27 above); the seer in *Orkneyinga Saga* XXXVI; Lodmund (p. 36 above); Hervor and Hord (p. 30 above).
40 H. R. Ellis, *The Road to Hel*, Cambridge, 1943, p. 69. Note especially the ride of valkyries described in a poem in *Viga-Glums Saga* XXI, which is expanded in the prose into a description of two troll-women with a trough, pouring blood over the district.
41 N. Lid, *Nordisk Kultur* (see 37 above), p. 38, mentions the hero riding with trolls on a crook-stick in *Thorsteins saga boejarmagns*, which resembles a well-known tale of fairies. See J. Simpson, 'Otherworld adventures in an Icelandic saga', *Folklore*, 77, 1966, pp. 1–4. This is a fourteenth-century saga.
42 *Flateyjarbók, Olafs S. Trygg.* I, 167–74, 207 ff.
43 Almqvist, op. cit., pp. 235 ff.

Hostile Magic in the Icelandic Sagas

44 *Egils Saga* LVII; cf. Almqvist, op. cit., pp. 215 ff.
45 Saxo Grammaticus, V, 134; Elton, p. 164.
46 *Gisla Saga* II; *Reykdaela Saga* XXV; *Bjarnar Saga* XVII.
47 J. A. Boyle, 'Kirakos of Ganjak on the Mongols', *Central Asiatic Journal*, 8, 1963, pp. 204–7; 'A form of horse sacrifice amongst the thirteenth- and fourteenth-century Mongols', ibid., 10, 1965, pp. 145–50.
48 Strömbäck, op. cit., pp. 34 ff.
49 *Landnámabók* S. 79, p. 112.
50 Ibid., S. 149; H. 129; p. 188.
51 Ibid., S. 289; H. 250, pp. 302–5.
52 The use by the Lapps of a staff with a brass ring fastened to it in the bear ceremony is mentioned by Schefferus (Karsten, op. cit., p. 116).
53 *Njáls Saga* CI; for other versions see S. Nordal, 'Þangbrandur á Mýrdalssandi' in *Festskrift til Finnur Jónsson*, Copenhagen, 1928, pp. 113–20.
54 *Landnámabók* S. 145; H. 116; p. 186; cf. Strömbäck, op. cit., pp. 77 ff., giving Lapp parallels.
55 Grima of Greenland (p. 22 above) is said to be a healer, as is also Egil Skallagrimsson (p. 33 above), and Heid from Biarmaland (p. 28 above) while one witch provided salves and bandages (p. 28 above).
56 Strömbäck, op. cit., p. 24.
57 E. Holtved, 'Eskimo Shamanism', in *Studies in Shamanism* (ed. C. M. Edsman), Stockholm, 1967, p. 26.
58 Strömbäck, op. cit., pp. 40 ff.
59 See p. 35 above.
60 Assistants sometimes sing at the divination ceremony (Strömbäck, op. cit., pp. 118 ff).
61 A particularly good example of this is *Yngvars Saga* (ed. E. Olson), Copenhagen, 1912.

3
The Ominous Wood
An investigation into some traditionary sources of Milton's *Comus*

Margaret Dean-Smith

Milton's entertainment, composed at the instance of Henry Lawes for the Welcome at Ludlow of John Egerton, Earl of Bridgewater on assuming office as Lord President of Wales, had originally no other title than *A Maske*. Sir Henry Wootton, scholar, traveller and recipient from the author of the edition of 1637, 'viewed the performance with singular delight, struck by the pastoral mellifluousness of its lyric measures, and a certain Doric delicacy in the songs and odes . . .', rather (added Thomas Warton, writing more than a century later) 'than by its graver and more majestic tones'. To John Toland[1] there was nothing extant in any language resembling 'the peculiar disposition of the story, the sweetness of its numbers . . . and the moral it teaches'. Of these laudatory critics only one was an eye-witness and did not write with the hindsight which came to regard *Comus*, the title bestowed by Warton, as an early work by the author of *Paradise Lost*, less an entertainment of a recognised and recognisable kind than a moral exercise.

Much has been written about the 'mellifluousness of its lyric measures'; much, especially in America, of the 'graver tones' and of the 'moral which [*Comus*] teaches', some of it, to English ears peculiarly misguided.[2] Less has been written upon the 'peculiar disposition of the story' beyond adverting to its adoption of a theme which the convention of Welcome Entertainments could turn to personally allusive ends, namely the fable of the son of a sorceress baffled in his hereditary enchantments by the exercise of one or another of the stoical or Christian virtues.

It is the purpose of this study to look again at the 'disposition of the story', and to trace what Warton called 'the traditionary superstitions not yet worn out in the popular belief... not yet driven away by puritans and usurpers, [superstitions which] correspond with the complexion of Milton's genius, often appearing even in his elder poetry'. Warton's apprehension of Milton's genius was inevitably that of a Romantic, seeing him not as the puritan and libertarian polemicist of 1641–60, 'writing with his left hand', but as the heir of Spenser, the next great link in the continuum of Romanticism. In considering here those 'traditionary superstitions' which corresponded to Milton's genius[3] (that is 'corresponded' in the old meaning of the term) it must be remembered that to Warton himself, collector and connoisseur of medieval romances,[4] it was an article of faith that only the 'coeval texts' known to an author of the past enabled the critic to discern that author's meaning in the quotations and allusions which the reader was expected to recognise: or to perceive the sources of a plot borrowed without discredit from another work with which an audience might be assumed to be familiar. From Warton's discussion of *Comus* and its performance later critics have adopted the theory of its indebtedness, particularly in 'the sweetness of its numbers' to Fletcher's *Faithful Shepherdess*,[5] the pastoral written before 1611, which achieved success as the Queen's Twelfth Night entertainment and later at Blackfriars (performances more likely to have been seen by Lawes than Milton). More important to the theory of the influence of coeval 'traditionary superstitions' is Warton's own perception of the likeness in the plot or story of *Comus* to that of George Peele's *Old Wives' Tale*, the 'pleasant comedie' contrived from a number of popular tales jumbled together, performed by the Queen's Majesty's Players in 1595, and printed in that year. Inevitably Warton looked to the classical legend of Circe, which had furnished forth more than one court masque, but with the reservation that *Comus* himself (whom he saw as the hero, thereby reversing the convention of masquing, which gave the dominant place always to the noble and virtuous personifications and the subordinate to the ignoble or grotesque characters of the antimasque) was a 'deity of Milton's own invention'.[6]

At about the time when Warton was writing, and presumably unknown to him, a Scottish antiquary, Robert Jamieson, then (*c.* 1770) a child of seven or eight years old, was listening to stories told by 'a country tailor at work in my father's house, in a sort of formal, drowsy, measured, monotonous recitative, mixing prose and verse in the manner of the Icelandic sagas'. The collector of folk-tale and song in a later century will recognise the fidelity of this description, albeit given when Jamieson was in middle life, and like Jamieson would call the 'mixture of prose and verse *cante-fable*'. The tailor in this manner recited the tale of Child Roland and Burd Ellen and, pleased by the child's interest, enlarged upon the wonders of Elfland and its inhabitants. In 1814, in his contribution to *Illustrations of Northern Antiquities* Jamieson wrote down what he could remember of the story in the form in which the tailor had told it some forty years before. His purpose, however, was to identify it as the 'original' or precursor *'in puris naturalibus'* of the Danish verse-ballad Rosmer Hafmand contained in *Kaempe Viser*,[7] the Danish collection of heroic songs, translated selections from which Jamieson had published in his own *Popular Ballads and Songs* of 1806. In contributing to the *Illustrations*,[8] eight years later, he revised the selection, adding an historical note on the *Kaempe Viser*, a valuable if prolix, essay on the manner in which the ballads were sung or related and his recollections of the tailor's stories of the wonders of Elfland.

Jamieson's account of the Child Roland story, together with his belief that the *cante-fable* form ante-dated the verse-ballad, and was therefore 'proof' of antiquity, was seized upon by the folklorist Joseph Jacobs, not only to provide an 'English' fairy-tale in his collection of 1890, but as an essential element in his theory that here was the ultimate plot of *Comus* as well as the germ of the principal 'tale' in Peele's comedy. For later Shakespearean editors Jacobs supplied a source for the evocative words 'Child Roland to the dark tower came' which have touched poetic imaginations for more than three centuries, and to one such at least, Israel Gollancz, Jacobs' theory was tenable and the source of the phrase determined.[9] But a ballad-scholar of a later generation than Jamieson would not so much concern himself with the precedence in time of this or that version of a narrative ballad as with the diversity of the characteristics reflecting the traits and history of the engendering society in which it was current.

Together Jamieson and Jacobs provide a series of those traditionary tales or 'superstitions' to which Warton believed Milton's genius to be sympathetic, and which, on this ground, can be related to the 'maske', later known as *Comus*, devised for the Welcome to the

The Ominous Wood

Lord President of Wales; tales which, moreover, could be directed towards those personal and topographical allusions which an entertainment of this kind was expected to display. That they also could be identified in a rambling snatch of Edgar's feigned madness the court audience at Whitehall on St Stephen's night and the public at the Globe in 1606 might be presumed to recognise. The Child Roland story in some form was, therefore, known before this; whether the *Kaempe Viser* of 1591 was concurrently known and circulated in Britain cannot be proved, though this is not impossible or even improbable since James VI and I had married a Danish princess, daughter of the queen who had commissioned it. Jamieson seems to have assumed that it was, and that the ballad which, in 1814, he designates 'The Second Ballad of Rosmer Hafmand', in which the two principal characters are called Proud Eline and Roland, inspired the lines in *Lear*. He expressed this view in 1806 (Vol. 1., p. 217) in the annotations to the first of the Merman ballads to be translated, but it was not until his 'dissertation' in *Northern Antiquities* that he proposed that the 'Scotish legend' ante-dated the Danish ballad. In the present examination of the plausibly traditionary sources of the *Comus* plot it is convenient to ignore Jamieson's claim of its greater antiquity and to consider the Rosmer Hafmand ballads before Peele's *Old Wives' Tale* and the tailor's story after. But first it is necessary to look at Jamieson's own credentials.

Robert Jamieson, in 1799, was a young classical master in a school at Macclesfield when he began to concern himself with the collection of traditional poetry on an impulse of nostalgic recollection of the 'scenes of rural gaity and unsophisticated nature in which he first became acquainted with these ditties'. Through the Professor of Theology at King's College, Aberdeen, he was introduced to Professor Robert Scott of the same college, uncle of Anna Gordon Brown of Falkland, from whom he received 'upwards of twenty pieces . . . written down from her recitation'. Jamieson thus was unaware at the outset of the work of 'Mr Scott' (later Sir Walter), and the discovery of Scott's enterprise, ensuing as *Border Minstrelsy* in 1803, and the close resemblance of Scott's material to his own was painfully mortifying. He admitted, however, that Scott befriended and helped him and, visiting Mrs Brown at Dysart in 1800, he obtained from her and from her husband more than a dozen further pieces. Much of the contents of both volumes of the 1806 collection is indebted to her, an indebtedness which nearly two centuries later may constitute their chief value.

In or somewhat before 1805, Jamieson took up employment in Riga and there continued to gather material for his *Popular Ballads and Songs*, sending it to Scotland to be prepared for press by an unnamed friend. The consequences of this unsatisfactory procedure were all too evident: the collection is ill-arranged and the bibliographical and historical information is dispersed amongst textual notes attached to various pieces, introductions and correspondence with the editorial friend. To remedy work so 'un-digested' he determined on an 'appendix' to contain both new material and corrections to the old. This appendix is his contribution to *Northern Antiquities*, comprehending some twenty-eight new 'heroic and romantic ballads translated from the Northern languages', but the promised amendments are chiefly lavished on the Rosmer ballads, for by this time he was deeply enamoured of his belief that they were connected with the Child Roland story. He had already glanced at this connection in the notes appended to 'The Merman and Marstig's Daughter' (*Popular Ballads*, Vol. I, pp. 208-18)—by far the most dramatic account of the enticement of a mortal by a supernatural being—in which notes he paraphrased at length the ballad which he later called the Second in the Rosmer Hafmand series when it appeared in *Northern Antiquities*. But as he reprinted neither the First (*Popular Ballads*, Vol. II, pp. 202-9) nor Marstig's Daughter, the 'appendix' does not stand alone, and in order to follow the argument the reader must constantly turn back to the *Popular Ballads* of 1806.

Jamieson was an assiduous collector from a variety of sources, oral, manuscript and printed, who pursued a comparative method that seems to be in advance of his day. He was also a competent linguist, and a ready, perhaps too ready, versifier, with the keen ear which enables plausible imitation of the ballad-style. As an editor he was earnest, and by his own repeated self-justifications, scrupulous. But he was not by nature systematic and, like many another literary antiquary of lively curiosity, he could not resist the temptations of digression and of doubtful etymologies.

One supposes, for lack of better evidence, that he came upon the *Kaempe Viser* while living in Riga, but from a few scattered and derogatory comments on the work of 'Monk' Lewis he may have learned of its existence through the latter's *Tales of Wonder*. Although he included three translations from it in the first volume of *Popular Ballads* he offered no information about their source until a letter to his press-editor dated 'Riga. Dec. 31, Old Style, A.D. 1805-6', included in the second volume, pp. 84-98. He continued the description there given in a note appended to the ballad following, 'Skioen Anna', and revised the whole in more sober, less exuberant terms in *Northern Antiquities*, where he also remarked that the *Kaempe Viser* was known in Britain only by name, or had been mentioned 'by Northern antiquaries only in a manner unlikely to excite a lively interest'. It also seems that Jamieson worked from the enlarged edition of 1695, so that it is impossible to be certain that the Rosmer ballads, which he claimed inspired the lines in *Lear*, were contained in the original collection of 1591. But as he explains that the original 'One Hundred Heroic Songs' comprised 'the first centenary' of 1695, and is careful to give the page-numbers of the pieces selected for translation, he seems to assume that this 'first centenary' were indeed in print, and (more doubtfully) were known in Britain before Shakespeare wrote *The Tragedy of King Lear*. He also expects the reader to accept the fidelity of his translations.

Of the three *Kaempe Viser* ballads tossed, without explanation, into the first volume of *Popular Ballads*, two, namely 'The Merman and Marstig's Daughter' and 'Sir Oluf and the Elf-king's Daughter', appear from their pagination to come from the later part of *Kaempe Viser*,[10] the third, 'Elfer Hill', from the earlier. Neither 'Sir Oluf' nor 'Elfer Hill' has any connection with the Child Roland story but, whether he so intended or not, Jamieson draws 'The Merman and Marstig's Daughter' into the cycle of the Rosmer ballads by appending to it the long note referred to above. In the second volume of *Popular Ballads* he published 'Rosmer Hafmand or The Merman Rosmer',[11] 'the first in order of those mentioned in Vol. 1'. In *Northern Antiquities* he published 'The Second Ballad of Rosmer Hafmand' in full, 'The Third Ballad' and a revised version of the note originally contributed to the first volume of *Popular Ballads*, together with the tailor's stories of Child Roland and other adventures in Elfland, as nearly verbatim as he was able to recollect. All three Rosmer ballads come from the earlier pages of *Kaempe Viser*, but it is the later ballad of 'The Merman and Marstig's Daughter' which not only first caught Jamieson's ear and prompted comparison with 'Child Roland', but which, having itself the chill of contact with an evil, supernatural world, invests the other three with the same magic and lifts them into the company of such ballads as 'Tam Lin' and 'Thomas the Rhymer'.

The common theme of the Rosmer ballads (and also of 'Sir Oluf' and 'Elfer Hill') is of the dangers attendant on dealings between mortals and supernatural beings. The same theme runs through 'Child Roland', *The Old Wives' Tale* and *Comus*. The Merman, son of an enchantress, entices Marstig's daughter by false disguise just as Comus, another such, enticed The Lady. By passing 'wrang-gaites'[12] about the church, the Merman is enabled to enter consecrated ground; by passing widdershins about the hill Roland can enter the Elf-King's palace. In 'Child Roland' and *Comus* the ritual of un-spelling is the same. There is enough resemblance between the traditionary tales and the Maske presented at Ludlow on Michaelmas night to lend credence, on the one hand, to Warton's theory of the influence of such tales on Milton's imagination, and, on the other, to give substance to Jacob's belief that in Child Roland lay the germ of *Comus*.

The Danish Ballads

The abduction

> Now rede me, dear mither, a sonsy rede...
> How Marstig's daughter I may fa',
> My love and lemman gay to be.
>
> She's made him a steed o' the clear water,
> A saddle and bridle o' sand made she;
> She's shap'd him into a knight sae fair,
> Syne into Mary's kirk-yard rade he.
>
> He's tied his steed to the kirk-stile
> Syne wrang-gaites round the kirk gaed he;
> And when the Mer-man entered the kirk-door
> Awa the sma' images turned their e'e.

But the bride at the altar regarded him with delight, gave him her hand and her troth, and 'with fearless glee' danced out from the kirk at the head of the bridal train:

> And down they danced unto the strand,
> Till twasome now alane they be;

The Ominous Wood

> O Marstig's Daughter, haud my steed,
> And the bonniest ship I'll bigg for thee.
>
> And whan they came to the white sand
> To shore the sma' boats turning came;
> And whan they came to the deep water
> The maiden sank in the saut sea faem.
>
> The shriek she shriek'd amang the waves
> Was heard far up upo' the land;
> I rede gude ladies, ane and a'
> They dance wi' nae sic unca man.

Notice that in this, the only account in Jamieson's translations of the abduction by the disguised Merman, no human being, not even the priest, recognises the fair-seeming knight for what he is; only the 'small images' turn away and the small boats flee to safety before the water is upheaved as the Merman 'jawps it up i' the sky'.

The story of captivity, search and rescue continues in the 'Three Ballads of Rosmer Hafmand' or 'The Merman Rosmer', all close variants of each other, of which the first (*P.B.* II, p. 202; *K.V.*, p. 161) may, for convenience, be called 'Rosmer Hafmand and Lady Hillers' Daughter', the second—the longest and most circumstantial—(*N.A.*, p. 411; *K.V.*, p. 165) 'Rosmer Hafmand, Proud Eline and Child Roland', and the third (*N.A.*, p. 416) 'Rosmer Hafmand (or Ettin[13] Rosmer) Proud Eline and Child Aller'. This is the shortest of the three, the least germane to the comparison Jamieson wished to make with the tailor's story, and lacks the identity of brother and lover and the dramatic conclusion of the other two, but it is perhaps the nearest to Matthew Arnold's 'Forsaken Merman' which owes its inspiration to the Rosmer ballads.

The search and rescue

> *Bucke Been og Elver Steen*
> *Og fleer kand jeg icke nefne.*
> *De lode sig bygge sa haard en Knar*
> *Til Island monne de stefne.*
> *(Jeg bryder aldrig min tro).*

This is the opening verse of the 'Second Ballad of Rosmer Hafmand', which concerns the captivity of Proud Eline in the 'castle' of Rosmer Hafmand—a castle which appears to be within or on a hill, although beneath the sea—the search for her by her brother Child Roland, and her rescue by the Child who, meantime has become her lover. Jamieson translates it thus:

> Bow-houghs and Elfin-stane
> And fiel mair I canna name
> They loot them bigg sae stark a ship
> Till Island maun they stem
>   (I never will break my troth).

But the ship sails into rough water that roared 'like an angry bear', and is sunk by 'the laidly elves'. The building and sinking of a ship is common to all the ballads (in the third, Rosmer leaps from the sea to sink her as he has sunk 'to the ground' seven score ships before). It is by this means that Child Roland (or, in the other ballads, her three brothers or Child Aller) enter the Other Kingdom beneath the sea to search for their missing sister.

> 'Twas then the young Child Roland
> He sought on the sea ground
> And leading untill Eline's bower
> A little green sty [path] he found.
>
> Roland gaed to the castell,
> He saw the red fire flee;
> Now come o'me whatso God will
> It's here that I maun be.

In the first Rosmer ballad, the three sons of Lady Hillers come to 'a high castell', in the third, Child Aller, the King of Iceland's son, finds at the end of the green path a 'wee house' with a gilded roof, though this leads to, or later becomes a castle. Only in the second ballad is the castle of the Merman called a knock or hill, as in the tailor's story. When Roland enters the court or garth he sees:

> His sister, Proud Eline
> In menevair sae free.

But Eline's welcome is full of fear that Rosmer should return and cut him in pieces.

Only in this first encounter do Roland and Eline greet each other as brother and sister. When Rosmer, 'the lang-shanks Etin', enters complaining that:

> ... there's come in here
> A christian woman or man,

The Ominous Wood

Eline tries to pacify him by saying that a crow had flown over the house with a man's bone in its beak. 'To win him' she puts on 'a blue mantle' before she tells him:

> Here is a Child frae Island, come
> O' my near kin and land,

and for love of her the Merman swears never to drown anyone 'sae near a-kin', but to be 'his ward and warrant'. But from this time forward, brother or no, Roland is Eline's lover.

> Sae here in love and lyst [pleasure] fu' derne [secret]
> Scarce tha years o'er them flew,
> When the proud lady Eline's cheek
> Grew a' sae wan o' hue.
>
> About twa years he there had been
> But there maun be nae mair;
> Proud Eline lyle's wi' bairn by him,
> That wirks them mickle care.

Once more Eline 'stands before' Rosmer, this time to beseech his permission for the 'stranger page' to visit his own country; the guileless Rosmer (as he is in this situation), delighted at the departure of his unwelcome guest, offers to speed him on his way with a chest of gold and silver. But Eline removes some of the gold and hides herself in the chest, which Rosmer carries up from the sea's depths on his back, with Roland beneath his arm, saying as they reach the shore:

> 'Now I hae borne thee to the land,
> Thou seest baith sun and moon:
> And I gie thee this kist o' goud
> That is nae churlis boon.'

Roland, flown with success, rejoins:

> 'I thank thee Rosmer, thou gude fellow,
> Thou land'st me but [no] harm,
> I'll tell thee now, for tidings new
> Proud Eline lyle's wi bairn.'
>
> Then ran the tears down Rosmer's cheeks
> As the burn rins down the brae:
> But I hae sworn thee ward and warrant,
> Here drowning thou should hae.

> Hame to the knock syne Rosmer ran
> As the hart rins to the hind ...

but when he reaches the hill whereon or wherein his castle stood,

> No Eline could he find.

'Wroth and grim', he turned into 'a whinstane gray' and stands thus to this day:

> But proud Eline and Child Roland
> Wi' gaming, lyst and joy,
> Gaed hand in hand, wi' kindly talk,
> And mony an amorous toy.

Thus ends the most dramatic of the Rosmer Hafmand ballads. Comparison with the tailor's story of Child Roland which Jamieson regarded as its forebear (the folklorist today would probably regard each as a variant of the same tale, or of a similar theme, and lean towards Scandinavian rather than Scottish origins) shows eloquently the difference between folktale and balladry. In the one circumstantial detail and repetition are inherent characteristics; in the ballad of tradition, as Evelyn Kendrick Wells has demonstrated, there are no explanations, no circumstantial descriptions, no characterisation, no apology. The action moves from event to event with dream-like immediacy, and whereas the folktale is one of adventure, the ballad is one of adult emotions, without moral judgment.

> We shall see, while above us
> The waves roar and whirl,
> A ceiling of amber,
> A pavement of pearl.
> Singing 'Here came a mortal
> But faithless was she;
> And alone dwell forever
> The Kings of the sea.'

The interlude intituled a pleasant conceipte, The Owlde Wifes Tale

This entry in the Stationers' Register for 16 April 1595 is more nearly correct than the printed title of George Peele's *Pleasant conceited comedie*, later, in 1828, edited by Alexander Dyce, who

The Ominous Wood

owned one of the only four exemplars now known, and remarked upon 'parallel incidents' found in *The Old Wives' Tale* and Milton's *Comus*.

In date it stands between *Kaempe Viser* of 1591 and Shakespeare's *Tragedy of King Lear*, but, were it not for Dyce's perception of the parallel (which other writers have regarded as tantamount to derivation), one might not look for any connection with the 'romance' quoted by Edgar in the guise of Mad Tom; but when the principal 'tale' is extracted from the rest of the 'conceits' a parallel emerges not only with *Comus* but with the Rosmer ballads and the tailor's story of Child Roland.

The framework of the play, giving meaning to its title, is the chance meeting of three benighted strangers with Clunch, a smith, who guides them to his cottage where Madge, his wife, entertains them with 'fireside tales'. The centrepiece of these concerns the abduction of Delia, daughter of the King of Thessaly by the 'conjurer' Sacrapant. Like Comus, and like the Merman who abducted Marstig's Daughter, Sacrapant is the son of an enchantress, and succeeds in enticement by false disguise. She is sought by her two brothers. In their search they encounter Erestus, who tells a sad story of Sacrapant's evil enchantments which have given him the appearance of a bear by night and have driven his wife Venalia out of her mind. Erestus, by day appearing as an old man, directs the brothers, as the brothers in *Comus* are directed by the Attendant Spirit in the guise of Thyrsis, and the brothers in the tailor's story are directed by the Warluck Merlin. He advises them to 'fear no stranger, avoid no danger and blow a blast at every flame', adding that when the flame goes out their wish will be fulfilled. But, although the brothers attain the enchanter's castle, they are captured and enspelled, while Sacrapant relates how he has learned to change the shape of men and how he has stolen Delia in order to maintain the appearance of youth. He displays a light in a glass: until that glass is broken by 'one who is neither wife, widow nor maid' his life will endure; he can die 'only by a dead man's hand'.

There is no third or youngest brother to succeed, like Roland, where his elders failed, but a hero appears, 'a wandering knight', by name Eumenides. He accosts Erestus and is promised good fortune in a riddle which declares itself when Eumenides bestows his last pence on the burial of one Jack. Jack's Ghost thereupon attaches himself as liege-man to the knight whose purse is magically filled with gold. Together they set out for Sacrapant's castle. When they enter, the Ghost, now very much in the lead, bids his master be seated and remain mute, stuffing his ears with wool, that he may not hear Sacrapant's beguiling speeches, and when the conjuror appears, a fair young man, crowned with a wreath, the Ghost whom he cannot see, tears the wreath from his head, and snatches from him his sword of magic potency. Sacrapant's 'timeless date' is ended, and with the sword Eumenides digs for the glass which contains the vital spark of life and art. He finds, but cannot break it: it is broken by Venalia, who enters 'on the blast of a horn', and being mad is 'neither wife, widow nor maid', and the Ghost returns displaying Sacrapant's head grown old. Delia, her brothers and all other victims of his enchantment are restored. Delia and Eumenides embrace, but the Ghost of Jack demands half of Delia and hands the knight the magic sword; but having 'tried constancy' he leaps into the ground and disappears.

This is not a fairy-tale for a child, but adult fantasy compounded of romantic allusions comprehensible to an Elizabethan audience familiar with Apuleius and Ariosto, constructed upon the recognisable materials of folktale, legend and classical myth. Men are changed into beasts; enchanters assume what shape they will; the traveller in the mysterious country of the supernatural provides himself with the safeguards that enable his return to the land of sun and moon; riddles are wisely expounded, liberality and constancy rewarded; the spell-bound are liberated and all concerned go on their way rejoicing. It is venerable stuff, a common stock upon which any writer of the time could and did draw. That Milton did so draw is a more plausible conclusion than that, poverty-stricken in invention, he imitated or revamped an entertainment intended to amuse the educated at the expense of their contemporaries' credulity, their taste for rhodomontade and relish of impertinent low comedy. Dyce's 'parallel incidents' will suffice.

The tailor's story of Child Roland, Fair Burd Ellen, and the King of Elfland

The origin of the famous line in *Lear*, III, iv, is variously proposed as a 'romance', an 'old Scottish ballad', 'a ballad to be found in Child'.[14]

It is not a 'romance' in the accepted literary sense (though

The Ominous Wood

Browning's poem gives the impression of being an episode in a romantic tale of which the reader knows the beginning and end), nor is it listed amongst the English romances 'known to the early scholars', i.e. to scholars of the eighteenth and early nineteenth centuries. It is not a 'ballad', either English or Scottish, whatever Halliwell may have supposed, and it is not in Child's canon, nor in collections additional to Child. The only known form of the story is the *cante-fable* recalled and published in 1814. Neither Jamieson nor his works have achieved established fame in ballad-scholarship,[15] but the source-notes which Joseph Jacobs appended to his *English Fairy Tales* of 1890 have attracted serious notice, have recalled attention to this item at least of Jamieson's industry, and gained the admission, in agreement with Jacobs, that 'it is just possible that [the tailor's story] may be the ultimate original of the plot of Milton's *Comus*'.

When, at more than forty years' distance, Jamieson came to retell the tailor's story of Child Roland he attempted to do so as nearly in its original form as he could contrive, declaring that this, however imperfect but bearing 'the genuine marks of the age which produced it, and of the taste of those who have preserved it [would be] much more interesting to the historian or antiquary' than 'to have presented this Romance in a poetical dress'. Therefore, he tells his readers, he 'replaced some curious particulars with *Etcetera* through fear of being deceived by memory and substituting one thing for another'. But he was tempted by the opening words of the *cante-fable*, 'King Arthur's sons in Merry Carlisle' (where a later ballad-scholar would see only a familiar establishment of rank recognisable to a simple audience) to make allusions to Arthur's court, to call the 'claymore that never struck in vain' Excalibar, and to add Gwenevra to the only three names, Roland, Ellen and Merlin given in the original. Nevertheless, the story still has all the hall-marks of traditional narrative—the appearance of characters and sequence of events offered without circumstantial explanation, the incantatory repetition of phrases and the devices by which the teller could lengthen or shorten his tale at will. The hall of the King of Elfland, splendid beyond compare, is concealed within 'a round green hill, surrounded with rings from bottom to top', to be entered only by a magic formula; the twilight of Elfland is dispelled by a luminous jewel; the whole fantasy is true to fairy-tale and scarcely touched by the conventions proper to a 'romance'.

Having explained himself to the reader, Jamieson proceeds with the 'rude outline' of the tailor's story, which in the main elements of its plot corresponds to the Rosmer Ballads, *The Old Wives' Tale* and *Comus*, filling in a few gaps with phrases in parentheses.

The abduction

> King Arthur's sons o' merry Carlisle
> Were playing at the ba',
> And there was their sister, Burd Ellen
> I' the midst amang them a'.
>
> Child Roland kicked it wi' his foot
> And keppit it wi' his knee,
> And ay as he play'd out oer them a'
> O'er the kirk he gar'd it flee
>
> Burd Ellen round about the isle [sic]
> To seek the ba' is gane,
> But they bade lang and ay langer,
> And she camena back again.
>
> They sought her East, they sought her West,
> They sought her up and down,
> And wae were the hearts (in merry Carlisle)
> For she was nae gait found.

The story then lapses into prose, and describes how the eldest of the brothers consulted 'the Warluck Merlin', and learned that Burd Ellen had been carried away by 'the fairies', and was now in the castle of the King of Elfland, 'and it were too bold an undertaking for the stoutest knight in Christendom to bring her back'. Nevertheless, to liberate her might be possible to one 'who was instructed beforehand of what he is to do'. Inflamed by the glory of such an enterprise the eldest brother resolved to set out on the adventure, and after proper instructions from Merlin (which he failed in observing) he set out on the perilous expedition.

> But they bade lang and ay langer,
> Wi' doubt and mickle maen;
> And wae were the hearts (in merry Carlisle)
> For he camena back again.

Then the second brother likewise set out, likewise failed in observing the instructions given by Merlin, and again

The Ominous Wood

> ... they bade lang and ay langer,
> ... For he camena back again.

Child Roland, the youngest brother of the Fair Burd Ellen, then resolved to make the journey to Elfland and at length persuaded his mother, the good queen, to let him go. She gave him her blessing, and he girt on 'in great form and with all due solemnity of sacerdotal consecration, his father's good claymore that never struck, in vain, and repaired to the cave of the Warluck Merlin'. There he was instructed in those safeguards which might ensure his return to 'middle eard', the most important being that he should 'kill every person he met with after entering the land of Fairy, and should neither eat nor drink of what was offered to him in that country, whatever his hunger or thirst might be; for if he tasted or touched in Elfland, he must remain in the power of the Elves.'[16]

The search and rescue

'So Child Roland set out on his journey, and travelled "on and ay farther on", till he came to where, as he had been forewarned by the Warluck Merlin, he found the King of Elfland's horse-herd feeding his horses.' Of him he asked the way to the castle, and was directed to go on farther and ask the cowherd; whereupon Roland 'drew the good claymore that never struck in vain, and hewed off the head of the horse-herd', and went on farther till he came to the King of Elfland's cowherd who was feeding his cows; but the cowherd sent him on to the shepherd. The same question was asked, with the same result, in the same words, of the shepherd, goat-herd and swineherd (and possibly more of such for an audience that relished repeated incantations). At last he was referred to the hen-wife, who told him to go on, yet a little farther, till he came to 'a round green hill surrounded with rings [terraces] from the bottom to the top; go round it three times widershins, and everytime say "Open door! Open door! and let me come in", and the third time the door will open, and you may go in.' Whereupon Child Roland drew the good claymore, that never struck in vain, and hewed off the head of the hen-wife; then he went three times round the green hill, as directed, 'and the third time the door opened and he went in. It immediately closed behind him, and he proceeded through a long passage, where the air was soft and agreeably warm like a May evening, as is all the air of Elfland.'

In describing the palace within the hill the tailor had recourse to comparing it with the grandest building he knew, the cathedral of Elgin ('the Chanry kirk') from which, as Jamieson said, in all his life he had never been more than twenty miles distant', and its great west window. In size and splendour it was what Ben-a-chi is to the Knock of Alves. And there, in the light of the great carbuncle, hanging from the crystal roof by golden chains, which 'by the power of magic' continually turned about, was the fair Burd Ellen 'kembing her yellow hair wi' a silver kemb'.

Her reproachful greeting, like that of Proud Eline discovered in the Merman's castle forewarned Child Roland of his danger, and when he asked for food she silently brought it, compelled only 'by the power of magic'. But in time he remembered Merlin's instruction 'not to touch or taste' as the doors of the chamber burst open to admit the King of Elfland crying:

'Fi, fi, fo, fum'

(thus, said Jamieson he endeavoured to render the tailor's gesture of sniffing about)

'I smell the blood of a Christian man.'

Addressing him as 'Bogle of Hell', Roland drew the good—and consecrated—claymore that never struck in vain and felled the king to the ground, but spared his life on condition that he restored the two enchanted brothers and released Burd Ellen; whereupon the king brought a 'phial of bright liquor and touched the lips, nostrils, ears and finger-ends of the brothers, who awoke as from a profound sleep during which their souls had quitted their bodies and they had seen . . .' What had they seen? Jamieson breaks off with 'etc. etc.' and adds tamely that 'all four returned to merry Carlisle'. So through genuine forgetfulness or weariness of repetition the dramatic climax of the story is lost, where in *Comus*, when the brothers fail to seize the charming-rod and let Comus escape, the same climax is deliberately thrown away in order to create a second climax in conjuring the nymph Sabrina from her 'glassy, cool, translucent wave'.

As told by the country tailor, Child Roland, the Fair Burd Ellen and the King of Elfland is a child's fairy-story of brave adventure, innocent of adult emotion and without *raison d'être* for the abduction of Burd Ellen. The only hint of the baleful mystery which later inspired Browning, and of the relationship of Elfland to Christendom on the one hand and to Hell on the other lies in the consecration of the sword and in what has become, or had already become a nursery jingle—'I smell the blood of a Christian man'. Those parts of the tale memorable to Jamieson after more than forty years are those which could excite the response and wonder of a child. The assault upon innocence, the peril of the soul, criminal passion, deception and despair which severally or together are the animating design of *Comus* and the Rosmer ballads are lacking, yet Joseph Jacobs had the perception to see that in this tale could be 'the ultimate plot' of Milton's dramatic entertainment in which a young girl and her brothers were the chief participants.

By the time Jacobs came to edit his 'English' fairy-tales in 1890 Browning's poem had already imparted new life to Shakespeare's line and substance to the jejune story believed to have given it birth. It could even be that in supposedly remembering a mysterious and evocative quotation from *King Lear* the literate Victorian reader was, in fact, remembering the nightmare journey across marsh, stubb'd wood and plain, the ring of mountains, 'the round squat turret': and 'ranged along the hill-side the lost adventurers,' Child Roland's peers.

> ... In a sheet of flame
> I saw them, and I knew them all. And yet
> Dauntless the slug-horn to my lips I set:
> Childe Roland to the Dark Tower came.

Here, by accident, or more probably design, are the elements, transmuted, of *The Old Wives' Tale* and *Thomas the Rhymer*, achieving that same chilling and irreparable magic of Marstig's Daughter when the 'sma' images' turned away their eyes and the 'sma' boats turning came'. The childish fairy tale has assumed that degree of emotion which had inspired 'The Forsaken Merman'. But at the same time folk-tales were becoming established as fashionable nursery pabulum without warning to the consumer to beware imitations.

With these diverse promptings Jacobs set out to present 'a compilation for children, not an exact recension'. He was not, like Jamieson, concerned to preserve the traditional mode of story-telling, nor even the features of the original undistorted. His purpose was rather to demonstrate that Britain, no less than Germany, could provide fairy-tales for 'little people', and partly to present to those interested in myth and folktale—in 1890 a serious-minded public—material which, he claimed, was hitherto uncollected because of 'the gap between the recording classes and the dumb working-classes of this country'.[17] He was thus able to afford himself opportunity for an extensive and erudite *apparatus criticus*, which in turn provided an excuse for editorial alterations and embellishments such as comparison between Jamieson's 'Child Roland' and Jacob's 'Burd Ellen', as he chose to call the story, demonstrates. The result is an unhappy amalgam of the Teutonic and the Walter Scottish Romantic, with no magic and no evil left in it. Between this 'compilation' and *Comus* there is no resemblance beyond a vague mutual indebtedness to a common theme. It would not be worth remembrance but for the source-notes which have attracted the attention of scholars and have given significance to the otherwise little-remembered Robert Jamieson and to those Danish ballads that awakened his comparative sense and prompted his recollection of the Scottish tailor's story which appears to be their only traditional British counterpart.

As Jamieson had become enamoured of identifying the tailor's story of Child Roland and Burd Ellen with the Danish ballads of Rosmer Hafmand and Proud Eline Lyle, so Jacobs was enamoured of identifying it with Mad Tom's verse; for good measure borrowing also the term Etin which designated Rosmer as a being of superhuman stature, he compared it with the vernacular story of the Red Ettin and with the 'world-myth' of Jack the Giant-killer, riding off in many directions, and carrying the reader farther and farther from the supernatural element of the Rosmer ballads and its implied presence in the tailor's story. Himself carried away by the comparative mythology fashionable at the time and the enquiry into 'the science of fairy-tale', he nowhere compares the substance of the Rosmer and Roland tales with those traditional 'English and Scottish' ballads which Child had already published,[18] those which he had placed earliest in his collection and regarded as of greatest antiquity—namely those dealing with that same attempted commerce between the supernatural seducer and the innocent (or wise). It is this theme, rather than any 'world-myth' which links Child Roland in what Jacobs calls 'brilliant literary relationships' to *Lear*, to *The Old Wives' Tale*, to Milton's *Comus*. 'No folk-tale in the world', declared Jacobs, 'can claim so distinguished an offspring.'

> A Mask, presented at Ludlow Castle, 1634,
> on Michaelmas night
> before the Rt. Honble John Earl of Bridgewater . . .
> Lord President of Wales
> dedicated by Henry Lawes ('your attendant Thyris')
> to John Lord Viscount Brackley . . . 'in all rightful devotion to those fair Hopes and rare Endowments of your much-promising Youth, which give a full assurance . . . of a future excellence. Live, sweet Lord, to be the honour of your Name, and receive this as your own, from the hands of him who hath by many favours been long oblig'd to your most honour'd Parents . . . H. Lawes.'

Although the mask was presented 'to publick view' on the occasion of Lord Bridgewater's installation it lies somewhat aside from the Welcome Entertainments customary at such events. It is dedicated not to the Earl, the personage honoured, but to his son, Lawes' pupil, 'The First Brother', and not by Milton, the anonymous author, but by Lawes, whose apotheosis, 'so lovely and so much desired' it is. Lawes, in fact, does not spare the reader from his own achievements; a friend of Milton, it is assumed he invited the composition of a *pièce d'occasion*, of which he was the copier for 'my several friends' satisfaction', the composer of the songs, the presenter, and in the text, the principal actor in parts of protector, counsellor and virtually hero. In a drama whose conclusion was the presentation of his charges to the parents who had entrusted to him—Henry Lawes—the education of their youngest children, it is he, rather than Comus, enchanter and would-be seducer—who should dominate the scene, but this purpose in the 'device' is revealed only at the end, when the three children are about to enter the scene of ceremonial rejoicing after emerging from the dangers that have tested constancy and courage, the Attendant Spirit (who is in fact their tutor) guiding them:

> . . . on to holier ground . . .
> And not many Furlongs thence
> Is your Father's residence,
> Where this night are met in state

Margaret Dean-Smith

> Many a friend to gratulate
> His wish't presence...
> We shall catch them at their sport,
> And our sudden coming there
> Will double all their mirth and chere.

The humbler sort are in the midst of paying their respects 'with jigs and rural dance' as the Attendant Spirit, who is also presenter, composer and subject of the most graceful testimonial ever written, dismisses them with the song announcing the formal revels 'in such Court guise As Mercury did first devise'—in which pastime the children are to be allowed to join. In the second song, immediately following, he presents them, as the Two Brothers and The Lady, to their parents, the Presence, whom the company present has gathered to honour:

> Here behold so goodly grown
> Three fair branches of your own.
> Heav's hath timely tri'd their youth
> Their faith, their patience and their truth...
> To triumph in victorious dance
> O'er sensual Folly and Intemperance.

If the young people, following the expectation and obligation of their rank, were about to enter the service of the Court, as Grierson suggests, in that ominous wood, 'sensual Folly and Intemperance' were dangers they would certainly encounter.

So the poem thus moves on levels both of fantasy and fact, and occasionally almost topples from one to the other, when the Attendant Spirit, disguised as the shepherd Thyrsis, addresses the Brothers, and is addressed by them *in propria persona*. But it also moves on the level of allegory in order to sustain the argument on which so much learned ink has been expended—'such were the three worlds which Spenser, Shakespeare and Milton, were born to: London and Warwick, Heaven and Hell, Fairyland and Prospero's Island'—and Milton would not have been Spenser's disciple if he had not turned fantasy towards allegory. Heaven and Hell he leaves aside for another twenty years; the darker issues of traffic with the supernatural are not allowed to arise, for his fantasy is pagan. Great Pan is not yet dead; the son of Circe and Bacchus does not fear a Christian trespasser in the wood but one 'of different pace, a chaste footing near about the ground'.[19]

The Ominous Wood

The invention

When Milton accepted his friend's invitation (or was it an urgent request?) to compose a *pièce d'occasion* for the installation of the Lord President at Ludlow, there were certain requirements to be satisfied if this were to take the form of a Welcome Entertainment, or—as Milton preferred to call it—a Mask. The time was to be autumn, the hour night. Most Welcomes were outdoor summer fêtes, and the Masque, so-called, at Court had developed not only a strict form but called for resources in grandeur of dress and scenery not to be found elsewhere. The Welcomes, less restricted, and more often dictated by fancy and circumstance, by custom provided opportunity to many people of every social grade to pay respect to the illustrious guest. A 'testimonial' to Henry Lawes could comprehend only four persons, and only one of these feminine. Neither the number nor the balance of the sexes fitted the pattern of a masque, and while the Welcome, with its personally allusive speeches allowed something of a dramatic plot in the device, the circumstances and relationships of these four made a love-drama unthinkable. Some part must also be found for family and friends, some too, for tenants or citizenry, and some gratifying allusion to the virtues of the locality was expected.

When Jacobs declared that Milton must have known the story of Child Roland, and had adapted it to his purpose, he may be limited in identifying one example of a traditional tale, but that tale of brothers in search of an abducted sister, of her rescue from an enchanter through constancy, courage and good counsel, was, above all other possibilities in myth, or legend or romance that which would exactly fit the occasion, and could, by the aid of darkness, imagination and torchlight fall within the resources the castle hall could provide. The hall itself, dimly illumined by the torches which the rout carry by an older tradition of masking, could furnish forth 'the Stately Palace set out with all manner of deliciousness', and it would not be the first time that the table of a state banquet, 'spread with all dainties' was made to play a part in the fantasy of entertainment. The rout first enter 'glistening' in torchlight, then 'run to [their] shrouds within the brakes and trees': Sabrina 'rises' and sings. Very little of the mask depends on any visual effect whatever. The forest scenes throughout are evoked by words, and no part comes closer to the tailor's story, and the Elf-King's crystalline palace within the hill than Sabrina's sub-aqueous habitation beneath 'the silver lake' of Severn river, even to 'the golden comb'.

The device

While the device proper—the triumph of youth bred in virtue over intemperance and sensual folly—is disclosed only at the end of what is in effect dramatic narrative rather than drama in action, the long shadow of the plot is cast by the prologue-speech of the Attendant Spirit who, gracefully referring to the occasion on which

> A noble Peer of mickle trust and power
> Has in his charge . . .
> An old and haughty Nation, proud in Arms . . .

announces the coming of his children 'nurs't in Princely lore' to attend their father's state installation.

> . . . But their way
> Lies through the perplex't paths of this drear wood
> The nodding horror of whose shady brows
> Threats the forlorn and wand'ring Passenger . . .
> And listen why, for I will tell you now. . . .

Comus, son of Bacchus and Circe, 'now ripe and frolick, . . . roving the Celtick and Iberian fields' has here betaken himself, and to every traveller offers a charmed cup of mis-used wine, and so changes their countenance, 'the express resemblance of the gods, into some brutish shape'. Their home and friends forgotten they 'roul with pleasure in a sensual sty'.

Having set forth this simple allegory, the Spirit retires, and Comus enters with his rout of monsters, 'headed like sundry sorts of wild beasts, but otherwise men and women, their apparel glistening. They come in making a riotous and unruly noise, with torches in their hands': while Comus himself carries in one hand his glass, in the other his charming-rod. In preparation for nocturnal rites he calls upon Cotytto, goddess of debauchery to 'befriend us till the utmost end'; but scarcely have the dances begun when he cries:

> 'Break off, break off, I feel the different pace
> Of some chaste footing near about this ground . . .

The Ominous Wood

> '... some Virgin sure
> (For so I can distinguish by mine Art).
> ... Now to my charms
> And to my wily trains: I shall ere long
> Be well stock't with as fair a herd as graz'd
> About my Mother Circe.'

The abduction

Preparing a charm of 'magick dust' which will make his victim see him as a harmless villager (while in the eyes of the audience he is unchanged) Comus withdraws, and The Lady enters. She has become separated from her brothers, and lost in the darkness fears 'the rudeness and swill'd insolence' of what she supposes to be revelling peasantry. She 'hallows' to her brothers, calling on Echo to carry her voice; but her song brings into view Comus, in the appearance of a shepherd, who offers to find her brothers and to lead her to 'a low and loyal cottage'.

The search and rescue

As The Lady follows the pretended shepherd from the scene the Two Brothers enter. The Elder is hopeful, the Younger fearful for their sister's safety. For the purpose of the argument of the mask the three young people (the eldest, The Lady, being thirteen) are assumed to be older and more knowledgeable than their years, more apprehending of the dangers the wiles of Comus have in store, and the Elder Brother now reassures the Younger with the famous lecture on chastity: and the Younger replies 'How charming is divine Philosophy' when they hear a far-off hallow as the Attendant Spirit approaches. He is 'habited like a Shepherd' and they accost him eagerly as their father's servant Thyrsis. He tells them a sorcerer, 'great Comus', deep-skilled in all his mother's witcheries' has carried off their sister; as, after folding his flock he rested on a bank, he heard the roar of the monstrous rout and then cries:

> '... that might create a soul
> Under the ribs of death: but O ere long
> Too well I did perceive it was the voice
> Of my most honour'd Lady, your dear sister.'

Together they consider how to rescue her, and Thyrsis gives the

Brothers a magic herb 'of sovran use against inchantments', which will enable them to recognise Comus, no matter how disguised. Under its protection they must:

> Boldly assault the necromancer's hall,
> ... rush on him, break his glass
> And shed its luscious liquor on the ground:
> But seize his wand. ...

Like Roland with his consecrated sword and magic formula, and Eumenides, fortified by advice in a riddle and the cunning assistance of Jack's Ghost, directed by the magic herb and with the supposed shepherd as their counsellor, the Brothers set out to find the sorcerer against whose charming-rod their swords alone are useless.

The scene changes from dark to light, to the 'stately palace' whose grandeurs are but vaguely indicated. Therein is Comus: with him is the rout of monsters; soft music sounds, and near the table 'spread with all dainties' sits The Lady in the enchanted chair, 'chain'd up as if in alabaster'. She has set aside the fatal glass which holds no temptation for her, and she taunts him with his deception:

> 'Was this the cottage and the safe abode
> Thou told's't me of? ...
> Hast thou betray'd my credulous innocence
> With visor'd falsehood and base forgery? ...
> I would not taste thy treasonous offer: none
> But such as are good men can give good things
> And that which is not good is not delicious. ...'

Visible now in his true form and more subtle than the Brothers, Comus tries flattery of her beauty and the argument of *carpe diem*:

> 'There was another meaning in these gifts,
> Think what, and be advis'd, you are but young yet.'

But she counters with the old antithesis of *luxuria* and *sobrietas*, and an unchildish advocacy of equality in wealth. Suspicious that she is inspired by superior power, and that his own vital force is threatened, Comus again takes up the glass 'that will bathe the drooping spirits in delight' and offers it: 'Be wise, and taste.' But at that moment the Brothers rush in, wrest it from his hand and break it on the ground. Comus and his rout melt away: intemperance is quenched, but sensual folly, of which the children have only a bookish acquaintance, still lies in wait. The Attendant Spirit enters to conduct them out of danger, but the Brothers have failed to seize the charming-rod. The Lady is immovable in the enchanted chair and they cannot undo the spell.[20]

By this dramatic contrivance Milton is able to pay the expected tribute to the country of Lord Bridgewater's mission, and not only to Wales, but to his own master, Spenser 'the old Swain', and, by this reference, indirectly to the Countess of Derby, the children's grandmother, who had been one of Spenser's circle of Shepherds and Shepherdesses. In the Spirit's invocation to the nymph Sabrina which follows, Milton recalls not only the legend of the maiden daughter of Locrine, king of Britain, which Spenser had recounted in *the Faerie Queene* and Drayton in *Poly-Olbion*, but for the more serious-minded of his audience the significance, both pagan and Christian, of touching the seats of the five senses. Sabrina, drowned in the Severn was restored by the daughters of Nereus who

> ... through the porch and inlet of each sense
> Dropt in ambrosial Oils till she reviv'd
> And underwent a quick immortal change,
> Made Goddess of the River: still she retains
> Her maid'n gentleness. ...
> And as the Old Swain said, she can unlock
> The clasping charm and thaw the numbing spell.

The song of invocation, the scene of Sabrina appearing attended by nymphs provided also the tableau of pure beauty, the antithesis to that of the grotesque monsters, necessary to any entertainment pretending to the name of mask. It recalls, and was perhaps intended to recall the masque of *Tethy's Festival* contrived in 1610 for the creation of King James' son Henry as Prince of Wales in which the Queen and her ladies impersonated rivers, each allotted a river in some way associated with her, or with her husband's estate.[21]

Sabrina, Goddess of the Severn, 'rises, attended by water-nymphs', and commanding The Lady's attention sprinkles

> Drops that from my fountain pure
> I have kept as precious cure
> Thus I sprinkle on thy breast. ...
> Thrice upon thy finger's tip,
> Thrice upon thy rubied lip,
> Next this marble venom'd seat,
> Smear'd with gums of glutinous heat
> I touch with chaste palms moist and cold.
> Now the spell hath lost his hold.

The Lady, released from enchantment, rises from the chair, Sabrina and her nymphs 'descend'. Here is used neither 'a red liquor in a crystal phial' nor 'ambrosial oils', but water, *ex naturali qualitate* the ancient symbol of the Grace of the Holy Ghost.[22] Here, rather than anywhere else in the poem are united that 'triple heritage of the renaissance poet', the worlds of myth and fancy, of fact, and of his own religion.

In the deserted palace and its surrounding forest it is still night; under Heaven's protection the small company creep silently away

> Before the sorcerer us intice
> With some other new device,

and with the Spirit as guide leave the enchanted ground of the supernatural for the terrestial world of Ludlow Castle where innocent bucolic revelry is in progress, to be presented to their parents as worthy of 'deathless praise' and of an appropriate place in those courtly dances which properly conclude a state Welcome. These being ended the Spirit, who is also the Tutor, pronounces the Epilogue which summarises the allegory of the device:

> Love virtue, she alone is free,
> She can teach ye how to climb
> Higher than the Sphery chime:
> Or, if Virtue feeble were,
> Heav'n itself would stoop to her.

Thus is stated the Miltonic allegory in praise of Virtue in which alone true liberty resides with which the author has chosen to clothe a plot which is recognisably one of fairy-tale.[23] It is indeed the plot of many fairy-tales in which the enchanter's castle or the witch's cottage lies at the heart of the ominous wood. But in 'devising' a mask, be it for the Court's seasonal entertainments or for the occasion of a Welcome there are other considerations besides plot and allegory which the author is obliged to fulfil. The essential nature of the Welcome is compliment to the persons of honour, to heritage and to occasion, and it was customary to frame this compliment not only in a device that gratified the wits of the audience but to extend it in expository speeches that now make tedious reading and probably made tedious hearing. To this common form *Comus* is no exception.

But Milton, the democrat, pays no compliment to the person of the Earl of Bridgewater, now to be Lord President of Wales and representative of the King. Rather than flatter the royal office he flatters the country whose venerable history has given lustre both to the office and to the occasion. If the Attendant Spirit, in the person of Henry Lawes, is the champion of the piece, Sabrina, 'Goddess of the Severn', is the tutelary saint, though in so elevating her Milton has inverted the crude morals of the unedifying legend. And this legend, rather than some other is evoked solely for the honour of Wales; for the compulsion to exalt the Tudor dynasty was past by thirty years. Of all or any of the 'traditionary superstitions corresponding to the complexion of Milton's genius' this one alone has been generally recognised. Indeed, from previous use it could hardly escape recognition. Jacob's perception of the Child Roland story, as told to Robert Jamieson by a country tailor, as providing the plot of *Comus* has all but escaped notice in the literary eagerness to find it in *The Old Wives' Tale*, in *The Faithful Shepherdess*, in Book Two or Book Three of *The Faerie Queene*; Jamieson's 'identification' of Child Roland with the Rosmer ballads has escaped altogether. Those interested in the evolution or transmogrification of tales may observe the decline of ballad narrative, adult in emotion, unquestioning in its assumption of the existence and evil of a supernatural world, into a sly fireside tale which the knowing could interpret as they liked, and further into an epicene fairy-story told for the excitation of a child's innocent wonder. And they can ask themselves which of the tales Milton chose, if choose he did, for the plot of *Comus*, and why.

A distinguished author, recalling the Oxford of fifty years ago has written of the fashion then prevailing in academic circles of taking some 'great story' and tracing it back to its primitive origins, 'freeing the real story from successive accretions': the assumption being that the older form of the story was always the 'purer'. 'But invariably, by the time one had arrived at the oldest and purest form of the story, the story somehow had ceased to be great.' The power and the greatness were not in the story, but in the imagination of the poets who had made it their own. . . .[24]

But there still remains in the 'old' story, an element of greatness, beauty or magic on which the poet's imagination seizes. 'No folktale in the world', declared Jacobs in short-sighted enthusiasm, 'can claim so distinguished an off-spring' as the tailor's story of Child Roland. *Comus* is not Milton's masterpiece, nor *The Turn of the Screw*

Margaret Dean-Smith

Henry James's greatest work, but the enchanter's palace of crystal walls and all manner of deliciousness is as old as Marco Polo or the legends of Alexander the Great, as native to the Romantic era as Klingsor's magic garden. To corrupt the innocent, the contention of the angels dark and celestial for the soul of man is as immemorial as it is sempiternal.

Notes

1. John Toland, 1669–1772, deistical writer, author of a *Life of John Milton*, 1698, as well as of philosophical works.
2. Of comparatively recent studies A. S. P. Woodhouse's 'Argument of Milton's *Comus*' (*University of Toronto Quarterly* XI, 1941–2) is the most impressive in its comparison with *The Faerie Queene*, Books I and II, and its proposal that *Comus* is an exposition of the disciplines of Temperance under Nature and Virginity under Grace. This proposition is continued by the same author in the annual lecture to the Tudor and Stuart Club, 1949 (*ELH* XVI, 1949).
3. See E. M. W. Tillyard, *The Elizabethan World-picture*, 1943.
4. See Arthur Johnston, *Enchanted Ground*, 1964, chapter iv.
5. Few writers look farther for antecedents of the story of which Milton made 'peculiar disposition' than John Fletcher's *Faithful Shepherdess* (see *Works*, ed. H. Weber, vol. iv, 1812), itself derived from translations of Tasso and Guarini available at the turn of the sixteenth century. It is said to provide the scene of disenchantment (adapted to Geoffrey of Monmouth's legend of the Severn river), the triumph of chastity and verbal passages of 'lyric measures'. Warton's theory that Peele's *Old Wives' Tale*, in which two brothers seek their sister abducted by the enchanter Sacrapant, furnished the plot of *Comus* is shared by the literary historical W. W. Greg (*Pastoral Poetry and Pastoral Drama*, 1906, chapter vii) and, apparently an independent 'discovery', by Joseph Jacobs (*English Fairy Tales*, 1890, source-notes, pp. 238–45).
6. Greg, op. cit., however, proposes that Milton could have borrowed the name and character of Comus from Henrik van der Putten's *Somnium Puteani*.
7. *Kaempe Viser* or Heroic Songs: 'an Hundred Select Danish Songs concerning all manner of warlike and other singular adventures which have happened in this Kingdom with old Champions, illustrious Kings and other distinguished Persons from the time of Arid down to the present day...', originally published in 1591 by Andrew Vedel, a friend of the astronomer Tycho Brahe. A further hundred songs 'concerning Danish Kings, Champions and others, with notes both amusing and instructive annexed' were added and edited by the Rev. Andrew Syv (or Say) in 1695, 'from oral tradition and MSS'.
8. *Illustrations of Northern Antiquities* 'from the earlier Teutonic and Scandinavian Romances: being an abstract of the Book of Heroes and the

The Ominous Wood

Niebelungen Lay (by H. Weber): 'with Translations of Metrical Tales, Popular Heroic and Romantic Ballads from Old German, Danish, Swedish and Icelandic Languages' by R. Jamieson; and 'an abstract of the Eyrbiggia-Saga, being the early Annals of that District of Iceland around the Promontory called Snaefells', by Walter Scott; with notes, dissertations and glossary. Edinburgh, Ballantyne, 1814. The title harks back to Percy's *Northern Antiquities* of 1769, itself a translation of Mallet's *Histoire de Dannemarck* which contains as much of the legends of Asgard as of history.

9 Determined it may be, but the phrase does not occur in Jamieson's recollection of the story as the tailor told it: Jacobs, however, could not resist using it, in his embellished version for the *subterranean* palace of the King of Elf-land.
10 *Kaempe Viser*, pp. 759, 748; p. 170.
11 *Kaempe Viser*, p. 161; p. 165 et seq.
12 Jamieson's note on 'wrang-gaites' (Danish, *avet on*, i.e. *wrong-ways about*) says that it may also signify *backward*, but adds that what the Scots call '*widershins*', 'in a direction contrary to the motion of the sun', was of 'mighty efficacy in all incantations'.
13 Ettin (Etin), a demi-god or giant.
14 Jamieson himself (notes to 'Marstig's Daughter') calls it a 'romance'; Halliwell, *Nursery Rhymes and Tales of England*, 1845, calls it 'an old Scottish ballad', an opinion repeated in later reference-books.
15 See Arthur Johnston, op. cit., Appendix 2.
16 Notice the antithesis, as in the Rosmer ballads and *The Old Wives' Tale*, between 'the fairies' and an inhabitant of Christendom. Each was in mortal danger in the presence of the other. This antithesis, more subtly stated, is the argument of *Comus*.
17 Browning's 'Childe Roland to the Dark Tower came' (in *Men and Women*) appeared in 1855: Matthew Arnold's 'Foresaken Merman' (in *The Strayed Reveller and other poems*) in 1849: Grimm's *German Popular Stories*, the first of many translations and selections, in 1823. Browning's greatest debt is, perhaps to the manuscript version of 'True Thomas and the Queen of Elf-land'.
18 Published in England, as *English and Scottish Ballads*, in 1857–9.
19 C. S. Lewis, *The Allegory of Love*, 1938, p. 82.
20 Cf. Margaret Murray, *The Divine King in England*, 1954, chapter vi. In repeated reference to the chair, and its purification Milton may also allude to the position occupied by the Lord President as the King's deputy.
21 It is particularly this scene which literary scholars compare with, or even derive from Fletcher's *Faithful Shepherdess*.
22 See Nichols' *Progresses, Processions and Magnificent Festivities of James I*, 1823, vol. II, pp. 331 and 346 et seq., and *Somers Tracts*, 2nd collection, p. 211. The masque was written by Samuel Daniel, the scenery and costumes designed by Inigo Jones.
23 See *Lewis*, op. cit., p. 46.
24 Dorothy L. Sayers, *Begin Here*, 1940, p. 105.

4
Witchcraft at some Prehistoric Sites

L. V. Grinsell

By her critical and thorough examination of witchcraft and fairy-lore in the writings of Shakespeare and his contemporaries and immediate successors in three of her books,[1] Dr Katharine Briggs has placed all the relevant portions of the learned world in her debt, and provided a basis for much further work.

The purpose of this essay is to bring together some scattered fragments of witchcraft and fairy-lore associated with prehistoric barrows and megalithic monuments, expecially in France and Britain. In the nature of things this essay is very incomplete. Requirements for a more detailed study would be a more intimate knowledge of prehistoric sites in France and Britain than the writer possesses, and some knowledge of those in the Iberian peninsula, Germany and Italy where witchcraft was also rife; an equally extensive knowledge of the sites where witchcraft is supposed to have been practised in those countries; and a knowledge of the relevant foreign literature far greater than the writer possesses.

The book by Montague Summers, *The Geography of Witchcraft* (1927), is useful in that it describes the main regions which came under the witch scare (Italy, Spain, Germany, France and the British Isles), but unfortunately it provides no distribution maps. However, a general knowledge of the distribution of barrows and megalithic monuments in Britain, compared with the distribution of witch trials, shows that there is little relationship between them. Some areas, such as Essex, Huntingdonshire and Lancashire, which have abundant evidence of witch trials, have very few known prehistoric sepulchral sites, although some have probably been destroyed

Witchcraft at some Prehistoric Sites

by cultivation. On the other hand certain counties which contain large numbers of barrows and/or megalithic monuments, such as Derbyshire, Dorset, Gloucestershire, Sussex, Wiltshire and Yorkshire, have comparatively few witch trials. In parts of France, however, especially Finistère and Brittany, some correspondence between witches' meeting places and prehistoric monuments has been noted by several writers.[2]

In her books on witchcraft and fairy-lore Dr Katharine Briggs has noted[3] that witch-lore and fairy-lore are often inextricably interwoven, especially in Scotland. It is therefore advisable, when studying associations of witchcraft with prehistoric sites, to keep in mind fairy-lore connected with the same types of site. Any prehistoric site with fairy traditions should be closely checked for possible witch associations.

The earliest possible instance of witch cult at a British prehistoric site known to me comes from Somerset, and dates from 1514. John Panter, of the parish of Doulting just east of Shepton Mallet, was accused on 18 April that year of resorting annually to 'Mendepe' on the eve of St John the Baptist's day *ad consulendum demones* (to consult demons), and that he had answers from them which he related at length to William Joly of Shepton Mallet, and to others. The same day Agnes Panter (presumably his wife or sister) was examined on a charge of witchcraft. Now anyone going to Mendip from Doulting would strike the Mendip hills at Beacon Hill very near the location of a group of some ten or twelve Bronze Age round barrows (there were probably more in the sixteenth century); it seems quite possible that John Panter consulted his demons at these barrows.[4]

The earliest certain association of witchcraft with British barrows is revealed from *The Examination of John Walsh*, of Netherbury, Dorset (1566). This examination was conducted before 'Maister Thomas Williams, Commissary to the Reverend Father in God William bishop of Excester', on 20 August 1566, and was printed on 23 December that year. Walsh had been employed by one Sir Robert Drayton (of Drayton near Langport, Somerset?) for seven years, and for the five years between his death and the *Examination* of 1566 he had been practising physic and surgery on his own account. After six charges, we come to the following item:[5]

> Seventhly, he being demaunded how he knoweth when anye man is bewytched: he sayth that he knew it partlye by the Feries, and sayth

that ther be iii kindes of Feries, white, greene, and black. Which when he is disposed to vse, hee speaketh with them upon hyls, where as there is great heapes of earth, as namely in Dorsetshire. And betwene the houres of xii and one at noone,[6] or at midnight he vseth them. Whereof (he sayth) the black Feries be the woorst.

Walsh went on to explain that he used witchcraft derived from the fairies only for searching for stolen goods. It is clear that he sought his powers from fairies believed to inhabit some of the prehistoric barrows (of which more than 1800 still remain) on the hills and heaths of Dorset. Indeed a barrow has been located in Walsh's own parish of Netherbury.[7]

Another possible instance comes from the trial of Elizabeth Pratt of Dunstable, Bedfordshire, in 1667:[8]

> Elizabeth Pratt, when asked about two children of Thomas Heyward who were said to have been bewitched to death, accused instead three other Dunstable women. She said that 'the devill appeared to her about a fortnight since in the form of a catt, and Commanded [her] to goe to those three persons aforesaid to seeke the destroying of the two Children . . .' She said she was with them when they mett to bewitch the eldest childe of the said Heyward, and that they had two meetings about it whereof one was at the Three Knolls upon the Dunstable Downes, and the other a little lower upon the said Downes.

The 'Three Knolls' are of course the well-known group of Bronze Age barrows now known as the Five Knolls, three of which are bell-shaped and enclosed by the same ditch. Elizabeth Pratt was committed to Bedford Goal where her name occurs next to that of John Bunyan in the prison register.

From Scotland come the following instances of those accused of witchcraft describing their visits to fairies in fairy-hills:[9]

1623	Perth	Isabel Haldane told of a fairyland in a hollow hill.
1654		Jacob Behmen knocked three times at a fairy hill which opened and the fairies gave him white powder to effect cures.
1664		Isobel Gowdie's confession describes her visits to a Fairy Hill and the evil charms which she learned there.

In his *Secret Commonwealth of Elves, Fauns and Fairies*[10] Robert Kirk mentioned that 'there be many Places called Fairie-hills, which the

Witchcraft at some Prehistoric Sites

Mountain People think impious and dangerous to peel or discover, by taking Earth or Wood from them: superstitiously believing the Souls of their Predicessors to dwell there.' As is well known, his own death seems to have taken the form of entering a Fairy Hill from which he never returned. Although there may here be no connection with witches, fairies and witches are so intermingled in the Scottish tradition that it seems advisable not to exclude the Fairy Hills of Robert Kirk. What we should like to know is, how many Scottish Fairy Hills are barrows and how many are not.

Before leaving Scotland, it is well to mention that the spot in Fifeshire where Macbeth is supposed to have had his dramatic encounter with the three witches is marked by a standing stone called the Witches' Stone. The present writer is unaware whether it was set up in prehistoric times.

It is now opportune to examine various claims that relics connected with witchcraft have been discovered in prehistoric stone cists and barrows. Vague references to the finding of human hair in a stone cist on Whiten Tor (Dartmoor) and in another Dartmoor stone cist the location of which was not clearly stated,[11] are supported by the finding of two large coils of human hair in a stone cist on Soussons Common near Postbridge, Dartmoor, about 1902. They were submitted to F. T. Elworthy, author of *The Evil Eye* (1895), who pronounced them to be witchcraft relics comprising the casting of a spell on the former possessor of the hair.[12] A barrow on Weaver's Down near Liss, Hampshire, contained a hollow tree-trunk coffin in which are said to have been the remains of black and red hair.[13] In this instance the finders apparently saw no reason to doubt that the hair was contemporary with the tree-trunk coffin which was most probably Early Bronze Age.

At the time the Dartmoor discoveries were made, it seemed inconceivable that human hair could have survived from the Bronze Age; and therefore the possibility of origin from medieval or later times was rightly considered. However, in the peaty soils of Dartmoor human hair might well survive from the Bronze Age; but whether in the form of the 'large coils' described from Soussons Commons is an open question. The problem can be solved only by the scientific examination of any hair discovered in a Dartmoor stone cist under modern conditions. Meanwhile the discovery in Denmark and elsewhere of hair and textiles in Bronze Age barrows, and in the Danish bog-burials of the Iron Age, must lead us to keep an open mind until the next discovery of this kind has been made on Dartmoor.

In August 1961, James Dyer excavated a kidney-shaped barrow on Galley Hill, Streatley, north of Luton, Bedfordshire. In addition to Neolithic and later burials, it contained a pit four feet in depth, in which were traces of a wooden post (perhaps of a gallows), a piece of Cistercian ware probably fourteenth or fifteenth century, a horse's skull, and a chalk dice with 6 uppermost. The horse's skull and dice were thought by Dr Margaret Murray to be relics of witchcraft.[14]

One or two witchcraft relics are described as having been found either at or near the long barrow known as Wayland's Smithy on the Berkshire Downs. In 1939 the late G. B. Gardner exhibited before the Folklore Society, and afterwards published in *Folklore*, an object described by him as a witches' moon-dial used at midnight. It is said to be of human bone with seven sections corresponding to the Seven Hours of Dread. It is said to have been found near Wayland's Smithy.[15] In Birmingham Museum and Art Gallery is a modern human skull said to have been found near Wayland's Smithy, reputed to have been owned by Mary Chalmers, a woman skilled in the curing of cows and sheep, who lived at Little Moreton near Didcot and died on 4 June 1810.[16]

Finally let us turn to France, where the folk traditions connected with prehistoric monuments were comprehensively assembled by Émile Nourry under the pseudonym of Pierre Saintyves between 1930 and 1936.[17] Unfortunately his work contains also a considerable number of traditions connected with natural features, and it is often difficult to decide from the context whether a particular tradition relates, for example, to a megalithic monument or to a natural agglomeration of glacial erratics or other large stones. In other words neither folklorists nor French peasants can always be expected to distinguish between ancient monuments and natural features resembling them—a distinction that often defeats the experienced archaeologist.

Saintyves began his enquiry by issuing a questionnaire which included the item, 'has the vicinity of a megalithic monument been used as a meeting place for witches' sabbats?', and this question was enough to attract quite a number of replies which can probably be considered representative. The information assembled relates largely to the areas of high concentration of megalithic monuments

Witchcraft at some Prehistoric Sites

in north-western France, especially Finistère, the Morbihan, Côtes-du-Nord, Ille-et-Vilaine and the Manche.[18]

Some of the prehistoric monuments betray their popular association with the witch cult by their names, such as a menhir at Vaumort (Yonne) called La Pierre du Sabbat or La Pierre aux Sorciers (i, 48);[19] a dolmen in the province of Nord called La Cuisine des Sorciers (the witches' kitchen) where witches are said to have prepared their love potions (iii, 238-41); a barrow at Wallonie (Brabant) known as Le Lieu du Sabbat (iii, 245) where witches are said to have held their sabbats. Others are named from a special kind of witch known as a Groach, as Le Dolmen de la Groach and Le Menhir à la Pointe de la Groach both in Finistère (iii, 326, 333), and a dolmen at Locmariaquer in the Morbihan known as Daul er Groach (iii, 481). An *allée couverte* in the same province is known as La Maison des Boudiquets, boudiquet being either a fairy or a witch, and incidentally illustrating the close connection between fairies and witches in French folk tradition (iii, 354). There are dolmens in the Morbihan known as La Vieille Femme de Concoret and La Roche à la Vieille, both said to be named from an old fairy or witch and illustrating the same connection (iii, 472, 475). In the Manche province is La Rocque ou le Coq Chante, said to be haunted by a witch who guards treasure buried there (iii, 179). Fairies or witches are said to dance around several megalithic monuments (i, 282; iii, 216-17). The needs of those with a taste for the gruesome are supplied by sites such as La Pierre Sanglante (Liège) where witches are said to have slaughtered children (iii, 249), and the Dolmen des Issières (Yonne) where a witch is said to have been burned (i, 282). The writer has been unable to relate any of these sites to known witch-cult locations as he knows of no publications on the geography of sites of the witch-cult in France.

There are occasional instances in France of prehistoric flint arrowheads being known as witches' stones, and prehistoric stone axes being known as witches' fingers (i, 237; ii, 245-6).

The late G. B. Gardner, author of *Witchcraft To-day* and sometime owner of the Museum of Witchcraft at Castletown in the Isle of Man, founded a modern revival of witches' covens and seems to have had a tendency to hold them occasionally at or near well-known prehistoric sites already replete with folk tradition. This seems to be the explanation of a witch's split-ended hazel wand, used at one of these latter-day witches' covens at the Rollright

L. V. Grinsell

Stones (Oxon) on 1 May 1955. The object is now in the Museums of Witchcraft at Boscastle, Cornwall. It will be recalled that the folklore of Rollright, recorded near the end of the last century by Sir Arthur Evans,[20] includes the tradition of a witch, in some accounts named Mother Shipton, who appeared before a minor King in the area and said:

> Seven long strides shalt thou take, and
> If Long Compton thou canst see,
> King of England shalt thou be.

The King took seven strides forward, but at the last stride a mound of earth appeared before him and obscured his view of Long Compton. The Witch then said:

> As Long Compton thou canst not see,
> King of England thou shalt not be.
> Rise up, stick, and stand still, stone,
> For King of England thou shalt be none,
> Thou and thy men hoar stones shall be,
> And I myself an eldern tree.

Finally, there remains the problem of trying to identify, from objects found accompanying primary and secondary burials in barrows and other burials of Neolithic and Bronze Age, witchdoctors of those periods. A Danish Bronze Age grave yielded the claw of a lynx, bones of a weasel, vertebrae of snakes, horses' teeth, a rowan twig, charcoal of asken, and iron pyrites, all interpreted as relics connected with witchcraft.[21] Clearly in such matters a good deal depends on the interpretation which the director of excavations decides to place on his finds. It is hoped that this aspect may be the subject of a future study.

Notes

1 *The Anatomy of Puck: an Examination of Fairy Beliefs* . . . (1959); *Pale Hecate's Team: an Examination of the Beliefs on Witchcraft and Magic* . . . (1962); *The Fairies in Tradition and Literature* (1967).
2 Alfred Maury, *Croyances et Légendes du Moyen Âge*, Paris, 1896, pp. 38–9; E. Delcambre, *Le Concept de la Sorcellerie dans le Duché de Lorraine* . . ., Nancy, 1948–51, I, pp. 149–53, quoted in H. R. Trevor-Roper, *The European Witch-Craze of the Sixteenth and Seventeenth centuries*, 1969, pp. 54, 127; P. Saintyves, *Corpus du Folklore Préhistorique*, 1936, indexes under Sorciers and Sorcellerie; esp. vol. iii, pp. 216, 238–40, 354, 472, 477, 521, 542.

Witchcraft at some Prehistoric Sites

3 *The Anatomy of Puck*, pp. 19, 99.
4 Aelred Watkin, *Dean Cosyn and Wells Cathedral Miscellanea*. Somerset Record Soc. vol. 56, 1941, p. 157; quoted in Keith Thomas, *Religion and the Decline of Magic*, 1969, p. 445, note 1.
5 Most of the pamphlet is quoted (but in modernised English) in B. Rosen (editor), *Witchcraft*, 1969, pp. 64-71. The passage here quoted in the original English is from M. A. Murray, *The Witch Cult in Western Europe*.
6 It is of interest that at Music Barrow and a barrow on Bincombe Down, Dorset, the fairies are said to make music at mid-day. L. V. Grinsell, *Dorset Barrows*, 1959, p. 56.
7 Information from Mr N. H. Field. The site is north of Emmanuel Cross, at National Grid reference SY 458991.
8 E. Curtis, *Crime in Bedfordshire 1660-1688*, Bedfordshire County Record Office, 1957, pp. 9-10.
9 K. M. Briggs, *The Anatomy of Puck*, pp. 99-102, quoting the original sources.
10 Written possibly in 1691, first published 1815, quoted from the 1933 edition, p. 79.
11 Mrs E. A. Bray, *Borders of the Tamar and the Tavy*, 1879, p. 99; *Trans. Devon Assoc.*, 22, p. 201.
12 F. T. Elworthy, *The Evil Eye*, 1895, pp. 71, 416; L. V. Grinsell, *Ancient Burial-Mounds of England*, 1953, p. 132; R. H. Worth, *Dartmoor*, 1953, p. 191.
13 *Proc. Hants Field Club*, 14, p. 195.
14 Information from Mr J. F. Dyer, M.A., F.S.A.
15 *Folklore*, 50, 1939, p. 190 and pl. VII.
16 L. V. Grinsell, 'Notes on the White Horse Hill region', *Berkshire Archaeol. J.* 43, 1939, pp. 135-9.
17 *Corpus du Folklore Préhistorique*, 3 vols, Paris, 1934-6.
18 Another megalithic site associated with witchcraft is the tomb known as Le Trépied, in the parish of St Saviour, Guernsey. 'It was a notorious meeting-place for Guernsey witches, the Friday night Sabbats being sufficiently important to be attended by the devil himself, and the place is repeatedly mentioned in the witch trials of the seventeenth century'.— (Sir) T. D. Kendrick. *The Archaeology of the Channel Islands. I. The Bailiwick of Guernsey*, 1928, pp. 188-9.
19 References in this form are to the above-mentioned *Corpus*.
20 Sir Arthur Evans, 'The Rollright Stones and their folklore', *Folklore*, 6, 1895, pp. 5-51.
21 R. L. Brown, *A Book of Witchcraft*, 1971, p. 76, quoting Arne Runeberg, 'Witches, demons and fertility magic' in *Commentationes humanarum literarum*, Helsinki, 1947, vol. 114, no. 4.

Note For a reference to two leaden curse-tablets found in a tumulus on Gatherley Moor, Yorkshire North Riding, see p. 92.

5

Some Instances of Image-Magic in Great Britain

Christina Hole

Wherever magic is, or has been, practised, there the making of images for good or for evil appears as a known and familiar part of that magic. This is a universal practice, found all over the world, amongst backward and civilised peoples, in antiquity and onwards through time down to our own day. It is based on the age-old notion that there is a secret sympathy between things that resemble each other, or have been in contact with one another, and that, because of this, a man can be physically or mentally affected by the treatment given to a figure made in his likeness, or to some other object temporarily identified with him. Thus, an image made of wax, or clay, or wood, or almost any other material, could be used to cure its original of disease, or to induce love, or unite estranged friends, or enable a barren woman to bear a child; and equally, it could be employed to cause fatal illnesses, pains, insanity, sexual impotence, failure in a cherished enterprise, or any other form of human misery that malice could devise. Human nature being what it is, it is perhaps not surprising that all the evidence points to a far greater use of image-magic for purposes of the latter kind than for beneficial ends.

If those who practised it with evil intentions were commonly professional witches, they were not necessarily so. Sometimes they were quite ordinary people who were driven by rage, or fear, or malice to attempt a charm that was familiar, at least in theory, to almost everybody, and not beyond the powers of any one with sufficient strength of purpose. Some forms of magic, obviously, were too intricate for the amateur, calling for a high degree of

Some Instances of Image-Magic in Great Britain

occult knowledge on the part of the magician, but image-making was comparatively simple. It was not difficult to construct a rough effigy of wax or clay, name it for the detested enemy, stab it with thorns, or nails, or pins, and then destroy it slowly by roasting or melting it before a fire, or burying it and leaving it to rot in the ground. No great skill or long practice in magic was needed for this work, only strong hatred, and enough determination to carry the rite through to the end.

The magical image known in Scotland as the *Corp Creadh* was made of clay in the shape of a mannikin, and studded with pins wherever the maker desired the victim to suffer pains in the corresponding parts of his body. A curse was pronounced as each pin was rammed home. A slow death could be ensured by placing the *Corp Creadh* in a running stream, and for this purpose, it had to be made as hard as possible, so that it crumbled only slowly under the action of the water. As it did so, the person represented wasted away, and finally died. A Hebridean story recorded by R. C. Maclagan at the end of last century[1] shows how very simple this form of murder was believed to be. Two girls fell in love with the same man. He preferred the prettier of the two, and the other, filled with hatred of her rival, attempted to kill her by means of a *Corp Creadh*. She was not herself a witch nor, apparently, did she need to consult any one who was in order to find out what to do. She had only to remember the ancient traditions of her country and to act accordingly, and this she did. She made her image, pierced it with many pins, and hid it in a stream where it was not likely to be found. Thereafter, her victim's health steadily declined without apparent cause, in spite of all that her doctor and her family could do for her. She became so weak that she was unable to leave her bed; and it was locally believed that she would have died, had not a shepherd chanced to see the clay image in the water when he was searching for a strayed sheep. He recognised it for what it was, took it out of the stream, and destroyed it. From that moment, the ailing girl began to recover. The identity of her enemy was discovered when she, seeing that the first image had failed, began to make another, and was found doing so.

Sometimes the *Corp Creadh* was buried in earth instead of being immersed in water. A rite of much the same kind was known in some parts of Ireland, only there the image was not made of clay, but was formed from a sheaf of wheat twisted to resemble a human body. Pins were run into the joints of the stems, and a heart was made for the effigy out of plaited straw. It was necessary for the maker to go first to the church and say certain prayers there with his back to the altar; then, when he had fashioned the image, he buried it in the Devil's name near the victim's house, in wet soil, if the latter's death was to be a quick one, in dry soil, if it was to be slow and painful. In an account of this ritual published in 1895,[2] the writer says that 'only a few years ago', evidence of such an attempted killing was heard in the police court at Ardee, Co. Louth. A woman of that district made a sheaf-figure to compass the death of an enemy, and buried it in damp ground, where it would decay quickly. Her guilt was discovered when she was detected by the relatives of her victim, going by night to the burial-place and dowsing it with water in order to hasten the end.

This was amateur magic. There was nothing amateur about the 'picture of clay to destroy the Laird of Park's male children' which Isobel Gowdie described in her confession at Auldearne in 1662.[3] It was made of clay broken down to the fineness of meal, sifted through a sieve, mixed with water, and diligently kneaded until it was of the right consistency. Five witches took part in the preparations; as they worked, they repeated words which the Devil himself had taught them:

> . . . we pour water among this meal,
> For long dwining and ill heal.
> We put it into the fire
> That it may be brunt both stick and stowre.
> It shall be brunt with our will,
> As any stickle upon a kill.

When the clay was ready, it was moulded into a little figure that had 'all the marks of a child, such as head, eyes, nose, hands, feet, mouth and little lips. It wanted no mark of a child; and the hands of it folded down by its sides.' It was thrust into the fire until it was hardened and a little shrunken by the heat, and thereafter it was brought out every other day, dampened with water, and roasted again, 'some times one part of it, some times an other part of it', until the child it represented was dead. Afterwards, the image was laid in a cradle to preserve it from harm, and set aside until it was wanted again. 'Till it be broken', said Isobel Gowdie, 'it will be the death of all the male children the Laird of Park will ever get.'

Some Instances of Image-Magic in Great Britain

Janet Breadheid, who had helped to make it, told her examiners that when one child had perished, the witches waited until another was born in the same ill-fated family; and then, 'within half a year after that bairn was born, we would take it [the image] out again of the cradle and clout... and bake it and roast it at the fire until that bairn died also.'[4]

Seven hundred years earlier, in the tenth century, an unsuccessful attempt is said to have been made on the life of King Duff of Scotland by means of image-magic. He fell ill of a mysterious ailment that could not be diagnosed or cured. Some careless words uttered by a girl caused suspicion to fall upon her own mother, and when a search was made, this woman and two or three others were found roasting a waxen 'picture' of the King before a small fire. As soon as the figure was destroyed, he recovered. This story is related by Hector Boece in his *Scotorum Historia*, written in 1527, and repeated by some later chroniclers, but it is, nevertheless, a somewhat doubtful tale which seems to owe more to legend than to verifiable history. Another case of image-magic in the same period is better authenticated. An Anglo-Saxon charter of about AD 963 records the forfeiture of some land at Ailesworth in Northamptonshire by a widow and her son who were accused of making an effigy of one, Aelsi, father of Wulfstan, and driving iron nails into it. The woman, in whose room the figure was found, was drowned at London Bridge. Her son saved his life by timely flight, and was outlawed.

Some very curious happenings in Coventry came to light in 1324, when a man known as Robert le Mareschal of Leicester made a voluntary statement before the Coroner. During the November of the previous year, he had been lodging with a certain John de Notingham, who was a professed magician. That he, Robert, also had some skill in magic is evident from the fact that when, 'on the Wednesday before the feast of St Nicholas', (that is, on 30 November 1323), some twenty-seven burgesses and tradesmen of Coventry came to discuss a business proposition of a rather unusual nature, they saw, and talked freely to, both John and his lodger. The names of these visitors, and in some cases their trades, were listed in Robert's subsequent statement, and so we know that they were all respectable citizens of good standing, amongst whom were two or three hosiers, a mercer, a girdler, one 'who serves Alice la Honte' (perhaps as her steward or agent), and an apprentice at court. Their errand might have been expected to be equally respectable, but it was not.

They began by demanding an assurance from both magicians that they 'would keep their counsel'—a very necessary precaution, since what they had to propose was a simple matter of witchcraft, murder, and high treason. The required promise having been given, the leader of the band, Richard le Latoner, went on to explain that they were all weary of the oppressive exactions laid upon them by the Prior of Coventry. 'They could not live', he said, 'for the harsh treatment that the prior of Coventry had accorded them, and did, from one day to the next, and for the support which our lord the King, monsieur Hugh Despencer, Earl of Winchester, and monsieur Hugh Despencer, the son, gave the said prior, to their destruction, and that of the town of Coventry.' What they now asked was that John de Notingham should, by his necromancy and magical arts, kill the King, the two Despencers, and the Prior, and also the seneschal and the cellarer of the monastery. If these murders could be satisfactorily arranged, they were prepared to pay £20 to John, together with his maintenance in any English religious house he chose, and £15 to Robert.

To this coldly villainous proposal the two men agreed, apparently without hesitation or any twinge of conscience. They were each paid a sum of money on account of their fees, John receiving eleven marks and Robert four pounds. They were also supplied by the burgesses with two ells of canvas and seven pounds of pure wax, from which the necessary images were to be fashioned. Thus equipped, they retired within a few days to a lonely house about half a league from Coventry, and began at once upon their secret task.

It took them from early December until almost the end of the following May to bring it to the verge of completion. By late April the six images were nearly ready, and with them a seventh that had been specially made for the purpose of testing the efficacy of the others. This was a figure of a man named Richard de Sowe who apparently lived not far from the house where the magicians were working. Nowhere in the account of these events is there any suggestion that anybody mixed up in this affair was at enmity with the unfortunate Richard, or wished to harm him. He seems to have been chosen simply because he happened to be handy. At midnight on 27 April a sharp-pointed spit of lead was driven into the forehead of this seventh image, and on the following morning, Robert went to Richard's house to find out what had happened to him. He found him completely demented, unable to recognise any one or remember anything, raving, and shrieking 'Harrow!' In this state the wretched man remained until 20 May, 'the Sunday before the feast of the Ascension'. Then John de Notingham pulled the spit out of the forehead of the image and ran it into the heart. On the following Wednesday, Richard de Sowe died.

By this experiment, the virtue of the other six images, made at the same time and in the same way, was satisfactorily proved. All that now remained to be done was to use them for the deadly purpose for which they were intended. But at this point something seems to have happened to make Robert le Mareschal lose his nerve. He may have been warned that curious rumours were already rising round the lonely house in the field outside Coventry, or perhaps the authorities were beginning to enquire rather too closely into the odd death of Richard de Sowe. At all events, he took steps to protect himself by resorting to the medieval equivalent of turning King's evidence. He 'appealed', that is, accused, John de Notingham and the twenty-seven burgesses of the felonious acts involved in the matter of the images. He appeared as 'appellor', first in the Coroner's Court, and later, in the Court of King's Bench, where the case was heard in 1325. The results of the trial were curiously inconclusive. John died in prison before it began. The burgesses were all acquitted. Robert himself was held in custody when the trial ended, but what happened to him afterwards is not known.[5]

In 1441, Eleanor Cobham, wife of the Duke of Gloucester and aunt by marriage of Henry VI, was accused of conspiring with others to kill the King by witchcraft, and of causing a waxen image to be made of him for this purpose. Her accomplices in the affair were two priests, Roger Bolingbroke and Thomas Southwell, and a woman named Margery Jourdemayne, who was known as the Witch of Eye. There can be no doubt that these three were all practitioners of magic of one kind or another, and that the Duchess did consult them for the furtherance of her own desires. What is less certain, though her judges did not think so, is whether her actions were in fact directed against the King's life, or were inspired, as she declared in her defence, simply by personal hopes that were devoid of any treasonable intent.

With one conspirator at least, she had apparently had an earlier connection. Margery Jourdemayne was a noted purveyor of charms and love-potions, and once, or so it was alleged, she had supplied such things to the yet-unmarried Eleanor Cobham, to enable her to win the Duke of Gloucester's love. In 1430, she had been imprisoned for sorcery, along with two clerks with whom she was temporarily associated; but evidently this was not a very serious matter, since all three had been released two years later, when they were able to find someone (in Margery's case, her own husband), to stand security for their future good behaviour. In the following nine years, nothing further was heard of her. Probably she continued to practise her craft quietly and profitably at Eye-next-Westminster, without attracting hostile attention. In the end, having been drawn once more into the affairs of the Duchess, she found herself facing charges infinitely more dangerous than any that had been brought against her in the past, and from which, this time, there was to be no escape.

Bolingbroke was a magician of a quite different type. He was a man of learning, known to his contemporaries as one deeply versed in astrology and magic. He confessed in 1441 that he had practised divination at the request of the Duchess, in order to discover what the future held for her, and to what rank she would ultimately rise. He admitted that in this he had 'presumed too far in his cunning', and so indeed he had, for his own safety and that of his accomplices. An attempt to divine the future rank of an ambitious woman whose husband already stood very near the throne was dangerous in the extreme, since it could easily be, and was in this case, construed as a treasonable enquiry into the length of the King's life and the identity of his successor. Over the instruments that he needed for his 'nigromancie', a secret Mass had been said by Thomas Southwell in Hornsey Park. This was a ritual designed to release supernatural power for the use of the magician. It was not necessarily as blasphemous in intention as it seemed, but it bordered upon the blacker forms of sorcery because it involved the perversion of holy things to the service of witchcraft. When Bolingbroke was arrested, his instruments were seized also, and later, they were publicly displayed round him, on a Sunday in July, when he was forced to stand in the view of all men, wearing his magician's robes, upon a high scaffold at Paul's Cross. Among them were many strange objects, including a wax figure which was said to be a representation of the young King.

Some Instances of Image-Magic in Great Britain

All the accused strenuously denied that they were guilty of treason or attempted regicide, though they could not deny that they had meddled with dark powers and forbidden practices. The Duchess declared that the image had nothing to do with the King, but was intended only to enable her to bear a child to her husband. Perhaps it was; magical images have been used for this purpose all over the world, and she was a childless woman. Her defence was not enough to save her, nor were those of her companions. She was condemned to do public penance on three separate occasions, walking bare-headed and barefoot through the streets of London, carrying a candle of two pounds' weight. The rest of her life was spent in prison, first at Chester, and afterwards in Peel Castle, on the Isle of Man. Margery Jourdemayne was burnt at Smithfield. Roger Bolingbroke was hanged, drawn and quartered; his severed head was exposed on London Bridge, and his limbs in the four cities of Oxford, Cambridge, Hereford and York. The most fortunate of the conspirators was Thomas Southwell, for he died in prison before a worse death could overtake him.[6]

In 1469, Thomas Wake, a Northamptonshire squire, accused the Duchess of Bedford, the Queen's mother, of having contrived the marriage of Edward IV and her daughter, Elisabeth Woodville, by witchcraft. That marriage had taken place five years before at Grafton, very secretly, no one being present at the ceremony except 'the spouse, the spousesse, the duchess of Bedford, her mother, the priest, and two gentlemen and a young man who helped the priest to sing'.[7] The secrecy doubtless seemed necessary at the time, for Edward was well aware that so unequal a union was unlikely to be popular with his more powerful subjects, and all the less likely because the lady's first husband, Sir John Grey, had died fighting on the Lancastrian side. When the fact of the wedding became known, it caused general astonishment, and there were even some who found the whole affair so amazing that sorcery seemed to be the only possible explanation. That Thomas Wake was one of these is doubtful, for his accusation bears all the marks of a malicious slander, and it is perhaps significant that he made it during the Earl of Warwick's rebellion, when Edward was temporarily a prisoner and safely out of the way. In support of his statement, he produced a leaden figure of a man-at-arms which he said the Duchess had made for magical purposes; and he called upon John Daunger, the parish priest of Stoke Bruern, to bear witness that she had also made two other images, one of the King and the second of Elisabeth. These, obviously, like many similar pairs before and after them, were assumed to be the sole cause of a marriage that might, perhaps, have been more simply explained by a young man's romantic passion for a beautiful woman.

The case was not heard until January 1470, by which time the rebellion was over, and Edward was free again. The accusation failed because John Daunger, the principal witness, very prudently refused to give the evidence demanded of him, saying only that Thomas Wake had asked him to do so. The Duchess was therefore able to clear herself of the slanderous charge without difficulty.[8] Nevertheless, the whole miserable tale was revived thirteen years later by Richard III, in an attempt to prove that Edward's marriage had been invalid, and that consequently his young son, being born out of true wedlock, had no claim to the throne.[9]

Richard Batte may have been another victim of false accusation. He was a surgeon of Burton-on-Trent, in whose family dissension seems to have been rife. In 1591, his wife's brother alleged that he had plotted the destruction of his mother-in-law and all her children by means of a 'picture of wax' which he had employed a local painter to prepare. Batte admitted that he had arranged for such a picture to be made, but denied the evil intention. He wanted it, he said, to cure one of his patients of dysentery. This may quite possibly have been true, for image-magic could be used to heal diseases as well as to cause them. The appropriate medical treatment could be given directly to the wax or clay figure instead of to the sufferer, or else the ailment might be magically transferred to the image and subsequently destroyed with it. Where the real truth lay in this case remain unknown, for the result of the charge against Batte is not recorded.[10]

The wax image found in Lord Derby's bedroom at Latham in April 1594, was very clearly not intended for healing purposes. The Earl was already ill when it was discovered, but witchcraft had not, as yet, been suspected. Stow tells us in his *Annales* that 'the causes of all his diseases were thought by the Physicians to be partly a surfeit, and partly a most violent distempering himself, with vehement exercise, taken four days together in the Easter week'. But on 10 April about midnight, a member of the household, one Master Halsall, found the deadly little figure concealed in the room. It was marked with spots, similar in appearance to those which appeared next day on the patient's sides and stomach. There was also a hair 'twisted through the belly thereof, from the navel to the secrets'. The effigy was immediately burnt by Halsall in the hope of destroying the spell, but 'it turned out contrary to his love and affection', and from then on the Earl grew steadily worse. A local wisewoman also tried to save him by spoken charms and magical lotions, but she was driven out of the chamber by the doctors, and her healing brews overset. Whoever it was that had made the image had his or her strongest ally in Lord Derby himself, who constantly 'cried out that the Doctors laboured in vain, because he was certainly bewitched'. And such being his unalterable conviction, he died six days after the effigy was found.[11]

What may have been the last surviving relic of a quarrel long since ended by the death of both the people concerned was discovered in 1960, when the house containing the offices of the Hereford Rural District Council was being repainted.[12] A small and ugly doll, dressed in a long, full gown of spotted material, roughly sewn together, and wearing a cap or bonnet upon its head, was found hidden away in an alcove in the cellar. In a fold of the skirt was a piece of paper on which was written the name of Mary Ann Wand, and the words: 'I act this spell upon you from my whole heart, wishing you to never rest nor eat nor sleep the restern part of your life. I hope your flesh will waste away and I hope you will never spend another penny I ought to have. Wishing this from my whole heart.' The handwriting and the appearance of the dress and cap suggest that the image may have been made at some time in the eighteenth century; but what bitter grievance, real or imaginary, inspired the maker, or what, if anything, happened to Mary Ann Wand, is no longer remembered by any one.

In some forms of image-magic, there was no actual figure. The victim was identified with something else, and that object was made the agent of the evil worked upon him. A peculiarly horrible method of breaking a supposed spell, once all too well-known, was to torture or destroy some living bird or animal, in the belief that the person who had cast the spell would suffer or die in the same manner. Zincke, writing in 1887, mentions a woman of Wherstead in Suffolk, whom he had known personally some forty-three years earlier. She was then old and bed-ridden, but in her younger days, she had been employed by his predecessor in the parish as a poultrymaid. The ducks in her charge suddenly ceased to lay, and she, concluding that they were bewitched, roasted one of them alive in her oven. It is not altogether clear from Zincke's account whether this revolting act of cruelty was intended as a sacrifice to Satan, or some older spirit, for the redemption of the rest of the birds, or simply as an attempt to destroy the witch and the spell altogether. She was probably aware that a similar rite had been performed in the same county about a hundred years before, apparently with very striking results, and perhaps she expected that the consequences of her own act would be equally final. Some sheep were thought to be bewitched in the neighbourhood of Ipswich. One of the afflicted animals was therefore roasted alive as a counter-measure; it was suspended over the fire by its four feet, and these were the only part of its body that were not entirely destroyed. Immediately afterwards, a local woman was found dead in her own house. She had been burnt to death, and only her hands and her feet remained unconsumed.[13]

An East Yorkshire story recorded by Addy is that of a girl who used magic of this kind in order to force an unwilling man to marry her. She drove a number of pins into a live frog, and then put it into a box, and left it there until it was dead. When the corpse had withered to a skeleton, she extracted from it a certain small, key-shaped bone—the same bone, presumably, as that used by some horsemen to obtain magical power over their horses—and attached it to the young man's coat without his knowing that she had done so. At once, he began to suffer the same pain and torment that the frog has suffered, and what he afterwards described as 'queer sensations' which he could not understand. At the end of a week, when he could endure no more, he went to the girl and told her he would marry her, though he knew they would never be happy. A similar spell was used to recall a faithless lover at Curbar, in Derbyshire, but in this case the pin-studded frog was buried alive, and no bone was afterwards taken from it. The man suffered excruciating pains in all his limbs, and was finally driven by them to return to the girl he had deserted. She dug up the frog and removed the pins from its body, after which the lover's torments ceased, and in due course the pair were married.[14]

Sometimes a lighted candle was made to serve the purpose of an image. In 1490, Johanna Benet was charged before the Commissary of London with attempting the death of a man by means of a wax candle; as it burnt, so would the man it represented waste away.[15]

Some Instances of Image-Magic in Great Britain

In 1843, a rather similar accusation was made against a Norwich woman during the hearing of a prosecution for assault in that city. A Mr and Mrs Curtis alleged that Mrs Bell had bewitched the former, causing his arms and legs to be 'set fast' so that he was unable to move. Mrs Curtis had seen her light a candle and stick numerous pins into it. She had then put dragon's blood and water into an oyster shell, together with some of her own nail-parings, and repeated a form of words over the shell. As soon as she had completed this ritual, Mr Curtis's affliction began.[16]

An absent person could be summoned from a distance by thrusting pins into a lighted candle and pronouncing his name over it. A girl who wished her lover to come to her could make him do so by sticking two new pins into the candle in such a way that they pierced the wick and formed a cross, saying as she did so,

> Its not this candle alone I stick,
> But —'s heart I mean to prick.
> Whether he be asleep or awake,
> I'd have him come to me and speak.

At some time after the flame had reached the pins, the young man would appear. William Henderson quotes a story, told to him by a Buckinghamshire informant, of a girl who did this with very unfortunate results. The lover came, but in no loving mood. He said he had done so only because he could not help himself, that he knew she had worked 'some devilment or other' upon him, and that no words could describe what she had made him suffer. He then left her, and never spoke to her again.[17]

A summoning spell in which an apple was employed was recorded in Warwickshire during the early years of the present century. A man named George Bailey, who lived at Wimpstone, said that one very snowy morning he had gone on business to the house of a woman carrier who traded between Audley and Coventry. This woman claimed to have uncanny powers, and on this occasion she told her visitor that she would prove to him that her claims were genuine. She would, she said, summon her sister, who lived ten miles away, and make her come to the house immediately, notwithstanding the fact that she had no normal means of communicating with her. She then took an apple, ran twelve new pins into it, repeated some inaudible words over it, and put it into the fire. The weather was then very bad and the snow deep; it was not a day on which any one was likely to undertake a ten-mile journey without some very urgent reason. Nevertheless, about noon, the sister arrived. She could not explain why she had come, except by saying that, a few hours before, she had suddenly been visited by a strong feeling that she must do so, and had been quite unable to resist the urge.[18]

It was sometimes thought sufficient to write a man's name on a piece of paper and nail it to a tree in order to kill him. As the paper was slowly destroyed by the wind and the weather, so the owner of the name would decline and perish. In Yorkshire, if a newly-born child was weakly or deformed, it was believed that some enemy had harmed it by pricking its name with pins on a pin-cushion. To save the child, the cushion had to be secretly stolen and denuded of its pins. These were withdrawn, one by one, and transferred to a dead calf's heart, which was then buried in the churchyard.[19] From time to time, metal tablets, inscribed with the victim's name and, usually, a detailed curse, have been discovered, buried in the ground, and sometimes in a grave. In 1899, a leaden cursing-tablet of this sort was dug up at Lincoln's Inn. On it were cut invocations to the spirits of the moon, and the wish that nothing that Ralph Scrope might undertake should ever prosper or succeed. This Ralph Scrope lived in the sixteenth century, and was one of the Governors of Lincoln's Inn between 1570 and 1572. Who his enemy was, or what he had done to earn such bitter hatred, is unknown but, as in the case of Mary Ann Wand's image, the mute testimony of that hatred has long outlasted them both.[20]

We know a little more about the origin of the two leaden tablets found about 1789 on Gatherley Moor, in the North Riding of Yorkshire. They were buried in a tumulus near the Roman road; on both, certain planetary symbols and nine rows of figures had been scratched, together with a curse directed against several members of a family to which, if we may judge by similarity of name, the ill-wisher apparently belonged himself. The wording varied a little on the two tablets. On one was written, 'I do make this that James Philip, John Philip his son, Christopher Philip and Thomas Philip, his sons, shall fle Richemondshire, and nothing prosper with any of them in Richemondshire', and on the other, 'I did make this that the father James Philip, John Philip and all kin of Philip, and all the issue of them, shall come presently to utter beggery and nothing joy or prosper with them in Richemondshire.' This second and more vicious malediction was signed 'J. Philip' on the reverse side. The Somerset Herald, J. C. Brooke, who was consulted when the tablets were discovered, said that the family in question was probably that of Philip of Brignall. In 1575, the property seems to have been held by James, the second of Henry Philip's two sons, in spite of the fact that his elder brother, Charles, was still alive and had two sons of his own. It is not known why Charles was thus passed over, or what family quarrel or injustice lay at the root of the matter. One of his sons was called John, and it is possible that he was the 'J. Philip' who wrote and signed the curse on the leaden tablet. Apparently the magic worked, at least partially. It is recorded that after James's time, the family ceased to prosper, and within two generations the direct male line had failed. The land passed into other hands through the marriage of a daughter.[21]

Notes

1 R. C. Maclagan, 'Notes on folklore objects collected in Argyleshire', *Folk-Lore*, vol. 6, 1895.
2 Bryan J. Jones, letter in *Folk-Lore*, vol. 6, 1895.
3 Robert Pitcairn, *Ancient Criminal Trials in Scotland*, vol. 3, 1833.
4 Ibid.
5 *Parliamentary Writs*, ed. F. C. Palgrave, 1827–30, vol. 2.
6 *An English Chronicle . . .*, ed. J. S. Davies, 1856 (Camden Society, vol. 64); *Three Fifteenth Century Chronicles*, ed. J. Gairdner, 1880 (Camden Society, n.s., vol. 28).
7 Fabyan's *Chronicle*, ed. H. Ellis, 1811.
8 *Rolls of Parliament*, vol. 6 (9 Edward IV).
9 *Rolls of Parliament*, vol. 6 (1 Ric. III).
10 *Historical MSS. Commission*, 12th Report.
11 John Stow, *Annales, or a General Chronicle of England, Begun by John Stow: Continued and Augmented . . . by Edmund Howes*, 1631.
12 *Hereford Times*, 22 January 1960.
13 Rev. F. Barham Zincke, *Some Materials for the History of Wherstead*, 1887.
14 S. O. Addy, *Household Tales and Other Tradition Remains . . .*, 1895.
15 W. H. Hale, *A Series of Precedents and Proceedings . . .* from *Act-Books of Ecclesiastical Courts in the Diocese of London*, 1847.
16 *Norfolk Annals*, ed. Mackie, vol. 1, 1901.
17 William Henderson, *Notes on the Folk Lore of the Northern Counties of England and the Borders*, 1866.
18 J. Harvey Bloom, *Folk Lore, Old Customs and Superstitions of Shakespeareland*, 1929.

19 R. Blakeborough, *Wit, Character, Folklore and Customs of the North Riding of Yorkshire*, 2nd ed., 1911.
20 *Proceedings of the Society of Antiquaries*, 2nd series, vol. 18, 1899–1901.
21 T. Whellan *et al.*, *History and Topography of the City of York and the North Riding of Yorkshire*, 1859.

6
The Jew as a Witch Figure

Venetia Newall

Racial prejudice is not an attractive subject but I believe that, if the study of folklore is to become meaningful in this country, it must turn its attention to matters of importance in our society. Too often, and I am afraid, not entirely without justification, the English folklorist has been regarded as an antiquarian romantic, who has turned his back on the contemporary situation, escaping from its pressures and its problems into an idealised Merry England filled with May poles, thatched cottages, and country folk in hand-made smocks, perpetually smiling.

As a natural corollary to this there has been a tendency to avoid offensive, embarrassing topics. It is my contention that such an attitude does our subject a great disservice. These materials should be brought out into the light of day and analysed. Much of what we are about to consider is both painful and highly distasteful. Precisely for this reason it provides us with an important social document, which should be of interest to sociologists, social workers, welfare workers and all those concerned with the improvement of race relations. Antisemitism, like all aspects of racialism, is a folkloric attitude, and a deeper grasp of its inherent features can be gained by relating it to those in general.

Anti-semitism in Europe is by no means a thing of the past. To quote only a few random examples: a poll taken in France during November 1966 showed that 10 per cent were anti-semites, 20 per cent exhibited anti-semitic characteristics, and less than a quarter of the population imagined that Jews were no different from people in general, 1 per cent supported the Nazi extermination policy, many thought the Jews too numerous in trade, and 38 per cent had stronger feelings on this point.[1] Persecution of the Jews in the Soviet Union has been well documented in current press reports. As recently as 1972 *The Times* carried a report that: 'The Chief Rabbi of Great Britain, Dr Immanuel Jakobovits, and his family, conducted a symbolic Passover service outside the Russian Embassy in London yesterday in protest against the oppression of Soviet Jews.'[2] During the period of Hitler's rise to power the *Daily Dispatch* observed: 'There is no doubt that at least nine-tenths of the inhabitants of the British Isles think the worse of a man if they are told he is a Jew.'[3] Again, the *East Anglian Daily Times*: 'The fact has to be recognized that Christians generally do not take kindly to the Jewish race ... Not a few Englishmen regard Jews with a vague unfriendly toleration not far removed from dislike ... and share ... the wonder expressed in the lines "How Odd of God to Choose the Jews".'[4] In 1936 the *New Statesman* observed that there was, among the Jews, 'a pushing and unsporting minority', and those who were 'money-seeking-at-any-price', the reason for this being that, 'the average poorish Jew had a different glandular make-up from the average poorish Englishman'.[5] This is almost reminiscent of the famous remark by the German Communist leader Ruth Fischer, when the Communists were seeking to collaborate with the Nazis in the early 1920s: 'You are against the stock market jobbers. Fine. Trample the Jewish capitalists down, hang them from the lamp-posts ... But ... how do you feel about the big capitalists?'[6] More recently Bernard Levin was able to write in the *New Statesman*:[7]

> 'You are an extremely dirty little Yid,' said the letter from the Midlands, 'and it is only people's politeness that prevents them from telling you so.' I felt greatly relieved that people are so polite, I can tell you; just fancy if they had been rude! ... I read a sample of these letters, chosen at random, and was struck by the extraordinary high proportion in which the dominant note was anti-semitism of an extremely violent kind, the majority saying that I ought to be put in a gas-chamber, or at any rate that it was a pity that I had not been ... If anyone doubts that it would have been possible to staff British concentration-camps, he can have my postbag after my next outrage. And it won't just consist of illiterate scrawls; if previous experience is typical, there will be plenty of expensive headed notepaper from the Montpelier Square area.

The Jew as a Witch Figure

The role which folklore can play in the formation of such attitudes is touched upon by Bruno Lasker:[8]

> The word 'Jew' always awakens in my mind a momentary feeling of unpleasantness. I have never had any experience with a Jew which would arouse this feeling and I was unable to account for it until I remembered a fairy tale which somebody read to me when I was small. In this story, the villain is a Jew, lying, thieving, and altogether a despicable character. The story must have made a deep impression on me: as I had never seen a Jew, my childish mind pictured them all like this one.

The subject of anti-semitism is so vast, and so much has been written about it, that it is impossible to give more than an impressionistic account, even of one aspect of it, in one short paper. What I have endeavoured to do is to isolate certain facets of the phenomenon which struck me as being peculiarly the province of the folklorist and which have relevance to the concept of the Jew as a witch figure. The legend of the Wandering Jew, a sinister concept traditionally associated in general with ill omen (Tale Type number 777 in the Aarne-Thompson Index), appears to be a folk narrative explanation of the Diaspora, arising from a misunderstanding of its historical and geographical significance.[9] The role played by the Diaspora in conjuring up ideas of hate is evident from the following remarks of the anti-semitic ethnologist Friedrich von Hellwald in an article published in 1872:[10]

> From an anthropological point of view, the Jew who lives in our midst stands quite as far apart from us as the Arab... The European feels, so to speak, instinctively in the Jew who stands over against him the foreigner who has immigrated from Asia... A further specific feature of Judaism is its extraordinary geographical extent and its remarkable power of adaptation... All over the world, in all climates, Jews live in content and prosperity, in spite of having in some places to suffer very hard civil and social pressure.[11]

Traditionally it is said that the Dispersion of the Jews was the result of a curse, a divine punishment for the murder of Christ, an attitude encouraged by Christian theology, which has tended to teach the dating of the Diaspora from AD 70, the year when Titus captured Jerusalem and destroyed the second temple. St Augustine's remarks are characteristic: 'The Jews, however, who refused to believe in Him and killed Him... were miserably despoiled by the Romans and were utterly rooted out from their own kingdom ... and were scattered over the whole world'.[12] Again, in a work published in America at the outset of the Nazi terror: 'The Jews as a nation refused to accept Christ, and since His time they have been wanderers on the earth without a temple or a sacrifice and without the Messias.'[13] And here are two quotations from Roman Catholic school books: 'That his blood be upon us and upon our children! And God, my children, has granted this terrible prayer of the Jews. For more than nineteen centuries, the Jewish people have been dispersed throughout the world, and have kept the stain of their deicide'; 'Until the end of time, children of Israel in dispersion will carry the curses which their fathers have called down upon them.'[14] A large body of material on this subject was collected by the late Professor Jules Isaac, work which led to a widespread revision of Catholic and Protestant religious instruction materials.[15] It is of some interest in this connection that, as late as 1947, it was necessary for the International Emergency Council of Christians and Jews, which met in that year at Seelisberg, Switzerland, to urge the churches to 'avoid promoting the superstitious notion that the Jewish people is reprobate, accursed, reserved for a destiny of suffering'.[16]

The legend of the Wandering Jew,[17] one of the most extensive and pervasive migratory legends, seems to have first appeared during the thirteenth century, when mass expulsions of Jews from Western Europe were in progress. Loewenstein, in his book *Christians and Jews*, comments:[18]

> Similar currents of collective psychology made their appearance in France after the defeat of 1940. Many Frenchmen began to talk of the Jews as a 'nomadic' people. Obviously this was an attempt to justify in advance the anti-semitic decrees to be promulgated by the Vichy government. It was also a convenient way for the French people to rid themselves of any sense of guilt, for surely it is in the nature of nomads to 'move on'. The anti-semitic decrees, therefore, could be regarded simply as the natural consequences of the migratory tendencies of the Jews.

Sir Thomas Browne describes the legend as follows:[19]

> The story of the Wandering Jew is very strange, and will hardly obtain belief; yet is there a fermall account thereof set down by Mathew Paris, from the report of an Armenian Bishop, who came

The Jew as a Witch Figure

into this kingdom about four hundred years ago, and had often entertained this wanderer at his table. That he was then alive, was first called Cartaphilus, was the keeper of the Judgment Hall, whence thrusting out our Saviour with expostulation of his story, was condemned to stay untill his return; was after baptized by Ananias, and by the name of Joseph; was thirty years old in the dayes of our Saviour, remembred the Saints that arised with him, the making of the Apostles Creed, and their several peregrinations. Surely were this true, he might be an happy arbitrator in many Christian controversies; but must unpardonably condemn the obstinacy of the Jews, who can contemn the Rhetorick of such miracles, and blindly behold so living and lasting conversions.

The Ellis edition of Brand's *Popular Antiquities* enlarges upon this account:[20]

No sooner was his doom pronounced than he found himself hurried from family and friends; compelled to be a restless vagabond on the face of the earth. At the end of every hundred years he is seized with a strange malady that terminates in a trance of several days duration; on emerging from which he reverts to the same physical condition as that in which he was when Jesus suffered, at which period he was thirty years of age... On Easter Sunday of 1542, two German students met him in a church in Hamburg, listening to the sermon with marked attention. He was very tall; with white hair reaching below the middle of his back, a beard below his girdle, and naked feet, though the weather was cold. Conversing with the students, he gave his name as Ahasuerus, and represented that he was a thriving shoemaker at the time of the Crucifixion. When Jesus fell beneath the weight of the cross against the wall of his house, he rudely repulsed him and, pointing to Calvary, said, 'Get on, blasphemer, to thy doom.' Jesus replying, 'I will stop and rest; but thou shalt march onward until I return!' Twenty years after he reappeared in Strasbourg, and reminded the magistrates that he had passed through the place two centuries before, his statement being verified by reference to the police-register of the city. He inquired after the students, and declared that, since his conversation with them, he had visited the remotest part of the East Indies. In 1604 he visited France. The 'True History of his life as taken from his own lips' was printed at Bordeaux in 1608, and his complaint, set to a popular air, was a favourite ballad. The learned Louvet saw him returning from mass on a Sunday at Beauvais, when, surrounded by a crowd of women and children, he recounted anecdotes of the Passion in an affecting manner. There are also vague accounts of his having been seen at Salamanca, Venice, and Naples, where he was a successful gambler. On 22 April 1771, he visited Brussels, where he sat for his portrait to illustrate the ballad composed on his interview with certain burgesses some centuries before.

Krappe, the author of *The Science of Folk-Lore*, believed the origins of the legend were semi-learned, owing something to the Arabic figure Al-Khidr, everlasting, wandering, bestowing rewards on the good and punishment on evil-doers, an influence which, he believed, could have been brought to Europe at the time of the crusades. It became, he says, an allegory of the Jewish people.[21]

Many writers, including Shelley, Southey, Wordsworth, Byron and Crabbe, have either utilised the legend, or made some reference to it. Various ballads were sold by pedlars in France during the seventeenth century. One begins:[22]

> Est-il rien sur la terre
>   Qui sont plus surprenant
> Que la grande misère
>   Du pauvre Juif-errant?
> Que son sort malheureux
> Paraît triste et fâcheux!

A seventeenth-century ballad is reprinted in Percy's *Reliques*:[23]

> When as in fair Jerusalem
>   Our Saviour Christ did live,
> And for the sins of all the world
>   His own dear life did give,
> The wicked Jews with scoffs and scorn
>   Did dailye him molest,
> That never till he left his life
>   Our Saviour could not rest.

During the sixteenth century there were reports of visits by the Wandering Jew from the leading cities of Europe.[24] Local variants were collected in Britain. At the beginning of this century a Glamorgan farmer described how a handsome stranger came to his grandfather's home to rent accommodation, courted his Aunt Winifred and in due course left, saying: 'It is my fate to win love; it is my doom never to marry.' Winifred pined away and died. Twenty years later the handsome stranger was seen in the cemetery by her grave and was declared by those who saw him to be the Wandering Jew.[25] Here the mysterious coming and going of a

The Jew as a Witch Figure

good looking stranger to the district is sufficient to start a rumour that the unknown man is the Wandering Jew.

In 1948 there were two reports that Ahasuerus had been seen in the Men's Lavatory at the main branch of the New York Public Library and George Anderson, who made a lengthy study of the legend, refers to a man he had actually met, who believed himself to be the Wandering Jew.[26] It would be interesting to know whether this particular form of mental disturbance was ever at all common and, if so, what part it might have played in the formation of the legend.

The tale of the Wandering Jew has not been confined to print and the spoken word. A series of engravings by Gustave Doré appeared in the nineteenth century, Jacques Halévy composed an opera, *Le Juif errant* in 1852, and there are dolls, puppets, coins and games of cards and dice which deal with the theme. Several plants were called the Wandering Jew: Kenilworth ivy, strawberry geranium and *zebrina pendula*, which grows rapidly, with or without sunlight.[27] In each case the names are not old and appear to date from the middle of the nineteenth century.

In Nazi Germany the legend was resuscitated with new and sinister force, for example in *Völkischer Beobachter*, the official party paper:[28]

> All the suggestions for a lasting status, a lasting regulation of Jews in Germany, fail to solve the Jewish question inasmuch as they fail to rid Germany of the Jews. And this is the whole point ... We must build up our State without Jews. They can never be anything but stateless aliens, they can never have any legal or constitutional status. Only by this means can Ahasuerus be forced once again to take up his wanderer's staff.

Here, in its most extreme form, is the concept of the Jew as eternal exile and wanderer, outside society and apart from it, an idea which must spring in essence from the traditional dislike of the stranger in the midst of a closely knit national, social or religious unit, particularly in the past, when opportunities for travel, and hence cultural exchange, were so much more limited. This notion appears in folklore in various forms. He is of immense stature; no ordinary man but a giant who strides across the world in Seven League Boots—this from Spain and Portugal.[29] In Swiss legend his shadow is half an hour long[30] and in France a mighty boulder was a grain of sand which fell from his shoe.[31] Sometimes he was a storm spirit: when a strong wind arose, peasants in nineteenth-century Brittany and Picardy would cross themselves, saying 'C'est le Juif-errant qui passe!'[32] He also spreads disease—bringing epidemics, famine, decay and desolation in his wake. These aetiological legends are especially associated with the bleak mountainous regions of France, Germany, Switzerland and the Tyrol[33] and purport to explain the sinister appearance of regions perpetually covered in ice and snow.

Sometimes he inhabits the far-flung regions of the universe. In Italian belief he is a sea-monster chained to the ocean floor,[34] or an earth-spirit, living inside the ground and eternally digging a pit which will reach to hell.[35] In Lithuania he is of timeless age, the grandson of Jacob, and in Spain and Portugal he outlives Methuselah,[36] an element stressed by association with the scenery which he sometimes blights. There is a French legend that he used to travel from Italy to France across fields of ripening grain, but, when he returned, God had removed them and put in their place forests of pine trees. The next time everything was covered with snow and ice:[37] '"Bah!" dit le Juif, "la neige et la glace fondront; je repasserai l'an prochain." Mais Dieu l'entendit et dit: "Rien ne fondra et jusqu'au jour de jugement dernier la neige y restera." Voilà pourquoi le Juif Errant ne voyage plus d'Italie en France.'

Sometimes he speaks to the local people, giving evidence of his great age. At Saint-Briac, France, he remarked that on his previous visit a thousand years ago a huge forest grew there.[38] Here he is older than the scenery, the terrain, older, almost, than time itself.

His supernatural qualities and attributes are also linked with the environment and physical geography. In Denmark and Sweden moss grows on his mantle; a rock in the Black Mountains is called *Judenstein* because he walks round it on his journey through the area; and his tears, sometimes of blood, formed the black lake near Zermatt, in Switzerland.

We have already noted that in the Lithuanian variant he is Jacob's grandson, and there is a talmudic legend 'The Man in the Moon has Jacob's Face'.[39] Jacob's translation to outer space provides a link with a folk tale from Brittany, which specifically associates the Wandering Jew with the Man in the Moon,[40] condemned to remain there collecting sticks with which to burn the earth on the day of judgment. In popular tradition the Man in the Moon is

The Jew as a Witch Figure

often a Sabbath breaker, an explanation which no doubt originates with the biblical account (Numbers XV: 32) of the man who gathered sticks on the Sabbath and was stoned to death by the children of Israel.[41]

Unlimited in space, age, time, location and size, the isolation of the Wandering Jew is underlined by the theme, common to many versions of the legend, that he cannot remain still, but must always pace perpetually to and fro. 'He is as restless as the Wandering Jew' is a Hungarian saying[42] carried to its most extreme form in the association of the Wandering Jew with the birds of the air. There is a Lancashire tradition that the whistling golden plover embody the Wandering Jew: they are said to be the souls of those who assisted at the Crucifixion and were doomed to wander forever after.[43] Here is an aetiological legend purporting to account for the curious whistling cry of these and other types of bird, which fly overhead uttering an eerie, almost human, sound which struck fear into the hearts of those who heard them. Also known as the Seven Whistlers, they foretold death and disaster. 'Seven Whistlers are souls of Jews who crucified Christ' is Motif A1715.3 in Stith Thompson's *Motif Index of Folk Literature*.

The Seven Whistlers are also associated with the death hounds that accompany the Wild Hunt.[44] In northern Europe the storms and gales of winter gave rise to a belief in supernatural beings passing through the air, making a terrible noise; Jacob Grimm compared them to a ghostly army.[45] Here again the moral element is often very pronounced: the shades are those who in some way fell outside the Sacraments of the church—unbaptised babies, those who died a violent death or committed a major sin and have been banished forever into the sky, the traditional domain of evil spirits. Grimm refers to a twelfth-century German poet who uses '*daz wuetunde her*' (*das wütende heer*) of the Jews who took part in the Crucifixion.[46]

The connection between the Wandering Jew and the Wild Huntsman is attributed to the medieval legend of a Jew who refused Christ permission to drink from a horse trough while carrying the Cross to Calvary, and ordered Him to drink instead the water from a hoof print in the ground.[47] A variant formerly current in Oldenburg said that the Wandering Jew was permitted to rest from mid-May until July, a period of repose also granted to the Wild Huntsman.

In the Middle Ages the Wild Hunt was also called Cain's Hunt,

Cain being another progenitor of the Wandering Jew. When Cain murdered his brother, God said to him (Genesis IV: 10–15):

> What hast thou done? The voice of thy brother's blood crieth unto me from the ground. And now art thou cursed from the earth, which hath opened her mouth to receive thy brother's blood from thy hand. When thou tillest the ground, it shall not henceforth yield unto thee her strength: a fugitive and a vagabond shalt thou be in the earth. And Cain said unto the Lord, My punishment is greater than I can bear. Behold, thou hast driven me out this day from the face of the earth; and from thy face shall I be hid; and I shall be a fugitive and a vagabond in the earth; and it shall come to pass that every one that findeth me shall slay me. And the Lord said unto him, Therefore whosoever slayeth Cain, vengence shall be taken on him sevenfold. And the Lord set a mark upon Cain, lest any finding him should kill him.

It is worth quoting this familiar passage at some length, for it sets out certain major mythical concepts which later came to be associated with the Jews as a race: the eternal wandering, the shedding of blood, the curse, and the mark of Cain.

The themes of the wandering and the curse have now been touched upon. With the mark of Cain the notion of being set apart from society is given tangible physical embodiment. As a national and religious minority the Jews were obliged to wear the Jew badge, an outward and visible sign of their cultural differentiation. This mark, degrading by intent and later to be revived by Hitler, was first adopted by the Fourth Lateran Council in 1215 and to the public at large it stigmatised those who wore it as a race of outcasts.[48] If a Jew was caught without the sign, the informer was allowed to keep the relevant article of clothing from which it had been omitted.[49] The badge was ostensibly to prevent intermarriage and size, colour and shape were left for the ruler of each state to determine. In England it was at first white, altered to yellow by Edward I, and the age at which it became obligatory wear was seven.[50] For English Jews this appears to have been sufficient but, in the later Middle Ages in Austria, Hungary and Germany, the *Judenhut* was prescribed. This was a special hat, usually red, the brim shaped to resemble a pair of horns. The demoniacal implications of this item of headgear need not be enlarged upon, and there is additional evidence of alleged links between satanism and Jewry. Christian clergy convicted of sorcery were obliged to wear a piece

The Jew as a Witch Figure

of yellow felt remarkably suggestive of the 'Jew badge', and a Hungarian law of 1421 required anyone charged with sorcery to stand all day in a public place, following his first conviction, wearing a Jew's hat.[51] The social effect of all these various rulings was to brand the Jew and mark him as a ready target for insults. The stage directions for several mystery plays from Germany and France stress the point by insisting that Jews should be *'jüdisch gekleidet'* or *'avec rouelle et bonnet cornu'*.[52]

From the objects forced upon the Jews to mark them out as a nation, we can turn to alleged physical features purporting to set them apart from the rest of society, and here again I would stress that the subject matter under consideration is highly distasteful. In medieval folk tradition, and later, the Jews, much like witches, were held to be ugly, malodorous, animal-like, blind, deformed or mal-functioning in some respect. Motif A1662.1 in the *Motif Index of Folk Literature* is: 'Why Jews smell bad: rubbed Christ's body with garlic'. With commendable reservations for his day and age, Sir Thomas Browne observed on this subject:[53]

> that the Jews stink naturally, that is, that in their race and nation there is an evil savour, is a received opinion we know not how to admit ... [it] is ... much received by Christians that this ill favour is a curse derived upon them by Christ, and stands as a bridge or brand of a generation that crucified their Salvator ... But this is a conceit without all warrant; and an easier way to take off dispute in what point of obscurity soever ... thus therefore, although we concede that many opinions are true which hold some conformity unto this, yet in assenting hereto, many difficulties must arise: it being a dangerous point to annex a constant property unto any nation, and much more this unto the Jew; since this quality is not verifiable by observation; since the grounds are feeble that should establish it, and lastly; since, if all were true, yet are the reasons alleadged for it, of no sufficiency to maintain it.

Readers of *The Brothers Karamazov* will recall that a chapter entitled 'The Odour of Corruption' describes the atmosphere of scandal which rapidly builds up when the corpse of a loved and respected priest begins to stink shortly after his death: 'to expect putrefaction and the odour of corruption of the body of so great a saint was an utter absurdity'.[54] The bodies of the sanctified were supposed to emit a sweet fragrance. By contrast the devil often smells in popular belief, generally of brimstone, and it was also a traditionally accepted Christian viewpoint that the Jews stink, but they were supposed to lose their smell when baptised.[55]

Curiously, perhaps because it represents so basic a part of our normal living pattern, food, and habits connected with it, has been and still is capable of arousing intense feelings. An old rhyme goes:

> On Easter Sunday be the pudding seen
> To which the Tansy lends her sober green.

This dish was a Christian adaptation of the bitter herbs customarily consumed at the Passover Seder. John Aubrey observes: 'Our tansies at Easter have reference to the bitter herbs; though at the same time 'twas always the fashion for a man to have a gammon of bacon, to shew himself to be no Jew.'[56]

The ritual prohibition against eating the flesh of the pig appears in Motif A1681.2 of the *Motif Index*: 'Why Jews do not eat pork', and in an unpleasant rhyme sung by London children:[57]

> Get a bit of pork
> Stick it on a fork
> And give it to a Jew boy, Jew.

The Opies, who collected these lines, believe that they may at least be traceable to 1792, since Leigh Hunt, who attended Christ's Hospital at that date, mentions a similar rhyme in his autobiography.

'There can be no doubt', writes Ernest Krausz in his recent study 'that anti-semitic prejudices have contributed vastly to Jews keeping themselves to themselves.'[58] But anti-semitism itself must have been fanned by the seeming strangeness of Jewish custom in the Middle Ages. Everything about it was so different. As early as the time of the ancient Romans we find such writers as Tacitus, Horace, Juvenal and Martial ridiculing the observance of the Sabbath, circumcision, and the prohibition against pork, features which were regarded in themselves as indicative of social exclusiveness.[59] In fact the peoples among whom the Jews of Europe lived were woefully ignorant of their traditions and culture—in some areas perhaps partly the result of an inability to understand their language—hence the growth of grotesque and infamous legends, and the tendency to regard them with a superstitious dread. A parallel process was observable at the Reformation when Catholic

The Jew as a Witch Figure

priests were attacked by the Protestant reformers as 'the vilest witches and sorcerers of the earth'.[60]

Krausz quotes with approval Schermerhorn's observation that 'prejudice [is] a product of situations, historical situations, economic situations, political situations; it is not a little demon that emerges in people simply because they are depraved'.[61] This is undoubtedly so, but prejudice also arises from and is maintained by traditional thought patterns, and these are often expressed in folkloric form.[62] Hence the concept of the Jew as prototype of the outsider in Europe lay behind the medieval belief that the Ottoman invaders were in reality huge numbers of Jews, headed by Antichrist, intent on the destruction of European culture in its current form.[63] That the Jew was thus linked with Antichrist stemmed from the intense religious hatred aroused by this minority group which had refused to accept the predominant faith.[64] Thomas Aquinas and Albertus Magnus both claimed that Antichrist would be born in the Jewish tribe of Dan,[65] and medieval French and German plays on this subject stress the same association between the Jews and Antichrist.[66] It was in fact necessary for the city council of Frankfurt to pass a special decree protecting local Jews during performance of *Herzog von Burgund*, a fifteenth-century German lenten play on the Antichrist theme by Hans Folz, so inflammatory was the material contained in it.[67]

The religious differences between the Jews and their environing neighbours are still underlined in certain calendrical observances which might well have been discontinued. In 1937 Violet Alford noted: 'In Urgel they follow up their pace-egging by turning into the Twelve Apostles and "Killing Jews" with sticks.'[68] On Holy Saturday on Zante Island in the Greek Archipelago it is still the custom to throw unwanted pots out of the window: 'For the joy of Christ and the shame of the Jews', biting a key at the same time and saying: 'My head is iron, the Jew's head is but a hollow case.'[69] Here, so it would seem, is a folk interpretation, by re-enaction, repudiating the sin of heresy. In his book *The European Witch-Craze of the Sixteenth and Seventeenth Centuries*, Professor Trevor-Roper refers to 'the persecution of heresy as social intolerance' and draws attention to the similarity between persecution of Jews and persecutions of witches as representatives of social nonconformity.[70] The explicit or implicit identification of witch and Jew is a very common one: to this subject let us now turn.

In the early days of the church the inflammatory sermons of Chrysostom at Antioch (AD 387) accused the Jews of sacrificing their own children to devils.[71] Gregory of Nyssa, another fourth-century preacher, attacked them as 'companions of the devil'[72] and St Bernard of Clairvaux takes up the theme when he refers to 'a race who had not God for their father, but were of the devil'.[73]

With this foundation to build upon it is not surprising to find Jews and the devil closely linked in medieval drama and literature. In the 'Prioress's Tale' Chaucer observes:[74]

> First of our foes, the Serpent Satan shook
> Those Jewish hearts that are his waspish nest.

Plays like *Le Mystère de la Passion* show devils and Jews working together, and the Chaumont Christmas play represents Jews on the stage in the form of devils.[75] In one of the *Exempla* of Jacques de Vitry[76] (who was ordained in 1210), a Christian calls on the devil and a Jew appears. Similar themes occur in the representational arts. A thirteenth-century sketch from the Forest Roll of Essex (1277) is captioned '*Aaron fil diaboli*'.[77] A sixteenth-century series of prints, '*Juden Badstub*', shows Jews helped to bathe by the devil, and here we may compare Motif G303.16.19.33: 'Task for devil: washing a Jew to rid him of the evil smell'. '*Der Juden Synagog*', a seventeenth-century print, shows the devil taking part in the synagogue ceremonies.[78] In Crete the medieval 'Jew badge' took the form of a devil carved in wood, which had to be attached to the front door. Again, we may compare Motif G303.3.1.15: 'Devil appears as a Jew' (Spanish), an association of ideas implied, as already noted, by the obligation, through a decree of the Vienna Council in 1267, to wear a horned hat: *pileum cornutum*. More typical alleged demonic attributes of the Jew included horns or a tail, and they are represented thus, for instance, in the stained glass of Auch Cathedral and in the *Calvary* of Veronese in the Louvre.[79]

As a natural corollary to this, the Jews enjoyed an international reputation for practising magic. In the eleventh century Byzantine Jews who converted to Christianity were obliged formally to renounce 'all their witchcraft, incantations, sorcery, soothsayings, amulets, and phylacteries'.[80] Sometimes they were executed for supposed sorcery: twenty-four were burnt for this alleged crime at Frankfurt-on-Oder in 1579. Earlier, in 1240, the Synod of Worcester declared that: 'Such as consult Jews for the purpose of finding out

The Jew as a Witch Figure

by magic about their life and actions, they shall be brought before the bishop to be punished.' This statement invites comparison with the attitude of the peoples of Northern Europe towards the Lapps, another minority culture lacking a definable homeland. The ancient Norwegians supposed that they were skilled in sorcery and visited them secretly in order to learn from them; their medieval kings in fact prohibited journeys to Finnmark for this purpose.

Because of their reputation, Jewish amulets were greatly prized. The fanatical Chrysostom accused the Jews of proselytising by offering charms and certainly numbers of medieval amulets with Hebrew inscriptions were prepared specifically for use by Christians, perhaps because the unintelligible script lent them an aura of the supernatural.[81] It is even recorded that a fourteenth-century Bishop of Salzburg requested a *mezuzah* to fasten on the gateway of his castle, but the rabbi whom the Jew in question consulted, would not countenance the use of a religious object for such a purpose. Earlier, in the thirteenth century, a Viennese rabbi, Isaac ben Moses, was asked by a Regensburg Jew for permission to send wine to a Gentile: the man was very ill, and had requested it in the hopes of effecting a cure. Evidently he supposed that the wine possessed magical healing properties. Permission was granted but the outcome of the cure is not recorded.[82]

In the Middle Ages arraignment for sorcery was so frequent and caused so much loss of life, as well as sheer misery, to medieval Jewries, that rabbis often found it necessary to advise suspension of such important rituals as cleansing the house for the Passover, lest the Gentile population bring accusations of magical practices. Many traditional observances were affected by this atmosphere: some, like the funeral practices of 'binding the head' and 'overturning the bed' thus disappeared for ever.[83]

Accusations of sorcery assumed many different forms. Benevolent aspects included fortune-telling, interpretation of dreams, location of buried treasure, knowledge of the magical attributes of jewels, and rain-making.[84] Other charges, which also parallel the allegations made against witches, were of a more threatening nature. Jews were said to be capable of transformation into a cat, the traditional witches' familiar[85] and to have the power of summoning up demons and evil spirits. The most famous is enshrined in the folktales of the Golem—a Hebrew word meaning 'embryo'—a robot created by Rabbi Loew of Prague in the sixteenth century.

It might be said to represent the literal embodiment of the indomitable human spirit, the desire of the underdog, down-trodden and persecuted, to outwit his tormentors. The Golem was brought to life by a charm, the *Shem*, which was placed in its mouth, or hung about its neck. Thus equipped, it often served as a champion of the Jews, walking invisibly and preventing Gentiles from depositing dead children in the Jewish quarter, as sometimes happened, and thus frustrating charges of ritual murder, which were rampant at this time.[86] We may see a parallel to this in the traditional Lappish cycle of Stallo legends, in which a stupid giant is repeatedly outwitted; the Lapps, a short-statured race, have spent their lives in political dependence upon four countries across whose territories they extend—Sweden, Finland, Norway and Russia—and the giant may reflect their opinion of their neighbours.

In numerous ghost stories the Jew appears as will-o'-the-wisp[87] and Jacob Grimm describes a spirit called Jüdel, which was dangerous to children:[88]

> If the Jüdel wont let the children sleep, give him something to play with. When children laugh in their sleep, or open and turn their eyes, we say 'the Jüdel plays with them'. Buy, without beating down the price asked, a new little pot, pour into it out of the child's bath, and set it on the oven: in a few days the Jüdel will have sucked every drop out. Sometimes eggshells, out of which the yolk has been blown into the child's pap and the mother's caudle, are hung on the cradle by a thread, for the Jüdel to play with, instead of with the child.[89] ... in a lying-in room lay a straw out of the woman's bed at every door, and neither ghost nor Jüdel, can get in.[90] ... when cows growl in the night, the Jüdel is playing with them.[91]

Trachtenberg observes:[92]

> In some sections of Germany, into the 19th century, a spirit known as the Jüdel was believed to make its home in the oven, from which it sallied forth to attack the inmates of the house, the children in particular. An antidote against it was to smear the mouth of the oven with pork, thus locking it in. The Jüdel was evidently a folk representation of the wicked Jew, whose egress could effectively be blocked with pork!

In English tradition the Cornish tin mines were haunted by Jews called 'the knockers', old smelting houses were known as 'Jew's houses' and blocks of tin found in the bogs were 'Jews' tin'.[93]

The Jew as a Witch Figure

Here the Jew features as both ghost and bogeyman, with which Gentile children are threatened, superstition being used for a social purpose, to reinforce the fundamental tenets of society.

Another means of social control to coerce children into good behaviour was representing to them the image of the bogey who would eat them up. Napoleon was said to be a cannibal and the Puritans spread similar stories about the Cavaliers and Prince Rupert of the Rhine.[94] Cannibalism, especially of small children, was a common notion, genuinely believed in. Witches were often supposed to be cannibals[95] and there are echoes of this in Shylock's 'pound of flesh', International Tale Type 890 and Motif J1161.2, which made an earlier appearance in the thirteenth-century poem, *Cursor Mundi*.[96]

Overtones of cannibalism also appear in the infamous ritual murder charge. Calumnies of this type are commonly flung at cultural and racial minorities. The Romans accused the early Christians of ritual murder long before it was imputed to the Jews, and the Catholics made similar allegations about groups of heretics.[97] Anti-European riots in China in the latter part of the nineteenth century involved accusations that the missionaries murdered Chinese children and prepared magical potions and medicines from different parts of their bodies.[98]

Accusations that the Jews stole Christian children and crucified them after torture on Good Friday and Easter Sunday were especially prevalent in the twelfth and thirteenth centuries. England possesses a number of so-called 'child martyrs' of this type. The alleged ritual murder of William of Norwich is recounted in the *Anglo Saxon Chronicle*, and the authorities at Norwich Cathedral thought it necessary to issue an eight-page refutation of the legend,[99] obtainable by present-day visitors. A similar tale is told of Hugh of Lincoln. Chambers concludes his account in the *Book of Days*[100] by noting that 'the most remarkable proof of the firm hold which this story had taken upon men's minds in the middle ages is the existence of a ballad ... which has been preserved orally down to our own time, and is still recited from time to time in Scotland and the north of England.' The ballad 'Sir Hugh' or 'Jew's Daughter' is recorded in the Child collection as possessing twenty-one variants, and Chaucer recounts a version in the 'Prioress's Tale'.[101] There is a contemporary Anglo-French ballad extant,[102] but the first English examples date from the eighteenth century, and were carried by English settlers to the United States, where they appear as 'The Jew's Garden'.[103] Child cites parallel accusations of this type as occurring in the nineteenth century in Russia, Germany, Greece, Turkey and Hungary.[104] In fact in Central and Eastern Europe from 1880 to 1945 there are as many instances of the accusation as in the whole of the Middle Ages.[105]

A ritual murder allegation in Corfu in 1891, involving an eight-year-old girl, roused the German divine Hermann Strack to speak out once again. Strack, who was Regius Professor of Theology at Berlin University, wrote in the Preface to his great apologetic work *The Jew and Human Sacrifice*:

> I have made it my special business to let the facts speak for themselves ... The facts I have had to bring forward are, for the greater part, of a very loathsome kind. But, in order to cure the terrible disease of superstition, we must first of all *know* the disease... My exhortation to our Christian priesthood, to our whole Christian people is: up and gird yourself for battle, not only against unbelief, but also against superstition! When German Christendom, free from superstition, stands firm in true belief in the crucified Saviour, risen from the dead, the question, so far as concerns Germany, whether Christian blood is ritually employed by Jews, will be exploded and futile, for more reasons than one.

This is dated 1891. In 1900, in the Preface to the fifth edition, he was obliged to write: 'My publicly entering the lists on behalf of my conviction, and particularly my refutation of the calumnies against the Jewish religion, has procured me not only abuse in the daily Press, but also serious material damage. But I am none the less assured that it is my duty to go on as before.'[106]

A case which occurred at Kolin, Bohemia, in 1893 shows precisely how such pernicious folklore can arise. Marie Havlin, a chronically depressed girl who worked for a Jewish family in Brett disappeared, and a month later her body was found in the river. The anti-semitic newspaper *Polaban* at once declared that here was a case of ritual murder by the Jews, for stab marks were said to have been found on the body. This led to anti-semitic rioting locally. Following an autopsy, the burgomaster proclaimed that there were no stab marks on the body; that the girl had committed suicide by drowning. Despite this, a memorial stone was set up on her grave inscribed: 'Here rests Maria Havlin who died a martyr's death before the Jews' Easter. May God reward them for it!' Fortunately

The Jew as a Witch Figure

protests from the local Jewry were successful in obtaining the removal of the stone.[107] It is open to speculation in such a case, where the girl was a Catholic, and suicide therefore a mortal sin, whether the relatives were unwilling to accept the facts and turned instead to this traditional folk explanation, which could be seen not only as absolving her from sin, but surrounded her with an aura of sanctity.

Ritual murder accusations have continued into the twentieth century. One which occurred in Bessarabia in 1903 led to a massacre of Jews; others appeared in Poland in 1918, Lithuania in 1929, Bulgaria in 1934 and they were later revived by the Nazis.[108] The theme appears in traditional Jewish humour:[109]

> A great calamity threatened the little Ukrainian village. Shortly before the Passover holidays a young peasant girl had been found murdered. Those who hated the Jews quickly took advantage of the unhappy incident and went about among the peasants, inflaming them with the slander that the Jews had killed the girl in order to use her Christian blood for making *matzos*. The fury of the peasants knew no bounds.
>
> A report spread like wildfire throughout the village that a pogrom was in the offing.
>
> Dismayed by the news the pious ran to the synagogue. They rent their garments, and prostrated themselves before the Holy Ark. As they were sending up their prayers for divine intercession, the Shammes ran in breathlessly.
>
> 'Brothers—brothers!' he gasped. 'I have wonderful news for you! We've just discovered, God be praised, that the murdered girl was Jewish!'

The ritual murder charge was again made in a local newspaper published in Soviet Daghestan in 1960, stating that Jews need Moslem blood at regular intervals to use in their rituals.[110] The following report, which appeared in the *New Statesman* is also interesting in this connection:[111]

> In 1966 a mentally unstable woman, Maria Rykova, murdered a three year old boy. Since she was a Baptist, the people of Mtsensk, where the event took place, immediately connected Maria Rykova's tragic act with her faith and the murder of the little boy began to gain new and terrible significance. People of neighbouring villages and towns like Orel and Tula, soon spoke of dark blood rituals and Baptist murders in Mtsensk—a sinister echo of the anti-semitic myth

of the Protocols of Zion once deliberately spread by the tsarist Okhrana. As there are no Jews in Mtsensk, the crowds have turned upon the Baptists, another religious minority . . . [This] does not explain the sudden revival in Russia of the ritual-murder myth after half a century of anti-religious mass education.

A possible explanation of the traditional ritual murder charge could be that it arose from ignorance of the practice of ritual slaughter. The similar accusation of consuming human blood, which was adduced as a reason for the expulsion from Spain, is also a recurring feature of witch persecution. The consumption of animal blood, let alone human, is of course, diametrically opposed to Jewish observance, but folklore is frequently illogical in its operation. Reasons customarily advanced for this supposed practice are many and diverse. The blood was said to be used at various stages of the life cycle as an aphrodisiac, to ease labour pains, to make children fertile, to prolong life, and to cure the blindness once said to afflict all Jews at birth.[112] This last shows the Church's teaching rendered in its most literal form, from the examples in the visual and plastic arts—notably the blindfold synagogue sculpture on Strasbourg Cathedral—to the prayers appointed for Good Friday: 'which we offer for the blindness of this people'.[113]

The accusations, which were especially prevalent at the time of Passover and Easter, have left their mark on Seder ceremonial with the words: 'In every generation there are those who rise up against us to destroy us', and in occasional rabbinical advice to drink white wine rather than red, lest the red be mistaken for human blood.[114]

Folk tradition asserts that the Jews were afflicted with complaints like haemorrhage and haemorrhoids, involving loss of blood. The rationale for this was apparently a very literal interpretation of the concept of guilt and corporate responsibility supposedly advanced in Matthew XXVII: 25: 'His blood be on us, and on our children.' We need not be too surprised at such credulity when St Augustine himself was able to say: 'In consequence of the curses upon their fathers, the criminal disposition is even now transmitted to the children by the taint in the blood, so that the godless posterity suffers torment inexpiably through its violent coursing through their veins till they repentantly admit themselves guilty of the blood of Christ and are healed.'[115] Another common misconception, that Christian blood is applied to heal the wound of circumcision, may have been due to the fact that dragon's blood, a type of red gum, was sometimes employed for this purpose.[116]

One of the strangest accusations, stabbing a consecrated host and causing it to bleed, assumed by implication a belief in transubstantiation.[117] The doctrine was officially promulgated at the Fourth Lateran Council in 1215 and stories of this type were especially rife in the thirteenth and fourteenth centuries.[118] Christians convicted of utilising the host for magical purposes were obliged to wear the yellow Jew badge, an interesting correlation. Strack notes that the appearance of a red substance on these wafers could have been a type of bacteria, unknown till 1819.[119]

Misunderstanding of Jewish custom runs like a connecting thread through many of the folkloric aspects of anti-semitism. Thus the pig, a forbidden animal according to Mosaic law, was associated in the popular mind with the Jewish people. The *Judensau*, carved on a fifteenth century Frankfurt bridge, represents the animal feeding her children, while the devil looks on. The Nazis made use of this theme: *Der Stürmer*, no. 3, 1934, carried on its front page the drawing of an enormous sow labelled 'Jewish Publishing House'.[120]

The *Oxford English Dictionary* cites the Hebrew word Sabbath as the origin of the witches' Sabbath,[121] and witches' synagogues are referred to by the inquisitor Boguet.[122] An attribute which the Jew was supposed to share with witches and other enemies of society was possession of the Evil Eye.[123] This notion was a particular feature of German belief. In the area between Darmstadt and Heidelberg there was a tradition that when someone very ill wished to die quickly, a Rabbi was asked to pray for his recovery.[124] In Spain one spat after saying 'Jew', this being a usual method for warding off evil,[125] and in East Friesland it was unlucky to meet a Jew first thing in the morning. If he was the first to enter one's house, or even to look through the window on a Monday—the first day of the week—it meant that everyone in the family would be unlucky for the next seven days. At one time the Jew could be indicted.[126]

Other destructive and witch-like activities of which the Jews were accused including causing earthquakes,[127] raising storms,[128] especially at sea, and spreading the plague—the Black Death which took such a dreadful toll of human life in the fourteenth century.[129] We see reflected here our ancestors' fear in the face of natural phenomena, the workings of which were not perfectly understood.

Without adequate vessels or safety equipment, and lacking the navigation guides, the radios and metereological reports of today, mankind used to be virtually helpless against the raging sea. When Charles V's attack from the coast against Algiers in 1541 was a failure, it was said that a Jewish magician had raised the storm which routed his ships.[130]

Men feared not only the violence of the elements but the inexplicable spread of epidemics and disease, at a time when the practice of medicine was in its infancy, and virtually nothing was known about diet, hygiene or infection. The plague came suddenly, bringing tragedy, social confusion, a high mortality rate and a shorter life expectancy:[131]

> Rich men trust not in wealth,
> Gold cannot buy you health;
> Physic himself must fade,
> All things to end are made;
> The plague full swift goes by;
> I am sick, I must die—
> *Lord have mercy on us*!

Hitler played on this ancient fear when he wrote in *Mein Kampf*: 'I discovered the Jewish activities in the Press... Here was a pestilence, a moral pestilence, with which the public was being infected. It was worse than the Black Plague of long ago.'[132] *Der Stürmer* of 17 April 1941 contains a picture of the Warsaw Ghetto before the walls were built, and a huge placard across the entrance reads 'Typhus-infected area. Transit-traffic only permitted'.[133]

Some of the calumnies framed against the Jews were astutely selected[134] since they revived these traditional associations, implicit and explicit, between Jew and witch. One of the most infamous was the notorious anti-semitic forgery, *The Protocols of the Elders of Zion*,[135] which relates, to the medieval slander that when Jews control the world they will persecute the Christians,[136] and to the modern fabrication that there exists a world-wide conspiracy of right and left-wing Jews, communists and capitalists, all supposedly working for the downfall of the rest of the world.[137] *The Protocols* purport to be the proceedings of a secret meeting held in the Jewish cemetery in Prague by the leaders of world Jewry, who were allegedly plotting the destruction of the non-Jewish world. Long discredited in court, the book is still widely read[138] and the general

The Jew as a Witch Figure

scene represented does carry certain overtones of a witches' Sabbath, particularly the night-time setting and the secret gathering in a cemetery.

Related to this is the menacing folk-figure of the Jewish doctor-sorcerer, which again takes its roots from the Middle Ages. Zedekiah, doctor to Charles the Bold in the late ninth century, was said to have swallowed a wagon-load of hay—horses, rider and all. He was also credited with the power of flying through the air, and of dismembering a man and reassembling the parts without doing him any harm.[139]

Conspiracy by Jewish doctors was a disreputable charge made by both Hitler and Stalin, but they were in turn reviving a common medieval accusation. In 1550 Ivan the Terrible was requested to admit Lithuanian Jews into Russia, and he replied: 'It is not convenient . . . for they import poisonous herbs into our realms.'[140] In 1610 the medical faculty in Vienna announced that Jewish doctors were obligated by their creed to kill one in ten of their Christian patients.[141] Such notions are not entirely unknown in our own country. Here as a quotation from the *Sunday Express*:[142]

> In Britain half a million Jews find their home. They are never persecuted and indeed in many respects the Jews are given favoured treatment here. But just now there is a big influx of foreign Jews into Britain. They are overrunning the country. They are trying to enter the medical profession in great numbers. They wish to practise as dentists. Worst of all, many of them are holding themselves out to the public as psycho-analysts. A psycho-analyst needs no medical training, but arrogates to himself the functions of a doctor. And he often obtains an ascendancy over the patient of which he makes base use if he is a bad man.

In the Middle Ages medicine and magic were closely connected, due to a belief, the result of insufficient scientific knowledge, that illness is brought about by the activities of evil spirits. Jewish doctors, who had travelled, and were able to read Greek and Arabic treatises on medicine in Hebrew translation, tended to be a little more skilled than their Gentile colleagues, and hence increased their reputation for practising sorcery. Luther, who seems to have suffered from an acute persecution complex, lived in constant dread of being poisoned by the Jews. He wrote hysterically: 'If they could kill us all, they would gladly do so, aye, and often do it, especially those who profess to be physicians. They know all that is known about medicine in Germany; they can give poison to a man, of which he will die in an hour, or in ten or twenty years; they thoroughly understand this art.'[143] The Jewish poisoner is a common figure in Elizabethan drama, Barabas, in Marlowe's *Jew of Malta* being perhaps one of the best known.

The most usual form that the accusation took was poisoning the wells: compare Motif 362: 'Plague from Jews' poisoning wells'. It seems to have appeared for the first time in Bohemia, in the twelfth century, and then with increasing frequency in the fourteenth century in Germany, France and Switzerland.[144] Sometimes the Jews were denounced as accomplices of the lepers, another minority group which inspired irrational fear.

Several years ago Aharon Meged wrote in the *Jewish Chronicle*: 'Many things have changed in the past 3,000 years, but the hatred for our people has remained constant.'[145] He echoes the words of Gustav Mahler: 'I have been thrice homeless: as a Bohemian in Austria, as an Austrian in Germany, and as a Jew throughout all the world; everywhere rejected, nowhere welcomed.' Racial hatred is irrational. It is also meaningless. This aspect is summed up in two jokes of a peculiarly Jewish type: 'A group of Nazis surrounded an elderly Berlin Jew and demanded of him, "Tell me, Jew, who caused the war?" The little Jew was no fool. "The Jews," he said, then added, "and the bicycle riders." The Nazis were puzzled. "Why the bicycle riders?" "Why the Jews?" answered the little old man.'[146] Again: 'A Jew was drowning in the Dnieper River. He cried for help. Two Tsarist policemen ran up. When they saw it was a Jew, they said, "Let the Jew drown!" When the man saw his strength was ebbing, he shouted with all his might, "Down with the Tsar!" Hearing such seditious words, the policemen plunged in, pulled him out, and arrested him.'[147]

When the Israelis defeated the Arabs in the Six Day War, it was a shock and a puzzle to militant anti-semites. How was such a thing possible? German neo-Nazi groups soon rallied and the *Jewish Observer* quotes the explanation that they produced, proving by lengthy and tortuous arguments that in fact the Israelis are not really Jews at all.[148] Almost comparable with this was the determination of *Berliner Zeitung* in East Germany to show that the Israeli victories were based on the country's status as true successor of Hitler:[149]

How then do the capitalists who rule Israel behave towards their

The Jew as a Witch Figure

Arab neighbours? They wage the same kind of aggressive war against them that Hitler Germany used when launching attacks on her neighbours. They justify their aggression with the same living-space-lie which the policy planners of Nazi Germany's aggressions used to employ. They do exactly as they have been done to by the German Fascists during the second world war.

The role of folklore in reinforcing stereotype is very considerable[150] and stereotyping is something of which we are by no means free in England. Jews, who sought refuge in this country from Tsarist oppression at the turn of the century, were accused of lacking morals and standards of cleanliness, charges which were officially investigated and refuted.[151] This is data which can be used with advantage by modern sociologists and others studying race relations, for similar remarks have been made in recent years about black immigrants. Notices stating: 'No Jews need apply' have been a common sight in England.[152] It is said of negroes that they smell, resemble animals—'Go back to the jungle where you came from'—practise witchcraft, and have some obscure link with the devil by virtue of their colour.

I believe that study of anti-semitic folklore of the past will help us towards a better understanding of the race problems with which we are faced today, so that we may avoid some of the mistakes which have been made in the United States. I cannot do better than conclude with the words of the Rev. James Parkes who has probably done more than anyone else to combat anti-semitism in this country:[153]

> Jews are unhappily not the only group which has been subject to unjustified hostility; and to understand this oldest and most pervasive expression of a widespread social evil is a help to understanding the same prejudice against different people of a different colour, a different religion, a different social stratum. Because so much of it stems from a bygone age, it helps also to remind us that humanity has a long memory, and that men may be heirs to ancient enmities of whose origins they are themselves unaware.

Notes

1 *The Times*, 29 November 1966.
2 *The Times*, 27 March 1972.
3 *Daily Dispatch*, 17 October 1932.
4 *East Anglian Daily Times*, 2 March 1934.

5 *New Statesman*, 7 November 1936.
6 Ruth Fischer, quoted by *Vorwärts*, 22 August 1923. Her remarks were intended to appeal to NSDAP supporters. See W. T. Angress, *Stillborn Revolution*, Princeton, 1963, p. 340.
7 *New Statesman*, 12 November 1965.
8 Bruno Lasker, *Race Attitudes in Children*, New York, 1929, pp. 163-4.
9 Antti Aarne and Stith Thompson, *The Types of the Folktale*, Helsinki, 1964, p. 268.
10 'Zur Charakteristik des jüdischen Volkes', *Das Ausland*, Stuttgart, 1872, nos 38, 40.
11 See also Norman Cohn, *The Pursuit of the Millennium*, London, 1970, p. 76.
12 St Augustine, *City of God*, London, 1963, pp. 318-19.
13 Francis B. Cassilly, *Religion: Doctrine and Practice*, Chicago, 1934, pp. 399-400.
14 Jules Isaac, *The Christian Roots of Antisemitism*, London, 1965, p. 13.
15 Jules Isaac, *The Teaching of Contempt*, New York, 1964, pp. 39-71.
16 Isaac, *The Christian Roots of Antisemitism*, p. 24.
17 See Sabine Baring-Gould, *Curious Myths of the Middle Ages*, London, 1884, pp. 1-32, 637-40.
18 Rudolph M. Loewenstein, *Christians and Jews*, New York, 1963, p. 46, note.
19 Sir Thomas Browne, *Pseudodoxia Epidemica*, London, 1672, 1st ed. 1646, pp. 432-3.
20 John Brand, *Observations on Popular Antiquities*, ed. Sir Henry Ellis, London, 1900, p. 779; E. Cobham Brewer, *Dictionary of Phrase and Fable*, London, 1896, pp. 680-1.
21 A. H. Krappe, *The Science of Folk-Lore*, London, 1930, p. 104.
22 R. Chambers, *The Book of Days*, London, 1869, I, p. 535.
23 Bishop Percy, *Reliques of Ancient English Poetry*, 1765, II, pp. 291-6.
24 Joshua Trachtenberg, *The Devil and the Jews*, New Haven, 1943, p. 40.
25 Marie Trevelyan, *Folk-Lore and Folk-Stories of Wales*, London, 1909, pp. 337-8.
26 George K. Anderson, *The Legend of the Wandering Jew*, Providence, Conn., 1965, p. 107.
27 Ibid., p. 93.
28 *Völkischer Beobachter*, 26 June 1933, quoted in *The Yellow Spot* (no author), London, 1936, p. 15.
29 Anderson, op. cit., p. 28.
30 Ibid., p. 84.
31 Paul Sébillot, *Le Folk-Lore de France*, Paris, 1904, I, p. 313.
32 Chambers, op. cit., I, p. 535.
33 Anderson, op. cit., pp. 79-80, 87.
34 Ibid., p. 87.
35 Ibid., p. 88.
36 Ibid., p. 28.
37 Sébillot, op. cit., I, pp. 218, 253; Anderson, op. cit., p. 85.
38 Sébillot, op. cit., II, p. 60.
39 Timothy Harley, *Moon Lore*, London, 1885, p. 2; Louis Ginzberg, *The*

The Jew as a Witch Figure

Legends of the Jews, Philadelphia, 1925, V, p. 275; T. F. Thiselton Dyer, *English Folk-lore*, London, 1884, p. 50.
40 Anderson, op. cit., p. 103; Sébillot, op. cit., I, p. 20.
41 Dyer, op. cit., p. 49.
42 Anderson, op. cit., p. 99.
43 Charles Swainson, *The Folklore and Provincial Names of British Birds*, London, 1885, p. 180; Ernest Ingersoll, *Birds in Legend, Fable and Folklore*, New York, 1923, p. 89; Edward Armstrong, *The Folklore of Birds*, New York, 1970, p. 217.
44 Ibid., p. 219.
45 Jacob Grimm, *Teutonic Mythology*, London, 1883, III, p. 919.
46 Ibid.
47 Anderson, op. cit., pp. 5–6; see also Baring-Gould, op. cit., p. 27; M. D. Conway, *The Wandering Jew*, London, 1881, p. 97.
48 Malcolm Hay, *The Foot of Pride*, Boston, 1951, p. 87; Israel Abrahams, *Jewish Life in the Middle Ages*, London, 1932, p. 318.
49 Ibid., p. 322.
50 Ibid., p. 319.
51 H. C. Lea, *Materials Toward a History of Witchcraft*, New York, 1957, p. 1253; H. R. Trevor-Roper, *The European Witch-Craze of the Sixteenth and Seventeenth Centuries*, London, 1969, p. 35.
52 Trachtenberg, op. cit., p. 13.
53 Browne, op. cit., pp. 236, 240–1.
54 Fyodor Dostoyevsky, *The Brothers Karamazov*, tr. David Magarshack, London, 1958, II, p. 386.
55 Israel Lévi, 'L'Odeur des Juifs', *Revue des Études Juives*, 1890, 20, pp. 249 ff.
56 John Aubrey, *Remaines of Gentilisme and Judaisme*, 1686–7, ed. James Britten, London, 1881, p. 88.
57 Iona and Peter Opie, *The Lore and Language of Schoolchildren*, Oxford, 1959, p. 346.
58 Ernest Krausz, *Ethnic Minorities in Britain*, London, 1971, p. 71.
59 James Parkes, *Antisemitism*, London, 1963, p. 68; James Hastings (ed.), *Encyclopaedia of Religion and Ethics*, Edinburgh, 1908, I, p. 594.
60 Keith Thomas, *Religion and the Decline of Magic*, London, 1971, p. 52.
61 Krausz, op. cit., p. 124, quoting R. A. Schermerhorn, *Comparative Ethnic Relations*, New York, 1970, p. 6.
62 See Norman Cohn, *Warrant for Genocide*, London, 1967, p. 21.
63 Hanns Bächtold-Stäubli (ed.), *Handwörterbuch des deutschen Aberglaubens*, Berlin, 1927–42, IV, p. 816.
64 Cohn, *The Pursuit of the Millennium*, pp. 77–8.
65 Anderson, op. cit., p. 38.
66 Ibid., p. 39.
67 Trachtenberg, op. cit., pp. 36–7.
68 Violet Alford, *Pyrenean Festivals*, London, 1937, p. 38.
69 George Megas, *Greek Calendar Customs*, Athens, 1963, p. 104.
70 Op. cit., p. 32.
71 Parkes, op. cit., p. 64.

72 Léon Poliakov, *The History of Anti-semitism*, London, 1966, p. 25.
73 Hay, op. cit., p. 56.
74 Geoffrey Chaucer, *The Canterbury Tales*, tr. Nevill Coghill, London, 1951, p. 196.
75 Trachtenberg, op. cit., pp. 22–3.
76 *The Exempla of Jacques de Vitry*, ed. T. F. Crane, London, 1890, pp. 124–5.
77 Trachtenberg, op. cit., pp. 26–7.
78 Ibid., p. 26.
79 See Cohn, *The Pursuit of the Millennium*, p. 78.
80 Trachtenberg, op. cit., p. 67.
81 See T. Schrire, *Hebrew Amulets*, London, 1966, pp. 69–72.
82 Joshua Trachtenberg, *Jewish Magic and Superstition*, New York, 1939, p. 3.
83 Trachtenberg, *The Devil*, pp. 88–9.
84 Ibid., p. 72.
85 Ibid.
86 Angelo S. Rappoport, *The Folklore of the Jews*, London, 1937, pp. 195–9; *Dictionary of Folklore, Mythology and Legend*, ed. Maria Leach, New York, 1949, I, p. 459.
87 Poliakov, op. cit., p. 144; Bächtold-Stäubli, op. cit., IV, pp. 808–18.
88 See also Hermann L. Strack, *The Jew and Human Sacrifice*, London, 1909, p. 276, asterisked note.
89 Grimm, op. cit., IV, pp. 1779–80.
90 Ibid., p. 1792.
91 Ibid., p. 1795.
92 Trachtenberg, *The Devil*, p. 243, note 5; Bächtold-Stäubli, op. cit., IV, p. 830; Fritz Kynass, *Der Jude im Deutschen Volkslied*, Greifswald, 1934, p. 57.
93 F. W. Hackwood, *Christ Lore*, London, 1902, p. 113; Robert Hunt, *Popular Romances of the West of England*, London, 1871, pp. 346–9; see also Motifs F456.1.1.1; F456.1.2.3.2; 'Knockers as ghosts of Jews'.
94 Strack, op. cit., p. 285; Eliot Warburton, *Memoirs of Prince Rupert and the Cavaliers*, London, 1849, I, p. 17; II, p. 89.
95 Alan Macfarlane, *Witchcraft in Tudor and Stuart England*, London, 1970, p. 213.
96 Conway, op. cit., pp. 122–3.
97 Loewenstein, op. cit., p. 90; Strack, op. cit., pp. 33–4.
98 Ibid., p. 83.
99 *Common Ground*, Autumn 1966, vol. 20, no. 3, pp. 23–4.
100 Robert Chambers, *The Book of Days*, London, 1862, I, p. 447.
101 See M. J. C. Hodgart, *The Ballads*, New York, 1962, p. 126; Motif 254.17: 'Murdered boy still sings "Ave" after his death'.
102 Leach, op. cit., II, p. 551.
103 Ibid.; Tristram P. Coffin, *The British Traditional Ballad in North America*, Philadelphia, 1963, pp. 107–9; Poliakov, op. cit., p. 125; Hay, op. cit., pp. 124–7; William Wells Newell, *Games and Songs of American Children*, New York, 1963, pp. 75–8.

The Jew as a Witch Figure

104 *The English and Scottish Popular Ballads*, ed. F. J. Child, New York, 1965, III, pp. 241–3.
105 James Parkes, *Judaism and Christianity*, London, 1948, p. 12.
106 Strack, op. cit., p. xvi.
107 Ibid., pp. 222–3.
108 *Common Ground*, Summer 1967, vol. 21, no. 2, p. 36.
109 *A Treasury of Jewish Folklore*, ed. Nathan Ausubel, New York, 1948, p. 441.
110 Parkes, *Antisemitism*, p. 155.
111 *New Statesman*, 15 July 1966.
112 Strack, op. cit., p. 202; Trachtenberg, *Jewish Magic*, p. 8.
113 *The English Missal*, London, 1933, p. 249.
114 Isaac Levy, *A Guide to Passover*, London, 1958, p. 53; Raymond Apple, 'Pesach and the Blood Libel', *Common Ground*, Spring 1972, vol. 26, no. 1, pp. 12–15.
115 Quoted by Strack, op. cit., p. 175.
116 Ibid., p. 202; Trachtenberg, *Jewish Magic*, p. 8.
117 Hay, op. cit., pp. 144–5; J. A. MacCulloch, *Medieval Faith and Fable*, London, 1932, pp. 161–2.
118 Ibid., p. 161.
119 Strack, op. cit., p. 60.
120 *The Yellow Spot*, London, 1936, p. 154.
121 Geoffrey Parrinder, *Witchcraft: European and African*, London, 1963, p. 40; Rossell Hope Robbins, *Encyclopedia of Witchcraft and Demonology*, New York, 1959, p. 28.
122 Henry Boguet, *An Examen of Witches*, London, 1590, p. 55, quoted by Parrinder, op. cit., p. 40.
123 Macfarlane, op. cit., p. 213; Rappoport, op. cit., p. 73.
124 Conway, op. cit., p. 90.
125 Ibid., pp. 89–90.
126 Ibid., p. 91.
127 Hay, op. cit., p. 37.
128 Ibid.
129 Parrinder, op. cit., p. 21; Parkes, *Antisemitism*, p. 66.
130 Trachtenberg, *The Devil*, p. 80.
131 Thomas Nashe, *In Time of Pestilence*, 1593.
132 Adolf Hitler, *Mein Kampf*, tr. James Murphy, London, 1939, p. 60.
133 See also *The German New Order in Poland*, London, n.d., p. 237 and illustration opposite p. 235.
134 See Paul Hilberg, *The Destruction of the European Jews*, London, 1961, p. 8.
135 See, e.g., *Protocols of the Meetings of the Learned Elders of Zion*, tr. Victor E. Marsden, London, 1936.
136 Trachtenberg, *The Devil*, p. 42.
137 Maurice Samuel, *The Great Hatred*, London, 1943, pp. 12–14; Loewenstein, op. cit., p. 47; Cohn, *Warrant for Genocide*, pp. 22–3.
138 Samuel, op. cit., pp. 20–4; *Common Ground*, Autumn 1967, vol. 21, no. 3, p. 31.
139 Trachtenberg, *The Devil*, p. 66.
140 Trachtenberg, *Jewish Magic*, p. 6.

141 Trachtenberg, *The Devil*, p. 97.
142 *Sunday Express*, 19 June 1938.
143 Trachtenberg, *Jewish Magic*, p. 6.
144 Hastings, op. cit., I, p. 595; Trevor-Roper, op. cit., p. 33; Strack, op. cit., p. 279, note †.
145 *Jewish Chronicle*, 16 June 1967.
146 Ausubel, op. cit., p. 17.
147 Ibid., p. 442.
148 *Jewish Observer and Middle East Review*, 13 October 1967.
149 *Berliner Zeitung*, East Berlin, 13 June 1967, just after the end of the Six Day War. Quoted in the *Wiener Library Bulletin*, Autumn 1967, n.s. no. 9, p. 21.
150 See Neil V. Rosenberg, 'Stereotype and Tradition: White Folklore about Blacks', unpublished doctoral dissertation, Indiana University, 1970, p. 60.
151 Krausz, op. cit., pp. 56–7.
152 Ernest Krausz, *Leeds Jewry: Its History and Social Structure*, Cambridge, 1964, p. 21.
153 Parkes, *Antisemitism*, pp. x–xi.

7
The Witch as Victim

Geoffrey Parrinder

The attitudes which were adopted towards people accused of being witches are reflected in a large part of the literature of witchcraft, with theories of the diabolical nature of the witches, but the feelings of the supposed witches themselves were less often considered though they must have been equally important. If the witch was a victim, voluntary or forced, that is worth consideration, and if he or she suffered much that also needs discussion. Two of the best explored fields of witchcraft are Europe and Africa, and it is instructive to note the similarities and differences of attitudes.

That witches were chosen or voluntary victims for society was the opinion of Margaret Murray in her theory of an ancient but surviving witch-cult. In her first book on the subject, *The Witch-Cult in Western Europe*, Murray argued that witches were members of pre-Christian or anti-Christian cults, the 'Dianic' rites, which is what the inquisitors had said, and she stated that these cults were 'confined entirely to villages and peasants'.[1] She reconstituted this religion, with its God or masked priest, and made it into a fertility cult similar to the synthetic 'near eastern religion' of Frazer's *Golden Bough*. In *The God of the Witches* Murray claimed that the Dianic fertility cult was the religion of western Europe from Neolithic times onwards, and now she found 'proofs' that it was shared by nobles and prelates and in Britain 'influenced the lives of all the people from the highest to the lowest'. Covens were organised, she said, though the word seems to have been used first in sixteenth-century Scotland, descending from the 'Royal Coven' to village groups. Murray now borrowed further from Frazer's theories, this time the 'dying god', who, according to her, ruled only for a set number of years before being sacrificed as a victim. She named William Rufus, Thomas Becket, Joan of Arc and Gilles de Rais as divine Dianic victims.

In her third witchcraft book, *The Divine King in England*, Murray made her most stupendous claim, namely that all the kings of England down to 1648 were divine priest-kings. They were royal victims who either ritually sacrificed themselves or were preserved only by the sacrifice of another victim of royal blood and power. In fact few English kings before Charles I did die violently and publicly, but there were always plenty of people dying suddenly near the throne and it did not need much ingenuity to bring in Lady Jane Grey, Perkin Warbeck, Anne Boleyn, Katherine Howard, and the rest. However the time and year of death were more difficult, the sacrifices in the old religion being asserted to have taken place in February, May, August or November, and the sacrifice being at the end of every seven years of the age or reign of the king. This was hard to fit in from William Rufus onwards, whose birth date was unknown, who reigned thirteen years and who was hated by his subjects.

Murray's theories strained credulity more and more as they developed and looked at today they appear fantastic. Far from transforming our knowledge of history, as was once claimed, she seems to have distorted and obscured understanding of the very different Celtic and Germanic religions which were the historic predecessors of Christianity in these islands. Rejected by most of the learned world, it is unfortunate that her theories have been influential at the popular level, encouraged by zealots like Hugh Ross Williamson. They stimulated the rise, or supposed 'revival', of witch cults with secret rituals and orgies which, in a decline of Christian faith, show a pathetic straining after the supernatural but with a marked absence of a sense of humour.

Murray's belief that the witch was a divine victim, a dying god, an instrument of Dianic fertility ritual, has no basis in fact either in Europe or Africa. But that people accused of witchcraft were victims of the fears and superstitions of society is beyond doubt, and their sufferings were particularly acute in Europe. Punishment of witches was much less cruel in Africa, and our notion of that continent as barbaric and fear-ridden and our own as humane needs considerable revision, as will be shown.

The Witch as Victim

'Think about the victim', is a protest commonly made when debating the death penalty for murder. In the history of witchcraft the accused were often thought to have committed evil and murderous deeds, but if it was all a tragic delusion then many innocent people suffered in vain and a thought may be spared for the victims. Records of witchcraft recount the supposed activities of the accused, their service of the devil, nocturnal assemblies and cannibalism, capture and summary trial. Only occasionally are there glimpses of the torture and death agonies of the victims. In one of the earliest records, that of Dame Alice Kyteler in Ireland in 1324, her servant Petronilla was flogged to make her confess and burnt at Kilkenny for the diabolical details she had supplied. Dame Alice was supported by some of the nobility and was conveyed over to England and disappeared. One writer even says that Dame Alice herself suffered death for heresy and was the first to die for that crime in Ireland.[2]

As the witch fever increased so did the cruelty or rather the tortures produced confessions which stimulated fears. The *Malleus Maleficarum* from 1486 gives instructions for investigating charges of witchcraft and backing up formal examination with torture. 'Torture is not to be neglected', even if a witch is so stubborn and 'insensible to the pains of torture that she will sooner be torn limb from limb than confess the truth'.[3] That is, the truth wanted by the inquisitors. The accused was stripped, searched for marks or tools of witchcraft, bound with cords, shown the instruments of torture, applied to an engine of torture, and this was continued day after day. Mental torture was also used, such as promising to spare the witch's life, or the lives of her family, if she confessed and then after allowing her a short relief getting another judge to pass sentence of burning. There was also the possibility of purgation by the ordeal of the red-hot iron or boiling water, but the *Malleus* declared these to be unlawful since the devil might enable the witch to pass through the ordeal unscathed. But from that time there developed not only the 'hot water ordeal', but also the 'cold water ordeal' which consisted in ducking the bound witch to see if the waters of baptism rejected her; if she drowned she was innocent.

The use of torture has been correlated to the growth of witch-mania and exaggerated confessions. Judicial torture had been allowed occasionally by Roman law, but it declined in the so-called Dark Ages and was revived by the Inquisition. England profited by her insularity in that torture was forbidden by common law and the Inquisition was unknown in this 'best of islands'. Even when the Inquisition was in decline, or its leaders sceptical of the reality of witchcraft as in Spain, the secular courts often took up the practice of torture. Lea, in his great *Materials toward a History of Witchcraft*, pointed out that some of the more obscene and extravagant confessions appeared first under torture, and they were absent from the confessions of English witches. There was no witch-mania in the Dark Ages partly, at least, because torture was not used to force confessions, and witchcraft beliefs gradually disappeared with the decline of torture from the seventeenth century. In our own days totalitarian régimes have not hesitated to reintroduce both crude and refined tortures and have produced confessions and obscene charges.

Tortures included crushing fingers and toes in a vice, the rack or ladder to stretch the body, and a crusher to squeeze it. There were beds of nails, seats of spikes, heated witches' chairs, pulleys to jerk the body in mid-air, boots to crush the legs and break the bones, the latter much favoured in Germany and Scotland. Finger and toe nails were pulled out, and needles rammed in up to their heads. Perhaps the most effective was the torment of sleeplessness, to which victims often succumbed after surviving cruder tortures, and its virtues have been rediscovered today by the thugs of totalitarian societies. Even in England, generally so tolerant, pressing to death, the *peine forte et dure*, was allowed in charges of treason, but not for witchcraft. But scoundrels like Matthew Hopkins, the self-styled Witch-finder General, used non-judicial torments, pricking with a bradawl to find the insensitive spot and particularly the *tormentum insomniae*.

If tortures were so harsh, death must have come as a happy release to the victims, though continental inquisitors continued to show their ingenuity in burning people alive and tearing their bodies to pieces, rather than use the more sober hanging which was the rule in England. When the witch-mania began at the end of the fifteenth century many lawyers were hostile to the notions of witchcraft beliefs, but in time they came to support the witch-hunters and became even more savage than the clergy. New laws were introduced, such as in Saxony in 1572, which decreed that even 'good' witches were to be burnt. Even if they had harmed nobody they had made pacts with the devil and were potential dangers. In

The Witch as Victim

Scotland, which did not benefit on this point from its links with the continent, a law in 1563 had prescribed death not only to good and bad witches but to those who consulted them. Elizabethan England preserved the distinction between good and bad witches, comparable to the difference between evil thinkers and actual poisoners, but James I of England had the law changed since he 'found a defect in the statute ... by which none died for witchcraft but only they who by that means had killed so that such were executed rather as murderers'.

The twenty-four Aberdeen witches of 1587, after being identified by pricking to find the devil's spot, were bound to stakes, strangled and their bodies burnt. It was said that the black reek and stench from the burnings hung over the burgh for weeks. A few whose guilt was not proven were branded on the cheek and banished, and some of the accused had already committed suicide in prison. The Lancaster witches in 1612 were undoubtedly a rough lot; they were accused among other things of plotting to blow up Lancaster Castle, and in the fierce religious controversies of that time and region it is understandable that the authorities were alarmed. These supposed witches were not tortured but the fury of the crowds, and the leading questions and browbeating of the magistrates, may well have led the bewildered old women into the confessions that in time they freely gave. They accused one another of unnatural practices, from eating mutton on Good Friday to concourse with devils in the shape of black cats and dogs. Some of the prisoners were acquitted after exhortations to forsake the devil, and one was condemned to the pillory on four market days and to remain in prison for a year without bail. Of the ten condemned to death, Thomas Potts in his account says tersely that they 'were executed the next day following, at the common place of execution, near unto Lancaster'.[4] There is no indication of their sufferings among the jeers and curses of the crowd, and no humane word of pity for them since they had been proved servants of the devil.

Pity the victims indeed! Whether in the countless holocausts on the continent, or the quieter but just as fatal hangings in Britain, the inquisitors seem not to have been stirred by any compassion for their victims. This was because they believed the witches to be guilty, to be in the pay of the devil and beyond all human care or divine offer of salvation. They did not stop to consider whether the inquisitors themselves might not be mistaken, and so guilty of great crimes. Only rare spirits like Johann Weyer and Reginald Scot, while accepting the reality of witchcraft, argued that all the activities for which witches were executed were illusions. The almost universal credulity explains why the records of the inquisitions were not interested in the emotions of the victims themselves. Why should they be? Only rarely do we come across an honest expression of feeling from an accused person himself, rather than a statement attributed to him by witch-hunters. This can be illustrated from the well-known letter by Johannes Julius, burgomaster of Bamberg, which was one of the worst places of persecution and whose 'witch-bishop' tortured and burned more than six hundred people. Julius under torture had confessed to renouncing God and serving the devil and implicated twenty-seven of his colleagues. But in the letter which he smuggled out of prison to his daughter Veronica he declared, 'you have here all my acts and confessions, for which I must die. It is all falsehood and invention, so help me God. For all this I was forced to say through fear of the torture which was threatened beyond what I had already endured. For they never leave off the torture until one confesses something; be he never so good, he must be a witch.'[5]

The emotions of the victims do not often come through in this way, many of them were illiterate and others were unable to publish their true feelings. The recorders of witchcraft write blandly of torture, devils and executions. Witch-cults, Dianic rites, diabolical plots, flying vampires, cannibalistic feasts, synagogues and sabbaths, all figure in theories invented by lawyers intent on gain or theologians sitting quietly in their studies. Only occasionally does there appear a protest such as that of the Jesuit Friedrich Spee, who was so revolted by the horrors in Würzburg that he wrote a book against the whole superstition. Not only did he attribute all the confessions of witchcraft to torture, but he spoke with great pity of 'the squalor of prisons, the weight of chains, the fear of the implements of torture, and the lamentations of the poor'.

It is a relief to turn from the large-scale wickedness of medieval and Renaissance Europe to the milder and more tolerant atmosphere of Africa, so wrongly dubbed the Dark Continent. Surely the adjective should have been used of Europe, and the name 'savage' so commonly employed, and still current in French writings, applies far more to our own ancestors than to those of Africa. Even

The Witch as Victim

Trevor-Roper in his recent study of witchcraft writes of Augustine's 'African credulity', a term more applicable to Europe.[6]

In the nineteenth century armchair anthropologists spun their hypotheses of the origins of religion and magic, using traveller's reports from Africa and other distant places to bolster up the most improbable theories. In this century anthropologists and other writers in Africa have been on the spot, learning languages and customs, and producing precise and particularist accounts of religions. It is now clear that, whatever other beliefs in religion or witchcraft may be held in Africa, these do not include dying gods, sacrificed kings or substitute victims. There is no devil in African belief, no 'horned god' or obscene ritual. Some societies had monarchs, others did not. Some rulers were almost absolute, but more commonly their powers were limited and controlled. They ruled for various periods of time, and it is not possible to fit their deaths into schemes for sacrifice or for stimulating the fertility of land and people. In any case they have no direct connection with witchcraft.

What is generally termed witchcraft belief in Africa holds that there are some people who have the power of harming others by spiritual means, using forces that are not possessed by ordinary folk or cannot be detected normally. Much sickness is attributed to witchcraft and in some places all or most death is held to be caused by it. Witchcraft is to be distinguished from magic, good or bad, and usually the witch is believed to use spiritual forces and not material medicines. Another distinction is that in many places, though not everywhere, most or all witches are thought to be women, whereas magicians are generally men. Witchcraft may be thought to be inborn or inherited, but magic manipulates tools and substances.

The mythology of African witchcraft, following on the attribution of sickness to witches, includes the provision of victims for consumption at cannibalistic feasts by bands of witches, their flying to the orgy at night, riding on or accompanied by bats, owls, fireflies and other familiars. The notion of a soul separable from the body allowed the development of the belief that witches leave their bodies asleep at home and not only fly off to orgies but attack other wandering souls in the process. Such points of similarity to medieval European belief justify comparison, but our concern here is with the practice of witch-hunting and the fate of the caught witches, to see how the victims fare in this other continent.

It is difficult to find out how people accused of witchcraft were dealt with in Africa in the past, because the records are absent or superficial. Modern times have brought restrictive laws upon the treatment of people accused of witchcraft or offensive sorcery, and it is not easy to discover how much this has altered African custom. The question is important because on the one hand some Africans and Europeans maintain that most witches used to be killed summarily when caught, but on the other hand some anthropologists think that this has been much exaggerated and even argue that the belief in witchcraft served a useful purpose in cleansing society. Have they forgotten the victims?

Stories are told by reputable writers about the practices of the past. J. Buxton, speaking of the Mandari of the Sudan, tells of the grandfather of a present diviner. This man, Munya, was killed for witchcraft or sorcery. He was asked into a village to rest, since a bush-pig was to be roasted. When the fire was going somebody said, 'Everything is ready, bring the pig.' Munya was seized, bound to some stakes and thrown on the fire. His family survived but his son moved away to escape suspicion of witchcraft and the taint still affects the diviner grandson, though he is generally well liked.[7] J. Beattie, on the Bunyoro, reports that 'it is said' that in the latter part of the nineteenth century many 'sorcerers' were tied up in dried banana leaves and burnt to death.[8] And V. W. Turner declares that 'in the past' Ndembu custom decreed that a witch or sorcerer should be punished to death by burning, or confiscation of property and expulsion from society.[9]

Different points of view are expressed by Evans-Pritchard in his classic study of witchcraft and oracles among the Azande, saying that in pre-European days witches could be killed but this happened rarely, unless a man committed a second or third murder, and for a first offence compensation could be accepted.[10] And Monica Wilson of the Nyakyusa reports that a supposed witch was rarely killed, but if a man was convicted of witchcraft and did not admit it he was compelled to leave his village and forfeit his property to the chief.[11]

In this century laws in many African countries have been formulated on post-Renaissance European models, not only directed against those who are thought to have been practising witchcraft but also against accusers of other people of witchcraft. Even the

The Witch as Victim

consultation of diviners has been penalised in some lands, which is like making fortune-telling a crime. In 1928 the laws of Kenya prohibited anyone to profess to exercise supernatural powers, which would have put some of the prophets of the Bible into prison. The result has been that divination is practised in secret, or in a neighbouring country to which consultants go. Generally people are accused of witchcraft at informal assemblies or local courts, but not in central courts. And only the highest court can pass sentence of death. Men and women accused of witchcraft may be fined, or expelled from their homes if the offence is thought to be grave and repeated. In some places not even that action is taken, as will be seen later.

Most African societies have witch-doctors or witch-finders whose function is to cure those who are thought to have been bewitched, and to find out the witches and neutralise their power. Such witch-doctors are public and respected leaders of the community and are not themselves witches, though they are thought to possess supernatural powers which enable them to deal with witches without danger. They proceed in a variety of ways, one of which is the ordeal, to be discussed presently.

Nowadays there are new witch-hunting movements, and it is sometimes thought that these arise and flourish because there is more belief in witchcraft today than in the past. Such a statement is incapable of proof because of our almost total ignorance of the incidence of witchcraft belief in bygone centuries. It is further suggested that modern times have brought so many new fears and troubles that witchcraft beliefs have increased in order to explain and alleviate these ills. To this C. G. Baëta has retorted that the troubles of the present century are probably no worse, and may be a good deal easier, than those of past eras which knew the slave trade, tribal wars, and high mortality, all of which upset tribal stability.[12]

New witch-hunting movements apply their own methods to accused witches. In the Bamucapi witch-hunts of the 1930s in East and Central Africa the accused were selected by mirrors, forced to confess their guilt, and purged by the administration of soapy medicines. They were told that the medicine would kill those who reverted to witchcraft after drinking it, and the further threat was added that the witch-finders would return and call witches to destruction by beating drums. In the Nana Tongo or Atinga witch-hunt, which spread from Ghana to Nigeria in the forties and fifties, the witches were detected by the Atinga men who went into trances after dancing. The witches were pointed out, or their guilt was further proved by submitting a chicken to an ordeal, the answer coming from the manner in which it fell to its death. The accused people, who were all women in Nigeria, were made to confess and pay heavy fines. One writer says that some women were tortured to make them confess and that two were beaten to death. It is pleasant to note that some women were freed by their sons, who fought the witch-hunters because they could not believe their mothers to be guilty of witchcraft.[13] Spotting and curing witches has also been practised in some of the independent churches who, since they could not ascribe sickness to the wrath of the ancestors, have tended to blame it on witchcraft. The prophets or officials of these churches have been credited with the powers of detecting witchcraft or unconfessed sin. Suspects, or sometimes whole congregations, have been passed before the officials and accused persons were obliged to confess. If they refused they were expelled from the church. The great emphasis placed upon adult baptism by full immersion comes in part from its value in cleansing from both sin and witchcraft.

The use of ordeals to determine witchcraft has been widespread in Africa, though many have now been suppressed or modified. The ordeal was supposed to prove the guilt of the accused person by killing him and the commonest ordeal was drinking poison, which an innocent person should vomit. Sometimes both the accuser and the accused drank poison, and the family concerned might choose a representative who vomited easily. It is difficult to find out how often the dose was fatal, but it certainly was at times. Those who claim that witchcraft belief was useful tend to forget that the poison ordeal might have convicted the wrong person. It is said that there used to be many ordeals among the Lele of the Congo and many people died, but the ordeal was suppressed in 1930. It seems that Lele ordeals were held only at intervals, when everybody who had been accused of witchcraft drank poison. Those who survived were then compensated by their accusers, but the relatives of those who died had to compensate the families of people who had died of witchcraft. Mary Douglas reports that after the collapse of Belgian administration in the Congo in 1959 there was an outbreak of poison ordeals and hundreds of people are said to have died.[14]

Other ordeals included dropping arrow poison in the accused

person's eyes, plunging his arm into hot water or boiling oil, making him lick a hot iron or walk over hot ashes. Not enough details are recorded to state whether such ordeals were always fatal or injurious. They were supposed to give the accused witch a chance if she had pleaded innocence, but if the ordeal harmed her she would be even more fiercely exposed to the anger of the crowd.

Nowadays, and perhaps to some extent in the past, ordeals are administered to animals, especially chickens. Sometimes fowls are kept for the specific purpose of subjecting them to ordeals, and the poison which is given is thought to prove that the oracle speaks through the fowls to indicate the guilt or innocence of the witch. Since the ordeal is given to the chicken, the accused person suffers no physical harm from the accusation, and this is important in considering the lot of the victim.

Evans-Pritchard says that in pre-European days Azande witches were very seldom slain and nowadays they may not even suffer.[15]

> I had certainly expected to find, not only that witchcraft was abhorrent to Azande, but that a witch, though not killed today owing to European rule, suffers social ostracism. I found that this was far from being the case. On the contrary, confirmed witches, known for miles around as such, live like ordinary citizens. Often they are respected fathers and husbands, welcome visitors to homesteads and guests at feasts, and sometimes influential members of the inner-council at a prince's court. Some of my acquaintances were notorious witches.

This would not be agreed upon everywhere and people accused of witchcraft often suffer in African societies. Nevertheless, the quotation reveals an important aspect of African belief. This is, that witchcraft is thought to be a power in many people, but it is often regarded as normally latent and only in need of checking when it becomes offensive. Even so, people may be accused of witchcraft or sorcery because of a mysterious illness, and they may be expelled from their villages but return home later when the sick person is better. J. R. Crawford says of the Shona that 'killings by witchcraft are usually soon forgotten, it is the killings by violence that become part of tribal or family history'.[16]

Both traditional witch-doctors and modern witch-hunting movements demand confessions from witches and this subject is as important in Africa as it was in Europe. Confession is often taken as proof of the guilt of the witches and evidence of the fact of witchcraft. If one tries to put oneself in the place of the accused person, and assume her innocence, several points emerge. Some people will confess to anything, for confession is good for the soul and it purges of known and unknown guilt. Others are surprised when accused, since they are ignorant of witchcraft activity, but if authority declares that they are guilty then they may accept the charge and confess to the deeds that witches are commonly supposed to indulge in. This is complicated by psychological ideas, for who knows what the soul has been doing when the body was asleep at home? Some confess under pressure, or mild torture, through fear or need for quiet. Those who refuse the accusation are submitted to an ordeal, or bring a chicken to undergo it for them, and may or may not be cleared. Relatively few protest their innocence to the end; they may still be beaten or expelled, and fewer still are regarded by the community as having proved their innocence and are able to carry on as if nothing had happened.

It is said by anthropologists that 'witchcraft accusations are not random'. This means that they arise out of the tensions of small societies and are not normally applied to people far away. Many accusations are made within the extended family and particularly against women who have fears and jealousies through living together. Co-wives, mothers-in-law, grandmothers, barren women, even healthy mothers, may all be accused if a child is ill or dies. It may be the child of another wife or their own, but with the high rate of infant mortality some scapegoat must be found for the mysterious death and there are women at hand who can be suspected of harmful influences. Other witchcraft accusations are made within the village community, with jealousies arising at work, in office or farm, and over social or natural misfortunes.

Some anthropologists have propounded a 'cathartic' theory to explain accusations of witchcraft, and they justify their continuance because they have relieved tensions and so helped social stability. Marwick, in a well known study of Cewa witchcraft, said that witchcraft beliefs helped to 'dissolve relations which have become redundant' and they 'blast down the dilapidated parts of the social structure and clear the rubble for new ones'.[17] In plain language this suggests that the witchcraft accusations, even if wrong, are useful in keeping the society well ordered. But critics of the cathartic theory have said that if witchcraft beliefs resolve some conflicts they

The Witch as Victim

produce others. They are spurious correctives of much more deep-seated troubles: disease, faulty family and social relationships, jealousy and fear. Rather than enabling people to take up their lives in a new atmosphere, they poison the air with lying accusations and become a drug which pollutes the system. Witchcraft beliefs have been compared to a safety valve, but Nadel says 'let us be clear that the engine which needs it has been badly constructed; nor is the safety valve itself safe'.[18]

The cathartic hypothesis, like many medieval theories of witchcraft, seems but the latest in a series of explanations which neglect the victim. People may not be killed for witchcraft today, but some were in the past. African witch-hunting was never organised on the colossal and diabolical scale of the European inquisitions, but it also had its cruelties and innocent victims. Poison ordeals were administered to people accused of ridiculous crimes, and the innocent died or were banished. Even today indiscriminate accusations, or baseless charges, are brought against many people, especially women, causing injustice and anguish. They disrupt society rather than cleanse it and make the continuation of harmonious contacts in families and villages more difficult instead of easier. Witch-hunters may regard ordeals and purgations as useful and important, but there is no doubt that from the point of view of the victim they are an unmitigated scourge. The victim's viewpoint shows that witchcraft belief is not a valuable cleansing agent, or a merely harmless delusion. It is a plague and a curse which has brought fear and pain to countless people, and its destruction is essential for truth and harmony, the sooner the better.

Notes

1. M. A. Murray, *The Witch-Cult in Western Europe*, 1921, pp. 12 f.
2. *A Contemporary Narrative of the Proceedings against Dame Alice Kyteler* Camden Society, 1843, pp. 3 f., 46.
3. *Malleus Maleficarum*, ed. M. Summers, 1948, vol 3, 13 f.
4. *The Trial of the Lancaster Witches*, ed. G. B. Harrison, 1929, p. 168.
5. H. C. Lea, *Materials Toward a History of Witchcraft*, 1939 ed., pp. 1175 f.
6. H. R. Trevor-Roper, 'Witches and witchcraft', *Encounter*, May 1967, p. 4.
7. J. Buston, 'Mandari witchcraft', in *Witchcraft and Sorcery in East Africa*, ed. J. Middleton and E. H. Winter, 1963, p. 111.
8. J. Beattie, 'Sorcery in Bunyoro', in ibid., p. 46.
9. V. W. Turner, *Ndembu Divination*, 1961, p. 11.

10 E. E. Evans-Pritchard, *Witchcraft, Oracles and Magic among the Azande*, 1937, p. 26.
11 M. Wilson, *Good Company*, 1951, p. 118.
12 C. G. Baëta, *Prophetism in Ghana*, 1962, p. 6.
13 E. G. Parrinder, *Witchcraft*, 1958 ed., p. 169 f.; *Witchcraft European and African*, 1963 ed., p. 173 f.
14 M. Douglas, 'Techniques of sorcery control in Central Africa', in *Witchcraft and Sorcery in East Africa*, p. 141.
15 Evans-Pritchard, op. cit., p. 114.
16 J. R. Crawford, *Witchcraft and Sorcery in Rhodesia*, 1967, p. 65.
17 M. G. Marwick, 'The social context of Cewa witch beliefs', *Africa*, 1952, pp. 232 f.
18 S. F. Nadel, *Nupe Religion*, 1954, p. 206. See also a criticism of the 'cathartic' theory in M. Douglas, op. cit., pp. 123 ff.

8

The Divine Hag of the Pagan Celts

Anne Ross

The sons of Mil advanced to a landing in Inber Slainge. The Tuatha Dé Danann did not allow them to come to land there, for they held not parley with them. By their *druidry* they caused it to appear to the sons of Mil that the region was no country or island, territory or land at all, in front of them. They encircled Ireland three times, till at last they took the harbour at Inber Scene . . . they held converse with Ériu in Usnech of Mide. She said to them, 'Warriors,' said she, 'welcome to you. Your coming has been long prophesied. The island will be yours for ever. *There is not a better island* in the world. No race will be more perfect than *your* race.'

'That's good,' said Amergin.

'We don't give thanks to *her* for that,' said Donn, 'but to *our* gods and to *our* power.'

'A gift to me, O sons of Mil, and the children of Bregan, that my *name* may be upon this island.'

'It will be its chief name forever,' said Amergin, 'that is, Ériu.'[1]

In the above passage from the Irish 'Book of Invasions', one of the eponymous goddesses of Ireland comes out to meet the invaders; recognising their supremacy she seeks to placate and to flatter them, and demands a favour of them. The land, the locality, were of first importance to the Celts, and this feeling for place has continued in the Celtic temperament down to the present day; it is thus not surprising that the Celtic goddesses tended to be particularly concerned with, or connected with the place or places in which they were venerated; and, by ensuring that the land would bear her name forever, Ériu does in fact gain a victory even in the moment of defeat: she makes certain that the memory of her cult will be enshrined in the *land* by the conquerors themselves. In another context she is reputed to have formed an army by magic, out of sods of earth in order to oppose the sons of Mil as they seek to take possession of the island; she also appears in her more sinister guise, as well as revealing her startling beauty to the invaders. At one moment they see her as a beautiful woman; at another, she has assumed the shape of a sinister, beaked, pale grey crow, this linking her with the trio of war-goddesses.[2]

Donn mentions 'our gods and our powers'. What can the tradition tell us of these? Deviousness may be said to be one of the most typical and enduring characteristics of the Celtic temperament; and duality one of the most fundamental aspects of their religion. The god is benevolent, but his malevolence is never far beneath the surface of his geniality; he may be portrayed with two faces, but both are sinister—one grimly so, the other with an upturned, but utterly unsmiling mouth. The deity, moreover, is never far removed from his cult animal. He may be encountered in the form of his sacred stag, dog, horse or bird as the case may be;[3] he may, on the other hand, appear in fully anthropomorphic guise, accompanied by his choice of companion from the bird or animal world. The goddess, for her part, is at once creator and destroyer, gentle and fierce, mother and nurturer. She may slay by means of her magical powers, or by her invincible weapons; she often claims the severed heads of those killed in battle as her just portion. The Irish tales are full of references to such beings, from the fearsome trio of war-goddesses, with their bird-form and their powers of sexuality and fecundity, to the stately goddesses symbolic of the divine sovereignty of Ireland, whose matchless beauty could change in an instant into an ugliness which no man but one with the courage and character to equip him for kingship itself could face; and whose repulsive sexual advances he could bring himself to accept without an obvious flinching.[4] The power of the woman was a reality in the early Celtic world. There are practical reasons why this should have been so, quite apart from the universally accepted magic associated with her capacity to bear and nurture children. She could achieve high status in Celtic society; and of her physical powers Diodorus the Sicilian commentator on the Celts, for example, says: 'The Gallic women are not only equal to their husbands in stature, but they rival with them in strength as well'. He also remarks:

The Divine Hag of the Pagan Celts

'Although their wives are beautiful they pay little attention to them.'[5]

Ammianus Marcellinus gives a graphic account of the powers of the female when he says:[6]

> Almost all the Gauls are of tall stature, fair and ruddy, terrible for the fierceness of their eyes, fond of quarrelling and of overbearing insolence. In fact a whole band of foreigners will be unable to cope with one of them in a fight, if he calls in his wife, stronger than he by far and with flashing eyes; least of all when she swells her neck and gnashes her teeth, and poising her huge white arms begins to rain blows, mingled with kicks like shots discharged by the twisted cords of a catapult.

Such comments find echo in all the remaining source material. For Britain, for example, Dio Cassius implies a similar state of affairs in his vivid description of Boudicca, powerful queen of the Iceni and leader in the great revolt of AD 60 which almost brought disaster to the Romans; Cartimandua, queen of the Brigantes was clearly a woman of similar powers and proportions.

The divine world of the pagan Celts would seem to have been conceived of as a direct reflection of their mundane society. As with the mortal woman, so with the goddess—powerful, given to magic and treachery, concerned with prognostication, highly fertile. Strabo does, in fact, refer to the great excellence of the Gaulish women in bearing and rearing children;[7] achieving their own desires as much by enchantment, incantations and spells as by their sheer physical strength. Moreover, the islands exclusively occupied by goddesses which are such a recurrent motif in the literary tradition are paralleled by the insular retreats of priestesses, and so had a basis in fact as well as belief. The terrifying power of such women is recorded by Strabo; quoting the ethnographer Posidonius, he says:[8]

> There is a small island in the ocean, not far from the land, lying off the mouth of the Loire; and the women of the Samnites inhabit it; they are possessed by Dionysius and propitiate the god with initiations and other sacred rites; and no man may land on the island, but the women themselves sail out from it and have intercourse with men and then return. It is their custom once a year to remove the roof of their temple and to roof it again the same day before sunset, each woman carrying part of the burden; but the woman whose load falls from her is torn to pieces by the others, and they carry the pieces around the temple.

A similar situation is suggested in a story in the prose *Dindshenchas* called 'Inbir n-Ailbine'. An Irish warrior called Ruad is voyaging across the ocean when he found[9]

> they were unable to voyage in any direction, just as if an anchor was holding them. So then Ruad went out over the ship's side that he might know what it was that was stopping them . . .; there he sees nine women, the loveliest of the world's women, detaining them, three under each ship. So they carried Ruad off with them and he slept for nine nights with each of the women. . . . And one of them became with child by him, and he promised that he would come again to them if he should perform his journey. Then Ruad went to his foster-son's house and stayed with him for seven years, after which he did not keep his tryst truly, but fared on to Magh Muirigh. So the nine women took the son (that had been born among them), and set out, singing, in a boat of bronze, to overtake Ruad, and they did not succeed. So the mother kills her own son and Ruad's only son, and she hurls the child's head after him.

Surely some reminiscence of the ghastly child-sacrifices which are so well-attested by the archaeological evidence for Celtic cults.[10] However, although many of the Celtic goddesses do reveal such qualities of fierceness and vengefulness, it does not apply to them all. Humans and gods alike could be seduced by more tranquil and gentle beings to a happier Otherworld where they could indulge in all the pleasures they would have desired in their mortal realms, and live with their divine companion in bliss and peace for as long as they themselves chose to do so.

There can, however, be little doubt that the goddesses whose powers would seem to have been especially great and enduring did possess this fundamental duality of personality and function, even if their *physical* appearance did not always alter to suit it. The great queen of Connacht in the Ulster Cycle of Irish tales, Medb, 'Drunk Woman', for example, was a powerful warrior, a ruthless insatiable woman—in fact Fergus Mac Ro-Each, 'Fergus son of Great Horse', the epitome of virility, was the only man who could hope to satisfy her sexual appetite; the long list of her various husbands indicates her supremacy in the sphere of female activity and power. Again, in the Welsh tradition, the goddess Ceridwen, with her varied transformations, jealously guards the secrets of her mysterious cauldron which confers poetic wisdom on anyone who should happen to sample its contents;[11] and a great supernatural female,

The Divine Hag of the Pagan Celts

such as the giantess in the story of Branwen[12] is often put in charge of such a magical vessel—whether it contain the gift of poetic powers, or the capacity to restore the dead to life or of seeing into the future. The well-known folk-motif of the power of the giant's mother—Grendel's mother, for example, who is much more dangerous than the monster himself[13]—must be a carry over from these early tales figuring the almost invincible qualities of the divine hag—the goddess in her most formidable aspect.

Cú Chulainn, the hero of the Táin, is alleged to have learnt his knowledge of arms from two powerful female war-goddesses, whose sexuality and maternal aspects are as strongly-developed as their skill in weapons and strategy. Scáthach, 'the Shadowy One', who would seem to have had her domain somewhere in the Scottish Highlands, taught him the use of arms 'until he attained mastership of feats with her'. He approaches the fierce queen in typically-heroic fashion: he is advised by her daughter Uathach, 'The Terrible One', how to gain access to her mother:[14]

> She advised him, if it were to achieve valour that he had come, that he should go through the hero's salmon leap to reach Scathach, in the place where she was teaching her two sons, Cuar and Cett, in the great yew-tree; that he should set his sword between her breasts until she yielded him his three wishes: namely, to teach him without neglect; that without the payment of wedding-gifts he might wed Uathach; and that she should foretell his future, for she was a prophetess.

She was, in fact, a typical divine hag. Scáthach had a queen named Aífe for neighbour, and there was bitter enmity between them. Cú Chulainn goes into single combat with her; he overcomes her by strategy:[15]

> Then he threw her from him to the ground, and over her held his naked sword.... 'My three demands to me' he said ... 'that you give hostages to Scáthach, nor ever afterwards oppose her, that you remain with me this night before your stronghold, and that you bear me a son.

Cú Chulainn has yet another encounter to face with a divine hag before he can return to Ulster: this one, with her birdlike characteristics has clear affinities with the war-raven goddesses and may indeed be a manifestation of one of them:[16]

As he went along the same road, he met an old woman on the road, blind of her left eye. She asked him to beware and to avoid the road before her. He said there was no other footing for him, save on the cliff of the sea that was beneath him. She besought him to leave the road to her. Then he left the road, only clinging to it with his toes. As she passed over him she hit his great toe to throw him off the path, down the cliff. He had forseen it, and leaped the hero's salmon-leap up again, and struck off the woman's head. She was Éis Énchenn, 'Birdhead', the mother of the last three warriors that had fallen by him.

The name, the blindness of the left eye, the hag-like form, all these characteristics link her with the basic divine warrior goddess who was clearly such a fundamental and widespread concept in the religion of the pagan Celtic world. And in the world of mankind, women did in fact take part in battle; the custom was allegedly stopped by Adamnan, as being heathen, and it certainly could not be reconciled to Christian ethics. The Church was always suspicious of women and never quite comfortable about them—the pagan women were too powerful and dangerous. St Patrick prayed against the spells of women, smiths and Druids—a powerful trio of magic-makers! The 'spells of women' (*brichta ban*) are also referred to in the Irish tales and were clearly believed in, and feared. This belief in the powers of magic in certain women has persisted in Celtic folk tradition. In one of the 'Journey Prayers' recorded by Carmichael[17] protection is invoked against:

> The woman on her knee,
> The woman at her evil eye,
> The woman with her spleen,
> The woman with her envy;
>
> The woman at the cattle of her herd,
> The woman at the young of her cows,
> The woman at the rearing of her flocks,
> Until it reaches the fibres of her heart.
>
> The woman frowning and foul, ...
> Until she reach the place whence she came.
>
> Each woman who is full of spleen and envy,
> Who sunders her blood, her flesh and gore,
> On herself be her spleen and her severing,
> From this day to the final day of the world.

The Divine Hag of the Pagan Celts

In this passionate invocation for protection on a journey, we seem to have a *double-entendre* as it were; the 'woman' is, no doubt, the universal witch-figure, mortal, but possessing super-normal and hostile powers. She is also likely to be one of the many local divine hags whom the traveller was likely to encounter on his lonely journey over the hills, herding her beasts, guarding the waters of her sacred well (Fig. 1), and adding to the hazards of an already

Figure 1 Altar to Coventina, from Coventina's Well, Carrawbrough, Northumberland

arduous passage.[18] This fear of and dislike of women because of their alleged unnatural powers goes right back in Celtic tradition. Giraldus the Welshman writing in the twelfth century, castigates the female sex and quotes Cicero in support of his own sentiments, when he says: 'And in the same manner, as we may gather grapes off thorns or figs off thistles, Tully describing the nature of women says, "Men, perhaps for the sake of some advantage, will commit one crime; but woman, to gratify one inclination, will not scruple to perpetrate all sorts of wickedness." '[19] and, in his dispraise of women he says: 'and in Ecclesiasticus, "There is no head above the head of a serpent; and there is no wrath above the wrath of a woman" ', and when, as in the Táin, the Mórrígan, the war-raven goddess, turns into a water serpent to attempt to hinder Cú Chulainn and so bring about his downfall, the combination is indeed a formidable one.

Duality is then at the basis of all Celtic thought; everything had, for them, a double meaning; many of their artistic forms are meant to be seen in two different ways; and also to possess a duality of significance—naturalistic and symbolic. In the literary motif of goddess into hag this trait is very obvious; it is seen most clearly in the stories of the conferring of the divine sovereignty of Ireland by such a deity on the king-elect (p. 162 below). In this context the goddess appears to the future king, and as a rule to his two brothers, in the form of a hideous old woman; the brothers reject her sexual advances with horror. The one who is to be king, however, accepts them, and thereupon the hag turns into the most lovely girl imaginable. She is the deified 'Sovereignty' of Ireland; she mates with the king-elect, thus bestowing his majesty on him and blessing him and his reign. She is beautifully portrayed in the tale known as 'Baile in Scáil', 'The Phantom's Frenzy'; the Phantom, is of course, the pan-Celtic god, Lugh (Lugus) himself. Conn, king of Ireland is met by a strange horseman who leads him to the Dumb Phantom's dwelling; the house was thirty feet long with a ridge-pole of white gold. Inside the house is a girl sitting on a chair of crystal and wearing a gold crown. In front of her is a silver vat with corners of gold. A vessel of gold stands beside her and in front of her is a golden cup. The Phantom is seated on his throne and no one has ever seen such a splendid being. The girl is the Sovereignty of Ireland; she gives meat and ale to Conn while the Phantom recites all the names of the future kings of Ireland until the last king is reached.[20] In Ireland

The Divine Hag of the Pagan Celts

the goddesses, as we have seen, were closely bound up with the land and a particular locality and as a result the concept of the deity of the territory—the *territorial* goddess—was one which received much notice in the tradition.

The description of the fearful, sexual war-goddesses in the story of 'The Destruction of Da Derga's Hostel' typifies the dual nature of this fierce trio. In one cubicle of the house of the formidable Da Derga,[21] called the 'Cubicle of the War-Goddesses', the three deities are described as being naked and on the ridge-pole of the house: 'their jets of blood coming through them, and the ropes of their slaughter on their necks'.[22]

The war-goddess, in single form this time, but still in her most horrific aspect, appears again in the same tale:[23]

> As Conaire was going to Da Derga's hostel, a man with black, cropped hair, with one hand and one eye and one foot[24] overtook them. . . . A pig, black-bristled, singed, was on his back, squealing continually and a woman, big-mouthed, huge, dark, ugly, hideous, was behind him. Though her snout were flung on a branch, the branch would support it. Her pudenda reached to her knees.

This description of the war-goddess in her most repellent form brings to mind the extraordinary carvings found in Ireland in particular, but also elsewhere in the British Isles, portraying a

Figure 2 Sheelagh-na-Gig from Lavey, Co. Cavan

hideous hag, whose features are often composed in a repulsive leer; her body is naked, and the often grossly-exaggerated sexual organs are indicated by the hands (Fig. 2). Some of these carvings must date to the earliest centuries of the Christian era, others are considerably later. Various interpretations for this strange group of figures have been put forward, but no really satisfactory explanation for them has been reached. I would like to suggest that, in their earliest iconographic form they do in fact portray the territorial or war-goddess in her hag-like aspect, with all the strongly sexual characteristics which accompany this guise in the tales; and that they are not 'pornographic' or 'erotic' monuments but have both a fertility and an evil-averting significance.[25] This would serve to explain why they are frequently to be found in association with Christian churches. Such figures could hardly have been built into religious buildings of the post-pagan period unless it was to canalise

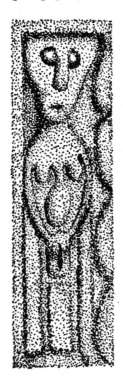

Figure 3 Sheelagh-na-Gig from Liathmor Old Church, Co. Tipperary

The Divine Hag of the Pagan Celts

the evil-averting powers they were believed to possess. If they were found on the site of the church[26] their powers could then be used for the benefit of Christians, once they had been purified as it were by Christian rites; and any latent paganism in the area would find a *double* satisfaction both in the continuing homage offered to this once-powerful deity and in her inclusion in the wider Christian pantheon as a still-vital protectress of the ground over which she was once sovereign. Just as the Romans allowed the veneration of native deities to continue in the Empire once they had been brought into the wider orbit of the official cults, so the Christian Church permitted the worship of local deities to continue in cases where it was possible to bless them and cause them to serve Christianity instead of paganism.

These strange apotropaic-fertility figures are known in Irish tradition as *sheelagh-na-gigs* (Fig. 3). A splendid example is housed in St Michael's church, Oxford, and dates probably to the Roman period; another was found in association with the priory at St Ives, Huntingdonshire; one is built into a church at Rodil, Harris in the Outer Hebrides; another is known from Yorkshire, and so on. This same concept of the powerful, fierce goddess also occurs in numerous iconographic contexts, where her sexual characteristics are, however, symbolised, rather than demonstrated in the frank manner of the *sheelagh* figures. For example, a voluptuous, naked female figure of the Venus-type, from Espeyran, (petite Camargue), stands with her right hand resting on a herm;[27] she thus dominates the severed male head in a manner which we can see paralleled elsewhere in the iconography, and recounted in the insular tales.[28] Found in a funerary context, this figurine would again have the *double* significance of fertility (symbolised by the female figure and the human head) and its power over death, which is also symbolised by the head. This iconographic group gains added significance when we come to consider the nature of the Irish seasonal goddesses who presided over *cemetery* sites in the ancient Irish world (p. 155 below). Another, a sinister, seated goddess from a grotto at Vence, near Marseilles,[29] has sharp, almost beaked features; she holds on her lap a severed male head; here we have the mother-goddess concept, but she holds, not a child, but a severed head, symbolic both of fertility and the Otherworld—and, in a war-like society which decapitated its enemies—death. (Fig. 4)

Human heads, taken in battle, were offered up to the Irish

Figure 4 Seated Goddess with severed head, from a grotto at Vence, Bouches-du-Rhône, France

war-goddesses; and the presence of similar bird-war goddesses in the wider Celtic world is suggested by such things as an inscription from Haute-Savoie which reads (C)athu-bodva 'Battle Raven' (Irish, Badb Catha),[30] and Gaulish personal names compounded from the word *bodb* 'crow'—for example, Bodocenus or Boduagnatus 'born or descended from the goddess Bodb'.[31] These personal names suggest the significance of this deity as an ancestor-goddess, a further link with her powers of fertility and generation. The raven-goddess appears as a stately draped woman on an altar from Sarrebourg with Sucellus, 'the Good Striker', the god with the hammer attribute, as her companion. A large raven stands below the two figures. She occurs with her raven attribute in two or three other Gaulish contexts, once winged.[32] Other figures suggestive of the divine hag with her bird-attributes are to be found in such contexts as the lid of the jar cover from Linwood, Hants, used by the New Forest potters in Roman times;[33] and even earlier in the form of the owl-goddess who adorns the terminals of the magnificent gold torcs found at Reinheim, Saarland, Germany.[34] They were recovered, together with other articles of inestimable value, from the burial of a powerful noblewoman, testifying yet again to the high social standing that could be enjoyed by women in the ancient Celtic world. Another later relief seems to suggest this same sinister concept; it is portrayed on a schist plaque, found at Bathwick, near Bath in 1966[35] in the form of three grim goddesses, having enormous eyes, but with the mouths omitted; they wear pleated dresses and have their hands folded across their chests and their total appearance is strongly suggestive of the Divine Mother in her more formidable manifestation.

Another great Irish goddess, Anu, was believed to nurture the gods themselves; and she may perhaps be compared with the stern goddess who adorns one of the plaques of the silver cauldron found at Gundestrup, Denmark.[36] She is flanked by a pair of eagles, and a raven perches on her right, outstretched fingers. A woman dresses her hair into tresses while another, wearing a long, ribbed knitted dress, sits on her bare left shoulder. She wears the sacred torc. Her breasts are bare; below the left breast lies a man, while a dog is stretched below the right. Here the goddess would seem to be related to the concept of the raven-goddesses especially in their maternal, nurturing aspect—nourisher of both the world of man, and of the animal kingdom. It is noteworthy that the Mórrígan's *breasts* are in fact commemorated in one of the stories in the prose *Dindshenchas:* 'Of the remarkable things of the Brug this: . . . the Bed of the Dagda in the first place. Thereafter the Two Paps of the Mórrígan.'[37]

Reminiscences of the terrible power of supernatural women seem to occur in some of the stories of the *Mabinogion*, underneath whose elegant, literary exterior lies a world of mythology and old belief. In the story of Culhwch and Olwen, with its strong undertones both of international story-motifs and ancient native tradition, Culhwch the young hero comes to the house of his mother's sister to seek aid in his search for the beautiful girl, Olwen:[38]

> They came to the gate of the shepherd Custennin's court. She heard the noise of their coming. She ran with joy to meet them, to try and throw her arms about their necks. Cei thrust a stake between her two hands. She squeezed the stake so that it became a twisted withe. Said Cei 'Woman, had it been I thou didst squeeze in this wise, there were no need for another to love me ever. An ill love, that.'

Many of the powerful territorial goddesses were described in the tales as having been taken over and made captive by invaders of Ireland, or as having been destroyed by them; or as having had a sanctuary of some kind created for them and conferring their names on it. Sometimes a seasonal festival was named after one of these goddesses. Temair, for example, who gave her name to Tara, one of the most sacred sites in Ireland, 'went to Ireland with her husband and every hill she would choose in Erin was given to her, and afterwards she designed on the hill of Tara a rampart and therein she was buried. Hence it is called Temair.'[39]

Here we have the founding of a royal seat and sanctuary attributed to a goddess; just as at Emain Macha (Navan Fort) near Armagh town, which recent archaeological excavations have shown to have been an important pagan sanctuary, the goddess Macha—Irish equivalent of the Gaulish horse-goddess Epona (Fig. 5), and the Welsh Riannon—was reputed to have given the fort its name in memory of her race against the swift horses of the king, Conchobor, and her death immediately afterwards on giving birth to the twins—Emain Macha, 'Macha's Twins'.[40]

The Mórrígan, the war-raven goddess, together with her two

Figure 5 Bronze of Epona with horses, from Wiltshire

The Divine Hag of the Pagan Celts

sisters, was the most terrifying of all the Celtic divine hags. In one of the *Dindshenchas* legends she was alleged to have given birth to a supernatural son called Meche; he had three hearts in his body with the embryos of serpents in the three; had he not been killed by the warrior Mac Cecht, the serpents inside the Mórrígan's son would have grown until they had destroyed the whole of Ireland. As it was, the hero burnt the serpent-ridden hearts and even so, the creatures in the river into which he threw the ashes, all died as a result of contact with them[41]—a fitting son for a goddess as malevolent and destructive as the war-goddess.

The Celtic goddesses, whether they had or had not hag-like aspects, did have strongly zoomorphic or ornithomorphic characteristics, and could either transform themselves into animals, or be transformed into animals, or had certain of these as their

Figure 6 Relief of horned god, goddess, three hooded figures and a ram, from Aquae Sulis (Bath), Somerset

Anne Ross

Figure 7   Relief of Verbeia with serpents, Ilkley, Yorkshire

particular attributes (Figs 6, 7). One story in the prose *Dindshenchas* for example, tells how a woman called Aige was transformed into a fawn, and chased round Ireland in this shape until she was finally slain; all that remained of her after her death was a bag of water. This was thrown into the river by her pursuers.[42] This would seem to have been a well-known motif connected with the cursing or transforming of supernatural women. For example, in another of the *Dindshenchas* tales, the Mórrígan herself curses another woman— Odras—for having bulled her cow on the goddesses' sacred bull; she curses her, and turns her into a pool of water. These examples from the Irish tradition would seem to bear some relationship to the famous Bath Curse—a curse on a lead tablet, written backwards, which reads, in translation: 'May he who carried off Vilbia from me become as liquid as water.'[43] Again, in the *Mabinogion*, a similar belief in transformation into liquid as a result of some shame or curse is implied in a passage in the 'Lady of the Fountain'. Cynon says: 'And when I came to the clearing the black man was there, and I confess to thee, Cei, it is a wonder I did not melt into a liquid pool for shame at the mockery I got from the black man.'[44]

The powerful goddesses sometimes gave birth to three sons at a single birth, according to the tradition. One such deity was the sinister Carman, after whom a seasonal festival was held. She had three grim sons, Dian, 'Violent', Dub, 'Black', Dothur, 'Evil'. In typical hag-goddess fashion:[45]

> by spells and charms and incantations the mother ruined every place. By plundering and dishonesty the men destroyed. ... So they went to Ireland to bring evil on the Tuatha Dé Danann by blighting the corn of this island upon them. To the Tuatha Dé Danann that seemed ill. So Ai ... and Cridenbel ... and Lugh Laebach ... and Be Cuille of their witches went to sing charms upon them ... and they parted not from them until they had driven the three men over sea. And the men left their mother Carman here as a pledge. ... their mother died of grief here in her hostageship and she asked the Tuatha Dé to hold her fair (*oenach*) at her burial-place, and that the fair and the place should always bear her name.

Another goddess who had a calendar festival named in her honour was Tailtiu. She was foster-mother to the great Celtic god Lugh (Lugus), and in her memory he allegedly established one of the most popular and enduring of the Celtic seasonal feasts —Lughnasad.[46] This was celebrated on, or about, 1 August. The chief importance of Oenach Tailten, celebrated at Teltown, near the junction of the Boyne with the Blackwater at Navan, was that it was a *cemetery*, not a royal seat—once again we have the concept of the goddess as guardian of the tomb. Another version of the legend associated the establishment of the calendar festival to the commemoration of Lugh's two wives, Nas and Búi; Búi was, in fact, another name for the Cailleach Bhéara. The prose *Dindschenchas* tells us that the two daughters of the son of the king of Britain were Lugh's wives. They died in due course, and Lugh gathered a great host together to lament them on the first day of August each year.[47]

The Cailleach Bhéara appears in the early literary tradition, and she is enshrined in modern Irish and Scottish Gaelic folk tradition.

Her especial geographical sphere was in south western Ireland; her longevity was legendary. She is, in origin, one of the numerous hag-goddesses, who, when their role as an active deity was terminated with the introduction of Christianity, became the familiar supernatural hag of folk belief—benevolent or malevolent as the case may be, or according to her mood, having marked local associations, and clearly defined fertility and pastoral connections. On Blaeberry Sunday, which was one of the many survivals of the Lughnasa festival in Ireland,[48] people used to resort to a rocky hillock close to Slieve Gullion in County Armagh, known as the Cailleach Bhéara's chair; she was believed to live in a deep chamber under the cairn on the top of the hill.

Such supernatural characters in Celtic tradition could be enumerated indefinitely; figures like Boand, wife of the Dagda, after whom the River Boyne was named;[49] Dub, wife of Enna, who got rid of her rival by chanting a 'sea-spell' over her and so causing her to be drowned.[50] Another story in the prose *Dindshenchas* tells of Crimthann, son of Lugaid who built a fort at Howth near Dublin; he went away with the witch or goddess, Nár, and slept with her for six weeks. In return for her favours she gave him many treasures including a chariot of gold; she was one of the divine people of Ireland—the Tuatha De Danann.[51]

Even when the goddess did not adopt hag-form, her supernatural powers enabled her to take on a different shape. This was sometimes done for sinister reasons, such as revenge; sometimes it was done in order to bring about the birth of some future hero. Dechtire, Conchobor Mac Nessa's sister, and fifty other girls disappear from Ulster. They return in the form of a bird-flock and destroy the vegetation on the plain of Emain Macha.[52] The girls hoped to trap the men of Ulster into following them, and this is what happened. They finally come to a superb house belonging to the god Lugh. He has mated with Dechtire and she gives birth to the semi-divine hero, Cú Chulainn. Heroes are often described as having been begotten by gods on semi-mortal women, or by heroes on supernatural females.

Cú Chulainn, born of a princess and a powerful god, is fated to encounter and combat with the divine hag on many occasions in his brief life. In the story of the Cattle Raid of Regamna, for example, the hero and his charioteer meet with a strange and frightening sight:

The Divine Hag of the Pagan Celts

They saw before them a chariot harnessed with a chestnut horse. The horse had but one leg and the pole of the chariot passed through its body, so that the peg in front met the halter passing across its forehead. Within the chariot sat a woman, her eye-brows red, and a crimson mantle around her. Her mantle fell behind her between the wheels of the chariot so that it swept along the ground.

This fearsome creature, who is accompanied by an equally horrific man, is, in fact, the dreaded war-goddess, the Mórrígan in hag form. Cú Chulainn, having been insulted by her, 'made a leap into the chariot. He put his two feet on her two shoulders, and his spear on the parting of her hair'. When she will not recite a poem to him he tries to leap again into the chariot:

Cú Chulainn prepared to spring again into the chariot; but horse, woman, man and cow had all disappeared. Then he perceived that she had been transformed into a black bird on a branch close by him. 'A dangerous enchanted woman you are' said Cú Chulainn.

This is the war-goddess at her most potent in the form of hag and bird at one encounter.

Cú Chulainn is brought into contact with certain divine hags again in the story of his approaching death. As he leaves Emain Macha on his last, tragic journey, he bids his nurse farewell:

Then he saw three Crones, blind of the left eye, before him on the road. They had cooked on spits of rowan-tree a dog with poisons and spells. And one of the things that Cú Chulainn was bound not to do was going to a cooking-hearth and consuming the food. And another of the things that he must not do, was eating his namesake's flesh. He refuses to approach the hearth and one crone says 'The food is only a hound. Were this a great cooking-hearth thou wouldst have visited us. But because what is here is little, thou comest not. Unseemly are the great who endure not the little and poor.'

The hero knows that all is up with him:[53]

Then he drew nigh to her, and the Crone gave him the shoulder-blade of the hound out of her *left* hand. And then Cú Chulainn ate it out of his *left* hand and put it under his *left* thigh. The hand that took it and the thigh under which he put it were seized from trunk to end, so that the normal strength abode not in them.

Although the Mórrígan appears so frequently as Cú Chulainn's opponent, she cannot bear to see his fate overtaking him; she acts as his protector by breaking up his chariot on the night before his fateful ride 'for she knew he would not come again to Emain Macha'—but in vain. Again, after his death, she comes with her two sisters and perches on his shoulder in the form of crows. 'That pillar is not wont to be under birds,' said Erc son of Cairbre.[54]

This is typical of the shadowy, sinister, ever-moving world of the pagan Celts, where the goddesses constantly take on or put off animal, bird, human or monstrous form, and influence the fortunes of mankind by their hostile or beneficent interference in the sphere of human action and destiny.

The divine hag often manifested herself as the spectral washer-at-the-ford; there it can be seen to be washing the clothing of someone about to die in battle.

These basic Celtic goddesses with their dual form of beauty and fertility, ugliness and destruction are, then, a well-attested type throughout the wider Celtic world, and the rites which accompanied their actual worship can be assumed from the archaeological evidence, and from veiled hints in the vernacular texts, to have been brutal and extravagant. Boudicca's fierce human sacrifices in honour of her goddess Andraste[55] support this supposition, and, although no dedication has as yet been found in the series of Romano-British temples found at Springhead in Kent, the remains of six-months-old babies, several of them decapitated and placed carefully in the corners of the buildings, together with a decapitated seagull, hint at the sacrifice of children at the foundation of the buildings, and are reminiscent of the child whose head was torn off by his mother in the Irish tale of Inber n-Ailbine (p. 142, above).[56] There also seems to be an echo here of the metrical *Dindshenchas* reference to the sacrifice of first-born children to the idol Crom Cruaich.[57] Skulls and bones of babies and young children have been recovered from many Celtic cult sites; and at the early La Tène sanctuary at Libenice in Czechoslavakia[58] where the burial of the priestess of the shrine was found, there were traces of child-sacrifice, and of the bloody rites connected with the diety or deities invoked there.

Such powerful deities would not only come into basic conflict with Christianity, but would inevitably continue to have a popularity amongst the people which the Church could not stem. Whenever possible the Christian Church would sanctify the more benign female divinities, such as Brigid, who survives in modern Scottish-Gaelic tradition in the role of midwife to the Virgin Mary. But where their reputation was too gruesome and anti-Christian,

The Divine Hag of the Pagan Celts

they would tend to be degraded into mere hags haunting specific localities or presiding over particular wells or megaliths which in themselves retained traditions of power and sanctity. Some of the later nuns, the Holy women, would, undoubtedly at some stage attract to themselves elements from popular belief about local supernatural figures. This would seem to have been the case with, say, Latiaran and her two sisters, so reminiscent of the trio of war-goddesses. At Cullen Well, Duhallow, Co. Cork, Latiaran Sunday was celebrated on, or before, 25 July. The well is situated beside the ruins of an old church in a grave-yard. A tree, said to have been planted by Latiaran, is situated close by the well. The feast was associated with the beginning of harvest, a time of plenty and celebration. A marvellous body of legend has grown up in connection with this ancient calendar festival. Latiaran, who is known only from the oral tradition, was one of three sisters, the other two being Lasair (Flame) and Inghean Bhuidhe (Yellow-haired Maiden).[59] The name Latiaran cannot be translated. These Christian ladies would seem, in origin, to have been local goddesses presiding over calendar festivals, and so here we have a conflation of pagan and Christian elements, a situation which must underlie so much of the Irish tradition. In other localities the names of the trio of Holy women differed, as is the case with groups of pagan deity-names. In Kerry, one of the sisters was known as Crobh Dearg (Red Claw); and Gobnait is alleged to have been one of the three in the region to the south of the Derry na Saggart Mountains. Each of the triads, however, attributes to a saint the three seasons—spring, summer and harvest. One legend records that the three sisters, Latiaran, Crobh Dearg and one other, went down, separately, into the ground, and at each place where they disappeared, a well sprang up, where people have paid rounds ever since. 'It is clear that these beliefs come down from a pre-Christian mythology.'[60]

J. F. Campbell in his great collection of Scottish Gaelic tales and traditions in the last century records several examples of the hag into goddess motif and vice versa. For example, in the story known as 'Nighean Righ fo Thuinn', 'The Daughter of the King under the Waves', we learn that

> The Finn were once together, on the side of Beinn Eudainn on a wild night, and there was pouring rain and snow from the north. About midnight a creature of uncouth appearance struck at Finn's

door. Her hair was down to her heels and she cried to him to let her in under the edge of his covering.

He refuses to allow her to come in, but finally Diarmad agrees and the story goes on:[61]

She went under the blanket, and he turned a fold of it between them. She was not long thus, when he gave a start and he gazed at her, and he saw the finest drop of blood that ever was.

Finn, like the other semi-divine heroes of the pagan Celtic world, often comes up against malevolent, hindering hags. In another tale, 'The Enchanted Cave of Keshcorran', Finn had been hunting with his men in Keshcorran and the ruler of the land there, Conaran son of Imidel, one of the Tuatha Dé Danann chieftains, took exception to this:[62]

As soon as he perceived that the hounds' cry now sounded deviously, he bade his three daughters (that were full of sorcery) to go and take vengeance of Finn for his hunting. The women sought the entrance of the cave that was in the mound, and there sat by each other. Upon three crooked and wry sticks of holly they hung many heathenish bewitched hasps of yarn, which they began to reel off lefthandwise in front of the cave. They had not been so long when Finn and Conan reached the cavern's edge, and so perceived the three hideous hags thus busied at its entrance; their three coarse heads of hair all dishevelled; their eyes rheumy and redly bleared; their three mouths black and deformed, and in the gums of each evil woman of them a set of sharpest venomous and curved fangs; their three craggy necks maintaining their heads on those formidable hags: their six arms extraordinarily long, while the hideous and brutish nail that garnished every finger of them resembled the thick-butted sharp-tipped ox-horn. Six bandy legs thickly-covered with hair and fluff supported them, and in their hands they had three hard and pointed distaffs.

The Celts certainly had the power to evoke horrific situations and beings, just as they could describe so exquisitely personal beauty and the perpetual loveliness of nature. These three terrors enchant Finn and his companions, and the story continues with the ultimate triumph of the Fenians over the hags. Such tales could be multiplied indefinitely.

Another monstrous female, akin to the Cailleach Bhéara, known in Scottish Gaelic tradition as A'Mhuileartach Bhuidhe, was also traditionally dispatched by Fionn and his warriors. She is described in Campbell's translation as:[63]

The Divine Hag of the Pagan Celts

> There were two slender spears of battle
> upon the other side of the hag
> her face was blue-black, of the lustre of coal,
> and her bone tufted tooth was like rusted bone.
>
> In her head was one deep pool-like eye
> swifter than a star in a winter sky
> upon her head gnarled brushwood,
> like the clawed old wood of the aspen shoot.

She says to the Fenians:

> Although I should get all the value of Eirinn,
> With her gold, and her silver, and her precious things
> I would rather have on board of my vessel,
> The heads of Osgar, and Raonaidh, and Coiril.

Another supernatural being, who must have originated as a local, pastoral goddess in the Scottish Highlands, was Cailleach Beinne Bric, who, like the numerous white ladies of English folk-tradition, was reputed to haunt a specific locality. She could be encountered driving her deer over the hills, or presiding over a potent spring—a folk-memorial to a once-powerful pagan divinity.

Such hags are met with in the stories of the Celtic saints, and it is, perhaps, noteworthy that the word *cailleach* 'hag' also means 'nun'. In the life of the Cornish and Breton saint, Samson of Dol, a sorceress, whose description resembles that of the Mórrígan, is described as having unkempt grey hair, *red* clothing (the colour of death), and grasping a blood-covered trident in her hand; in the life of the same saint we are introduced to a hairy horned hag, with a three-pronged lance, who allegedly flew through the woods.[64]

We can here detect a similarity between this flying hag and the figure of the horse-goddess Epona drawn on a tile from Roussas and dating to the fourth century AD. Here she has assumed hag-form, and she rides on the back of a horned, rein-wearing goose.[65]

Gerard Murphy, in his analysis of the *Duanaire Finn*[66] has appositely stressed the archaic nature of much of the content of modern Irish folk tradition, and this applies to the Celtic world in general: 'Many Irish folktale motifs are as old as the days of primitive Indo-European unity.'[67]

This is an important statement when one considers the archaic religious origins and the preservation in folk-entertainment contexts, of traditions concerning the nature and transformations of the gods and goddessess of the pagan Celtic world. The beautiful goddess, luring men to death, or to her Otherworld dwelling; the sinister, invincible triple war-goddess, with her strong sexuality, her hideous hag or bird transformation and her capacity to prognosticate disaster and preside over the dead and dying on the field of battle; the territorial goddess, unique in beauty, unrivalled in ugliness when she goes in hag-form to test the powers of endurance of the king-elect; the horse-goddess, beneficent, maternal, but fierce when opposed, mate of the king or chieftain-to-be in the form of a mare—all these powerful, diverse, yet basically homogeneous goddesses find some place in surviving folklore and superstition. They may figure as howling *banshees*, guardians of a particular family, wailing dolefully when death approached any of its members; as the hags of moor and mountain, washing the clothes of those about to leave this life for ever, herding their beasts on the hill-pastures, or glaring fiercely in the form of *sheelagh-na-gigs* from the wall of some church or other building. Whether taken over into Christianity as benign saints such as Brigid, or Latiaran and her two sisters, or preserved in some other form, it is clear that the Celtic goddesses had a long ancestry and an incredible longevity. Keats describes such a sinister, shadowy and fatally fascinating being in his poem 'La Belle Dame sans Merci', and his lines give faithful testimony to the enduring belief in her ruthless powers over mankind:

> Oh what can ail thee knight at arms,
> Alone and palely loitering?
> The sedge is withered from the lake
> And no birds sing.
>
> I met a lady in the meads,
> Full beautiful—a fairy's child
> Her hair was long, her foot was light,
> And her eyes were wild.

Notes

1 Tom Peete Cross and Clarke Harris Slover, eds, *Ancient Irish Tales*, Dublin, 1969, p. 18. All quotations from *Ancient Irish Tales*, copyright 1936, © 1964 by Holt, Rinehart & Winston, Inc., are reprinted by permission of Holt Rinehart & Winston, Inc., Publishers, New York.
2 Anne Ross, *Pagan Celtic Britain*, London, 1967, p. 205.
3 Ibid., chapters III and VII.

4 For fuller discussion of this theme of the king and the territorial goddess, see Rachel Bromwich, 'Celtic dynastic themes and the Breton lays', *Études Celtiques*, 9, pp. 439-74; P. MacCana, in *Études Celtiques*, 7, pp. 76 ff; 356 ff; 8, pp. 59 ff.
5 J. J. Tierney, 'The Celtic ethnography of Posidonius', *Proceedings of the Royal Irish Academy* vol. 60, section C, no. 5, Dublin, 1960, p. 252.
6 Ammianus Marcellinus, I, xv, 12.1 (Loeb edition, p. 145).
7 Tierney, op. cit., p. 268.
8 Ibid., p. 269.
9 W. Stokes, 'The prose tales in the *Rennes Dindshenchas*', *Revue Celtique*, 15, pp. 272-336.
10 See p. 158 of this chapter.
11 R. Bromwich, *Trioedd Ynys Prydein* ('The Welsh Triads'), Cardiff, 1961, p. 308.
12 G. and T. Jones, *The Mabinogion*, London, 1949 ed., pp. 30 f.
13 F. Klaeber, *Beowulf and the Fight at Finnsburg*, London, 1941, pp. 48 ff.
14 Cross and Slover, op. cit., p. 165.
15 Ibid., p. 167.
16 Ibid., p. 167.
17 Alexander Carmichael, *Carmina Gadelica* (ed. J. C. Watson), Edinburgh, 1940, vol. 3.
18 See p. 161 of this chapter.
19 Giraldus Cambrensis, *Itinerary through Wales*, London, 1944 ed., p. 27.
20 M. Dillon, *Early Irish Literature*, Chicago, 1948, pp. 107 f.
21 T. F. O'Rahilly, *Early Irish History and Mythology*, Dublin, 1948, p. 126.
22 For the sacrificial implications here see Ross, op. cit., p. 248.
23 Cross and Slover, op. cit., pp. 102 f.
24 A ritual posture.
25 It is a well-known and widespread belief that to expose the genitalia of either sex acts as a powerful apotropaic gesture.
26 Early churches must often have been built on pagan shrines or in their temenoi.
27 Human-headed pillar.
28 F. Benoit, *Le Symbolisme dans les sanctuaires de la Gaule*, Collection Latomus, vol. 105, Brussels, 1970, pl. I.
29 F. Benoit, *L'Art primitif méditerranéen de la vallée du Rhône*, Aix-en-Provence, 1955, pl. 2, 6.
30 Ross, op. cit., p. 244.
31 D. E. Evans, *Gaulish Personal Names*, Oxford, 1967, pp. 151 ff.
32 Ross, op. cit., p. 246.
33 Ibid., pp. 216 f.
34 Ibid., p. 217.
35 B. Cunliffe, *Roman Bath*, Oxford, 1969, p. 205.
36 A. O. Klindt-Jensen, *Gundestrupkedelen*, Copenhagen, 1961, fig. 22.
37 Stokes, '*Rennes Dindshenchas*', p. 293.
38 *The Mabinogion*, ed. cit., p. 110.
39 Stokes, '*Rennes Dindshenchas*', p. 279.
40 Cross and Slover, op. cit., pp. 208 ff.

41 Stokes, 'Rennes Dindshenchas', p. 304.
42 Ibid., p. 307.
43 Cunliffe, op. cit., pp. 65 f.
44 *The Mabinogion*, ed. cit., p. 161.
45 Stokes, 'Rennes Dindshenchas', p. 313.
46 See M. MacNeill's valuable study of this festival for all the comparative material and modern folk-survivals: *The Festival of Lughnasa*, Oxford, 1962.
47 Stokes, 'Rennes Dindshenchas', p. 318.
48 MacNeill, op. cit., pp. 160 ff.
49 Stokes, 'Rennes Dindshenchas', p. 315.
50 Ibid., p. 326.
51 Ibid., p. 332.
52 Cross and Slover, op. cit., p. 134.
53 Ibid., p. 334.
54 Ibid., p. 338.
55 D. R. Dudley and G. Webster, *The Rebellion of Boudicca*, London, 1962, pp. 68 ff.
56 Published in several recent volumes of *Archaeologia Cantiana*.
57 Edward Gwynn, *The Metrical Dindshenchas*, Royal Irish Academy, Todd Lecture Series, vol. 11, part 4, Dublin, 1924, pp. 19 ff.
58 A. Rybová and B. Soudský, *Libenice*, Prague, 1962.
59 MacNeill, op. cit., pp. 268 ff.
60 Ibid., p. 273.
61 J. F. Campbell, *Popular Tales of the West Highlands*, vol. 1, Edinburgh, 1860, pp. 403 ff.
62 S. H. O'Grady, *Silva Gadelica*, London, 1892, vol. 2, pp. 343 ff.
63 Campbell, op. cit., vol. 1, pp. 124 ff.
64 Ross, op. cit., pp. 227 f.
65 Ibid., p. 225.
66 'The Book of the Lays of Fionn', Part III, Irish Texts Society, vol. 43.
67 Ibid., p. 192.

Illustrations by Richard Feachem

9
Olaf Tryggvason versus the Powers of Darkness

Jacqueline Simpson

It has sometimes been suggested that one element—perhaps even a major element—in the complex concept of 'witchcraft' was a hostile view of pagan cults held by Christians, whereby pagan gods were degraded into devils, and their worshippers came to be regarded as malevolent sorcerers. Such hostility would presumably be at its strongest during the period of acute political and cultural conflict accompanying conversion of a heathen country, and would be reflected in traditions relating to that period known to later Christian writers. As Scandinavia was the last area of Western Europe to be Christianised, and as its conversion was a frequent topic of interest to Icelandic saga-writers of the twelfth and thirteenth centuries, I propose to examine some Icelandic accounts of King Olaf Tryggvason of Norway, to see how far his enemies are there identified with heathenism, magic and powers of darkness.[1]

Olaf was not the first Christian to rule Norway, nor was he able during his short reign (AD 995–1000) to complete a permanent conversion of his country; nevertheless, he exerted strong political pressure on behalf of the new faith, not only in Norway but in the Orkneys and Faroes, Iceland, and Greenland, all of which adopted it under his influence. Consequently he was remembered by the Icelanders as a person of particular importance in their history; when, in the last quarter of the twelfth century, Icelanders with clerical education began to write lives of Nordic Christian heroes modelled in part on those of European saints, it was only natural that Olaf Tryggvason should be the subject of one such saga. Later writers took up and elaborated the theme, weaving in many originally independent sagas and anecdotes about Olaf's contemporaries, several of which are undoubtedly chosen to emphasise the clash between Christianity and paganism in his reign. The chief stages in the process are as follows:

(1) *The Saga of Olaf Tryggvason* by Odd Snorrason, a Benedictine monk, written in Latin *c.* 1190; the Latin text is lost, but an Icelandic translation of the early thirteenth century survives in two versions.[2]

(2) A lost Latin *Saga of Olaf Tryggvason* by Gunnlaug Leifsson, another Benedictine monk, probably written *c.* 1200 and based on Odd's work. Sections of a lost Icelandic translation of Gunnlaug's saga were incorporated in the *Greater Saga of O.T.* (see no. 4 below); from these it seems chiefly notable for pious verbosity, but Gunnlaug may have been the first to add anecdotes about Olaf's followers clashing with heathen powers.[3]

(3) *Heimskringla*, Snorri Sturluson's history of Norway, completed *c.* 1235, naturally includes a section on Olaf. He draws much of his material from Odd, but re-handles it to fit his larger scheme and his stricter criteria of historical plausibility; edifying tales and supernatural marvels play less part in his work, though they are not entirely absent.[4]

(4) *The Greater Saga of Olaf Tryggvason*. This anonymous compilation, produced *c.* 1300, takes Snorri as its basic source, but also draws heavily on Odd and Gunnlaug, and expands its text by weaving into it a number of sagas and anecdotes on matters more or less closely related to Olaf's life.[5]

(5) *Flateyjarbók*. This massive manuscript, compiled *c.* 1380–90, includes a *Saga of Olaf Tryggvason* basically similar to the *Greater Saga*, but even further expanded by additional stories and anecdotes.[6]

Even Odd's saga, the earliest, is written almost two hundred years after Olaf's death, so there was ample time for folk-traditions to gather round his name, romanticising his career and over-simplifying the conflicts which marked his reign. These were largely due to the unwillingness of chieftains in remote areas to accept centralised government, to the long-standing rivalry between the royal line and the Earls of Hladir, and to rivalries within the royal line itself (as Snorri's account makes clear); religious conflict was only one element in a complex situation. Nevertheless, it was almost inevitable that tradition should emphasise this element, and tend to present Olaf's enemies as embodiments of paganism.

Olaf Tryggvason versus the Powers of Darkness

In the case of Olaf's immediate predecessor as ruler of Norway, Earl Hakon of Hladir, there are excellent historical grounds for regarding him as an ardent heathen, for a contemporary poem praises him for rebuilding temples and restoring sacrifices (abolished during a previous abortive attempt to Christianise Norway). Snorri says he worshipped Odin; Odd, that he worshipped the goddess Thorgerd Holgabrud, and won a great victory by sacrificing his young son to her. Thorgerd is an intriguing figure,[7] who resembles both the Valkyries and the bloodthirsty ogresses of heathen belief, and also some fertility goddesses; in later sources, such as the *Saga of the Jomsvikings* and the *Tale of Thorlief the Earl's Poet*, she is called by the derogatory terms 'she-troll' and 'hag' (*flagð*) and Hakon is said to have worked black magic by her help (see pp. 178–9 below). Most sagas, however, do not blacken Hakon's name by accusations of sorcery, but merely show him as the heathen sacrificer *par excellence;* Snorri says he was a good ruler in many ways, but dogged by ill-luck at the end, since it was fated that paganism must give way to the true faith. Hakon was killed treacherously by a slave while hiding from an uprising of farmers which coincided with Olaf's arrival in Norway.

Though Odd does not impute sorcery to Hakon, he does to another dangerous enemy of Olaf's, a certain Eyvind kelda; we have no contemporary sources from which to assess his character, but since he, like Olaf, was of the royal line, we may suspect that their enmity was essentially political. According to Odd, Olaf called an Assembly and decreed that 'all magicians (*fjǫlkunnigir menn*) and those who held the old faith should be banished, especially all those, whether men or women, whom Norsemen call wizards (*seiðmenn*). He made outlaws of them all, and decreed that they should be slain as if they were manslayers if this were proved against them.' So all who 'made use of devilish powers' prepared to go into exile; one was Eyvind kelda, 'a man of noble birth, being a descendant of Harald Fairhair in the third or fourth generation'. But Olaf, pretending to want Eyvind's friendship, invited him and the other wizards to a feast of reconciliation, made them drunk, and fired the hall; all died in the flames except Eyvind himself, who leapt out of the building 'by the craft of his devilish skills'. Some months later, Eyvind planned to attack Olaf with a large band of men, many of them magicians; Olaf was at Mass, and 'as soon as Eyvind saw the holy church, he and all his men went blind, and they walked backwards and forwards round the island'. Olaf had them rounded up; next day they were shipped out to a skerry and beheaded there, 'and ever since this has been called Sorcerers' Skerry (*Skrattasker*)'.[8]

In the first part of this story, the banishment of the wizards, Odd has been shown to be embroidering a statement in the lost *History of the Kings of Norway* by Sæmund the Learned (1056–1133), that Olaf called an Assembly 'and did not desist from preaching the true faith to the people until they submitted to baptism'.[9] Sæmund did not say that this Assembly was particularly aimed against wizards; Odd probably got this from a Norwegian writer, Theodoricus, who says that Olaf slew eighty persons of both sexes who were guilty of 'devilish wickedness' and were called *seiðmenn*, burning them inside a temple.[10] The terms used by Odd are interesting; *fjǫlkunnigir menn* (lit: 'men knowing much') is simply a euphemism for magicians in general, but *seiðmenn* are practitioners of *seiðr*, a specific form of magic which apparently resembled shamanism in the use of trances and the summoning of spirits as an aid to prophecy, and in many details of procedure.[11] The word *seiðr* can also refer to shameful and destructive magical practices; in Christian texts it can be a strongly derogatory term, and may have been suspect even in heathen times. What word was used in Odd's original Latin is of course unknown, but it is clear from the phrases 'devilish powers' and 'devilish skills' that he meant to blacken Eyvind and his companions as much as he could.

In *Heimskringla*, Snorri follows Odd closely as regards the first part of Eyvind's story; he calls him 'a wizard and a very great magician' (*seiðmaðr ok allmjǫk fjǫlkunnigr*), and says that Olaf banished wizards and 'those who use magic chants and actions' (*galdra ok gǫrninga*).[12] He adds the significant detail that Eyvind was a grandson of Rognvald rettilbein, whom he had previously mentioned in his *Saga of Harald Fairhair* as a notorious *seiðmaðr*, a son of Harald by a Lapp witch. This allegation of wizardry against Rognvald is supported by an old verse cited by Snorri, and the tale of King Harald and the Lapp witch is from a Norwegian source of c. 1190;[13] clearly, there was a deep-rooted tradition that this branch of Harald's family practised magic, though it is of course impossible to tell whether it was based on fact or on hostile rumour.

Snorri, unlike Odd, speaks of Eyvind kelda's escape from the burning hall as a simple, natural event. Moreover, he diverges sharply from Odd in his account of Eyvind's downfall, replacing Odd's edifying tale of the miraculous power of a church building by a story based on heathen folk-belief. He says that Eyvind and his companions, all wizards and magicians, landed on the island where Olaf was and worked a powerful spell, by which means Eyvind raised a thick mist and made a 'concealing helm' (*hulizhjalm*) to hide himself and his men from Olaf. But when they got near a farmstead where Olaf was, it became bright day, and the darkness he and his fellow magicians had made affected only themselves, so that 'they could see no more with their eyes than with the back of their heads, and went round in circles'. So they were caught, and left tied up on Skrattasker to drown.[14]

By omitting all mention of the church and the Mass, Snorri implies that it was Olaf's own strong personality and luck which caused Eyvind's spell to recoil on his own head, in accordance with the well-known principle that thwarted magic turns against its maker; the idea of Olaf's power against evil recurs in many tales, some of which will be discussed below. Mist, fog and darkness constantly appear in saga accounts of magic; the use of drowning is also well attested there as a means of getting rid of magicians without encountering the malevolence of their dying words or glance.[15] As for the 'concealing helm', this is a common term in sagas for any magic means of ensuring invisibility; originally it must have meant a concrete object worn for the purpose,[16] but in Icelandic the abstract sense is more usual. All in all, Snorri's version is far more folkloric than Odd's; it is closer to Nordic thought, and testifies to the strength of the tradition concerning Eyvind kelda's magic arts.

Another of Olaf's opponents mentioned by Odd was a powerful man named Hroald, living at Godey in northern Halogaland; he was a pagan, praying daily to the gods that he should neither be forced to accept the new faith nor driven from his lands—'and this man was so much deceived by the devil's temptings that the gods used to give him answers for his worship'. When Olaf tried to reach Hroald's home by sea, he was each time driven back by contrary gales, till his bishop stilled the winds and waves by throwing holy water on the sea; thereupon, Olaf captured Hroald and hanged him. Later Odd gives what is obviously a variant of the same story, in which a 'great magician', Hroald of Moldafjord, tries to bar Olaf's way by causing two huge, terrifying breakers to rise in a calm sea; but the king sails straight through, and catches and kills this Hroald too.[17]

In Snorri's work neither Hroald appears, but the same story is told of a rich farmer, Raud the Strong, who was a heathen sacrificer and magician, had Lapps ready to serve him at his will, and by his magic powers had favourable winds whenever he wished to sail. When Olaf tried to reach Raud's home he was hindered by constant fearful storms which affected that fjord only; eventually he sailed through, with his bishop standing at the prow in full vestments, with candles, incense, and holy water. Raud was killed by having a snake forced down his throat—a death which Odd says befell an unnamed man who argued against Olaf's preaching.[18] In this narrative Snorri has stressed the magic elements in Odd's accounts of both Hroalds, and has added a reference to Lapps; it is also worth noting that Raud's nickname *inn rammi*, 'the strong', very probably implies supernatural powers.[19]

Even more striking is the tale Odd tells about another of Olaf's opponents in Halogaland, a certain Eyvind kinnrifa, who refused to be baptised even when tortured with hot coals; he explained his obstinacy by saying:[20]

> My father and mother lived together a long while in lawful matrimony, but had no child. And as they grew old, they grieved at dying without an heir. Then they travelled to the Lapps with much money, and asked them to give them an heir by magic arts. The Lapps invoked the chief of the spirits that dwell in the air (for the air is just as full as the earth of unclean spirits), and that spirit sent an unclean spirit into that dark dungeon—for so my mother's womb may truly be called. And I am that very spirit, and in this manner I took flesh on myself, and afterwards showed myself in human form, and so was born into this world. I took the inheritance of my father and mother, and a great chieftainship. And this is why I cannot be baptized, for I am not a man.

This weird tale is most un-Nordic; rather, it is akin to medieval clerical speculations about the sexual powers of incubi or about the diabolical incarnation of Antichrist, or to Geoffrey of Monmouth's story of the begetting of Merlin. But the reference to Lapps is true to native beliefs; not only do they frequently figure as magicians in sagas, but some early Christian laws in Norway forbid people to travel to the Lapps to get help or prophecies from them.[21] Odd's account of Eyvind kinnrifa is followed by Snorri, though far more

Olaf Tryggvason versus the Powers of Darkness

briefly, but later it is radically altered by the compiler of the *Greater Saga of Olaf Tryggvason*. According to him, the Lapps explicitly denied that their skills could affect conception; they merely promised the parents that their next child would live, if they swore that he would serve Odin and Thor all his life. This they duly did, and the dying Eyvind declares himself unable and unwilling to break with Odin because he is 'dedicated to him in so many ways'.[22] It is unlikely that the compiler made this change for the sake of plausibility, as on the contrary he has a strong liking for the marvellous; probably he regarded the idea of a diabolical incarnation as verging on heresy,[23] and so substituted the safer motif of a vow to the pagan gods.

Finally in this group of incidents from Odd's work is that of Thorir hjǫrtr. He, like Hroald of Godey and Eyvind kinnrifa, came from Halogaland and persisted in heathen worship; eventually Olaf defeated him in battle, and he fled:[24]

> When one of the king's men saw that, he flung a spear at him, and it struck Thorir between the shoulders and pierced his chest-cavity, and he fell. Thereupon a large hart sprang up from his body in a mighty rush. When the king's hound Vigi saw that, he chased the hart and hunted it vigorously; and when the king saw that, he ran after them, far inland, and ahead of his men. He saw the hart and hound meet, and it was a hard fight; the hound bit the hart, but the hart gored the hound, and in the end both fell. The king came up and found the hart dead of many wounds; the hound too was not likely to live. Then the king's men came up, and he showed them the carcass of the hart, and it was already dry and extremely light, like inflated bellows.

Thorir's nickname *hjǫrtr* actually means 'hart', and so Snorri rationalises the story by saying that as Thorir fled Olaf shouted to his dog 'Vigi, Vigi, catch that Hart!', and that the dog stopped Thorir, who wounded him, but was killed by Olaf.[25] This eliminates the magic, in accordance with Snorri's frequent preference for rational accounts; it is followed by the *Greater S.O.T.* and by *Flateyjarbók*. But Odd's version is very close to genuine folk-belief, for it presents Thorir as a shape-changing magician of a common Nordic type, though with some interesting variations from the norm. Usually the shape-changer (*hamhleypa*) is said to lie in a trance while his soul goes off in animal form, often to attack an enemy; a well-known example is the legendary hero Bodvar bjarki, whose nickname means 'bear' and who appeared as a bear in battle while his body seemed asleep indoors.[26] If the animal form is injured, corresponding injuries appear on the man; if it is 'killed', it vanishes, and the man falls dead.[27] Odd's story is unusual in two features: that Thorir is dying, if not actually dead, when the hart springs from his body; and that this hart does not vanish when killed, but remains as a physical entity, though by no means normal flesh and blood.[28] On the other hand, it is not a mere magic garment like the skins which swanmaidens and werewolves put on and off at will; it has its own life, hard though it is to define its relationship to the dying Thorir. Odd himself was evidently troubled by the episode, not wishing it to be dismissed as incredible, while at the same time refusing to admit that so striking a display of magic could be objectively true; he comments:[29]

> If monstrous things and marvels such as have just been described are talked of, one may well think them incredible. Yet all men know that the Devil is always a foe of God Almighty, and so are those wretches who deny God. The Devil uses trickery and every kind of guile and deceit, and urges his unclean spirits against God's servants; he blinds their sight, and then in many ways tricks and deceives all their bodily senses. As for what we have related about such matters, and exemplary fables (*dæmisǫgur*) like these, we do not hold that these things happened in reality; rather, we think that they merely appeared to be thus, for the Devil is full of falsehood and wickedness.

The stories of the two Eyvinds, the two Hroalds, and Thorir, make it abundantly clear that the traditions about Olaf current in Odd's time tended to attribute various forms of sorcery to men who opposed him. But there is also one episode in which Olaf himself resorts to Lappish magic, though Odd represents him as unwilling to do so. Early in his struggle for the kingship, Olaf, preparing for a crucial battle, is advised by his men to consult a Lapp who could foretell its outcome and reveal the enemies' plans. He agrees, though declaring himself unwilling 'to visit men of this sort, or seek their aid'; on the way, he is almost sucked into a bog—a token, he tells his men, of how little one should trust such help. The Lapp will not let Olaf enter his house because of the 'bright spirits' accompanying him, but he tells him all he needs to know, asking as his only reward to be allowed to remain heathen. Later, the same Lapp heals the dog Vigi after the fight with the hart.[30] Such a story is in keeping with the general outlook of sagas, where

Olaf Tryggvason versus the Powers of Darkness

sympathetic characters quite often resort to diviners and seers (though not, of course, to harmful magicians). However, it is curious to meet it in the clerical Odd; presumably he found it a tradition too strong to ignore, and had to be content to tone it down as far as possible.

Besides showing Olaf in conflict with heathen men, Odd brings the gods themselves into the story—or rather, in accordance with orthodox doctrine, demons in the likeness of the gods. One Christmas Eve, 'the Devil himself, the foe of all mankind . . . took on human form' and visited Olaf as an old man with one eye, wearing a broad-brimmed hat. This stranger told Olaf about an ancient king buried close by, and answered the king's many questions well and learnedly, talking most of the night, despite the bishop's protests. Next morning the stranger had gone, but not before giving the cook some particularly good beef for the king's table. Olaf had the meat thrown in the sea, remarking 'I think that that stranger must have been the Devil in the form of Odin.' The shorter manuscript adds that a dog ate some of the meat and died. The Devil's plan, as Odd later explains, was to keep Olaf awake so late that he would oversleep and miss Mass on Christmas Day, and then to poison him with the meat, so that he would die in mortal sin.[31] The story makes an effective *exemplum* with a twofold moral: that one should not 'eat of the food offered to idols' (an idea readily applicable in the North, where sacred feasts were integral to the heathen cults), nor should one love tales of heathen kings and heroes, for these may turn the mind away from God's service.[32]

Olaf's second encounter with a god took place at sea; he took on board a handsome red-bearded man, who joked with him, and amused the men with boasts and boisterous jollity. When they asked him if he knew stories about the old days, the stranger replied:[33]

'The land we are sailing past was inhabited by giants in the old days, but it somehow happened that the giants were soon killed off, so that there were none left but two women. Afterwards, sire, it happened that human beings began to inhabit the land, men from the eastern regions of the world. These two women treated the men very oppressively, and made their lives a misery in many ways. Then, sire, these men decided to call on Redbeard to help them, and at once I drew my hammer out of my shirt and battered the women to death.'

Having said which, the red-bearded man leapt overboard, and Olaf said 'See how bold the Devil is, to appear before our eyes!'

This is, of course, Thor, whose great popularity towards the end of the Viking Age is reflected in several other stories which represent him as Christ's chief opponent in the North.[34]

The third of Odd's stories about supernatural beings is that of the Trolls' Assembly. Some of Olaf's men, being curious to see such an Assembly, slip away secretly into the mountains, where they overhear many trolls in a cave angrily discussing the trouble Olaf has caused them. The first tells how he used to live near Earl Hakon, who was his friend and gave him fine gifts, till King Olaf came. One day Olaf and his men were holding games nearby, and the troll could hardly bear the uproar and jollity, which tried his patience sorely;[35] so he joined invisibly in the wrestling, breaking a man's arm on the first day and another's leg on the second. On the third day the troll tackled Olaf himself:

> 'he gripped me unmercifully, and set his hands against my sides, and they would have felt no different if they had been made of red-hot iron. He began to crush me cruelly, and I could not hold firm against him; I escaped from his hands with much difficulty, and fled, badly burned, and came to this place against my will.'

The second troll tells how he took the form of a beautiful woman, 'and had a horn full of mead in my hand, in which I had mixed many evil things, and I meant to entrap the king that evening as he feasted.' But when the troll proffered the horn, Olaf struck him over the head and face with it, 'and so we parted'. The third troll says he too took on woman's form and went to the king's hall, where he magically made Olaf's foot itch, and then sat by him all evening stroking and tickling his foot. When Olaf went to bed, the troll went with him, still in order to stroke the itching foot, and then 'tried to destroy the king by devilish wiles.' But Olaf woke, and broke the troll's head with a book, so he fled; Olaf's foot had 'a nasty-looking spot, full of poison', which the bishop cut away from the flesh. Having heard the three trolls, Olaf's men return home, where the king confirms the stories, but rebukes them for taking such risks; he and the bishop then purify the whole region with holy water.[36]

The first troll's story is very Norse in its emphasis on physical strength; wrestling is a classic way to overcome a giant, troll or living corpse. But the burning heat of Olaf's hands is a motif limited to Christian contexts; one may compare the episode in *þorvalds þáttr víðfǫrla* where an elf complains that holy water

Olaf Tryggvason versus the Powers of Darkness

sprinkled on the rock inside which he lives has scalded him and his children, the heat by which an evil giant senses the presence of a Christian in *Þorsteins þáttr bæjarmagns*, or the complaint of a dead witch that the tears a pious woman sheds near her grave scald her (*Laxdæla saga*, ch. 76).[37]

The stories of the second and third trolls are no doubt inspired by the idea, so common in saints' lives, that demons can take the form of lovely temptresses. It has been suggested that a specific source for the whole episode may be found in a story in the *Dialogues* of Gregory the Great about a Jew who hid in a temple by night and overheard demons discussing how they had tempted Bishop Andreas to lust;[38] the later versions of the *Saga of Olaf Tryggvason* make clear, by the term 'unclean spirits', that all three trolls are to be identified as devils.[39]

However, the second troll's disguise as a woman bearing a horn of mead (a detail not paralleled in Gregory) may allude to a particular mythological figure, the Valkyrie who offers a hero a cup or horn of mead. When this scene is set in Valhalla, as it is in the tenth-century Norwegian poems *Eiríksmál* and *Hákonarmál* and on eighth- and ninth-century memorial stones from Gotland, the drink probably is 'a highly charged and significant symbol of the passing of the hero to the realm of the gods . . . a drink giving freedom from time and mortality'.[40] When a Valkyrie offers a horn to a hero at the outset of his career, as Sigrdrifa does to Sigurd,[41] it may symbolise the supernatural bond between them, whereby she will teach him magic lore and protect him in battle. There is a comparable concept in certain Irish tales in which kingship is conferred on the hero when he accepts a drink from an Otherworld woman called 'the Sovereignty of Ireland'. And to show that such ideas were not mere poetry but part of everyday cult practices, one can point to small figurines of women holding horns, found in Viking Age graves at Birka and elsewhere.[42] So if in fact the second troll's disguise is meant to suggest a Valkyrie, then this story carries the same moral as that of Olaf's encounter with Odin: the Christian king rejects the power which his heathen predecessors honoured, for that power is a deadly device of the devil.

It will be seen that Odd uses two types of story to dramatise his hero's conflict with paganism: in the first type real historical persons are represented as evil sorcerers, or even as a devil incarnate; in the second, gods and other supernatural figures are brought into direct contact with Olaf, either as tempters or as making physical attacks on him or his men—though Odd stresses that these 'gods' are nothing but demons. As Icelandic saga writing developed, both types, but particularly the second, were used in sagas about men (usually Icelanders) attached to Olaf's court.[43] Most of these are designed as entertainment with only the barest minimum of edification; in due course many of them, though originally independent, were included in the ever-expanding late versions of the *Saga of Olaf Tryggvason*, whose compilers evidently thought that even frivolous stories could illustrate the great theme of Christianity's triumph over heathenism.

The process may have begun as early as *c.* 1200 in Gunnlaug Leifsson's lost saga, if it is true that the story of Thorvald tasaldi (included in the *Greater S.O.T.*) comes from Gunnlaug.[44] This tells how Olaf sent Thorvald to summon a recalcitrant pagan, Bard, from whose home previous messengers had failed to return, and promised to protect him by his own *gipta ok hamingja*. *Gipta* is 'luck', and *hamingja* a quality of personal success and strength of character which great men were thought to have, and to be able to lend to others.[45] When Thorvald reached Bard's home, Olaf appeared to him in a dream and gave him a paper inscribed with the Names of God, telling him to wear it on his chest. So when Thorvald and Bard wrestled, Bard stumbled as soon as their chests touched, feeling someone trip him. Eventually Bard agreed to turn Christian and submit to Olaf. The story is rather diffuse and ill-written; on the whole, it is more interesting for its use of a well-known Christian charm than for its representation of heathenism.[46]

In contrast, *Hallfreðar saga* contains an episode in which an opponent of Olaf's is described in a way that reflects authentic traditions about heathen magic. This saga, one of the older thirteenth-century Family Sagas, concerns an Icelandic poet who, though devoted to King Olaf and converted by him, felt a troubled nostalgia for the old faith and refused to speak ill of its gods. Olaf plays a prominent role in the saga, the author of which was probably influenced by existing works about him, particularly Gunnlaug's; later *Hallfreðar saga* was woven into the *Greater S.O.T.*

The episode which concerns us here tells how Hallfred was sent by Olaf to find a certain Thorleif the Wise, who had refused Christianity, and punish him by killing or blinding him. Olaf promised to 'lay his luck and good fortune' on Hallfred for this

Olaf Tryggvason versus the Powers of Darkness

journey. Hallfred eventually came upon his quarry alone, for 'Thorleif had the custom, which was a frequent habit among men of old, of sitting out for long periods on a burial mound by his farm.' Hallfred tricked Thorleif into trusting him, and blinded him in one eye; however, he then relented, and did not finish the job as Olaf had ordered. The defeated Thorleif commented that Hallfred did not succeed alone, for the king's luck had helped him.[47]

The term 'sitting out' carries connotations of divination; the Norwegian *Older Gulathing Law* decrees death for those 'who do seers' journeys and sittings-out, in order to rouse trolls and thus do heathen deeds'.[48] According to the *Maríu saga*, one way of doing this involved the archaic divinatory method, known also among Greeks, Romans and Celts, of sitting on a hide. The would-be seer is advised to go to a secluded spot in a forest, lay a freshly flayed ox-hide on the ground, draw nine squares round it, putting power into them by devilish chants, and then sit on the hide till the devil arrives to reveal the future.[49] Thorleif's method, sitting on a burial mound, has a good many parallels in the sagas, and may very well have been widespread in heathen times, as the writer claims; its purpose seems frequently to have been to obtain knowledge and power by contact with the dead, and possibly also through the elevated isolation of the spot.[50] Appropriately, Thorleif's nickname *inn spaki* ('the Wise') is one which refers to 'the heathen wisdom which gives the power to see the future'.[51] Certainly, the author of *Hallfreðar saga* was following strong and authentic traditions when he chose this particular action to symbolise the heathenism of Thorleif.

Another story embedded in the *Greater S.O.T.* which is famous for its authentic glimpse of the cult of one of the old gods is the *Tale of Ogmund dytt and Gunnar helming*.[52] Its hero, Gunnar, quarrels with Olaf and flees to Sweden, where people worship a wooden figure of the fertility god Freyr, and by constant sacrifices 'fill it with such magic power that the Devil spoke to men out of this graven image'. The young priestess who acts as Freyr's 'wife' befriends Gunnar, and later asks him to accompany her when the image is driven round the country in a wagon for the good of the crops. The wagon gets stuck in a snow-drift, and the infuriated image attacks Gunnar for not pushing hard enough; it is on the point of killing him when he mentally vows to be reconciled with Olaf and become Christian. At once Freyr's image weakens and falls, the devil leaves it, and Gunnar can smash its empty wooden form. The story goes on to tell how Gunnar successfully impersonates the god for many months, makes the priestess pregnant, and at last returns with her to Norway, where they become good Christians.

It has often been pointed out that this story, despite its jocular tone, preserves correct information about Scandinavian fertility cults, since there is much evidence that images of fertility gods were carried round the countryside in wagons.[53] To the compiler of the *Greater S.O.T.*, its chief point must have been the doctrine that idols are mere 'work of men's hands', whose alleged powers are due to a devil which can be put to flight by Christian faith. The motif of a pious vow made in a crisis and associated with the thought of Olaf will be met with again; it became a popular means of injecting a moral into an otherwise frivolous adventure tale.

The story of Olaf reaches its greatest amplitude in *Flateyjarbók*, compiled *c.* 1380–90, where it is copiously interlarded with inset sagas and tales, originally independent, but capable of being associated in one way or another with Olaf's career. Several illustrate the theme of religious conflict, but since their purpose is patently to entertain, they will be treated more briefly than the earlier stories; they no longer reflect serious fear or condemnation of paganism, even if they still preserve motifs drawn from older beliefs.

The first such insertion is the *Tale of Thorleif the Earl's Poet*,[54] which is set in the reign of Earl Hakon and does not actually mention Olaf; it was apparently included because it shows Hakon in a ludicrous and evil light, and because it is an extended commentary on one sentence in Odd's *S.O.T.* There, Odd had said of Hakon: 'It is said that an Icelander composed a long and evil poem about him, made up of many evil and unheard-of things'—a phrase implying obscenity, or magic, or both.[55] According to the *Tale*, Thorleif, having a grudge against Hakon, visited him in disguise and recited at him a satiric poem (*níð*) of such virulence that Hakon was afflicted by violent itching between his thighs, the loss of his beard and half his hair, and an illness of many months which, it is hinted, deprived him of his virility. Later, Hakon retaliated by calling on the goddesses Thorgerd and Irpa to reveal the future and utter magic chants (*galldrá*) against Thorleif; he and they carved a figure from driftwood and put a human heart in it, by the 'magic and spells' (fjǫlkynge ok atkvæðum) of the Earl and the 'trollishness and prophetic powers' (trollskap ok fítónsanda) of the goddesses. This animated figure they sent to Iceland, where it killed Thorleif, and vanished into the ground.

A belief in the magic effectiveness of hostile, obscene and satiric verse is deeply rooted in heathen Nordic practice, several times referred to in sagas; it continued as a vigorous folk-belief well into the nineteenth century, in Icelandic legends about poets whose rhymes could kill vermin, affect the weather, lay ghosts, or bring disease or death on unpopular figures such as government officials.[56] There are good parallels in Celtic traditions.[57] The Icelandic accounts, both in sagas and more modern legends, show that this form of magic was considered useful and socially acceptable; it is used by sympathetic characters against oppressive enemies. The compiler of *Flateyjarbók* felt no need to apologise for this use of magic in a good cause; to him, as his introductory paragraph shows, the point of the whole affair is the downfall and damnation of Hakon.

Hakon's magic, by contrast, is presented in the blackest terms, and he himself degraded into a murderous sorcerer. The method he uses is interesting; it anticipates a motif which is common in later Icelandic folktales and beliefs, that of the 'sending'.[58] This was an apparent human being or animal sent by a sorcerer to hunt down and kill his enemies. It might be an entire corpse raised from the grave, or else a single human or animal bone magically endowed; it could change shape, appear and vanish, and could rarely be overcome by trickery or superior magic. Hakon's use of driftwood and a human heart is reminiscent on the one hand of these later necromantic 'sendings', and on the other of old mythological motifs: the creation of the first human pair from driftwood logs, or the making of a giant from clay and a mare's heart.[59] It is noteworthy that Hakon is here said to seek help from supernatural beings for his sorcery, rather than using his own skills alone; this is an unusual feature, and is the nearest any of these tales come to identifying heathen worship with heathen magic.

The next relevant story in *Flb. S.O.T.* is the *Tale of Thorstein Oxleg*,[60] which earns its place for several reasons: its hero is a historical personage who fought for Olaf in his last battle, and some of the fantastic adventures here attributed to him are designed to illustrate his devotion to Olaf's cause against monstrous foes, and

Olaf's ability spiritually to protect his men. The central episode is a fight between Thorstein and a whole family of supernatural beings variously referred to as trolls, giants and ogres. At the climax he is about to be slaughtered by a fearsome old she-hag when he makes a vow to become Christian and serve Olaf all his life; at once a ray of light blinds the hag, making her vomit and faint. Meanwhile a friend of Thorstein's (who had become separated from him) makes a similar vow; reunited, they complete the destruction of the trolls. A subsequent episode tells how Thorstein got his nickname by wrestling, at Olaf's request, against a terrifying ox worshipped by a heathen, and tearing its leg off.

The *Sǫrla þáttr*[61] is a curious reworking of mythological themes and of an ancient heroic legend about two kings, Hedin and Hogni, who die and revive night after night as they fight an everlasting battle over Hogni's daughter Hild.[62] According to the *Sǫrla þáttr*, this is due to the evil magic of a mysterious woman named Gondul (known elsewhere as a Valkyrie name), who is either an emissary of, or identical with, the goddess Freyja; she meets Hedin in a forest and bewitches him with a drink from her horn, and later works a spell to ensure the nightly resuscitation of the warriors. After 143 years this spell is broken by Olaf's follower Ivar ljómi (a historical figure); he intervenes at the request of the weary Hedin, who tells him that he can effectively 'kill' the dead, 'because you are Christian, and the king you serve has great *hamingja*'.

The *Tale of Nornagest* is sometimes regarded as another example of our theme,[63] for its story of an incredibly aged stranger who entertains Olaf and his court with tales about ancient heroes he himself once knew is certainly reminiscent of Odin's visit to Olaf, and indeed 'Gest' is one of Odin's many names. Nevertheless the whole tone is different; Nornagest is friendly to Olaf and sufficiently well-disposed towards Christianity to have been primesigned; eventually he accepts baptism, relights a candle on which his life depends, and so dies a good death. In fact, the framework and point of the story recall the twelfth-century Irish *Colloquy of the Ancients*[64], with its friendship between St Patrick and the aged heroes Cailte and Oisín, the Saint's delight in their tales, and probably (though the ending is lost) their final baptism and death.

There follows in *Flateyjarbók* the *Tale of Helgi Thorisson*.[65] Here the villains are Ingibjorg, daughter of the giant-king Gudmund of Glæsisvellir—known from several sources as the lord of a beautiful but dangerous Otherworld—and two emissaries of his, named Grim. Ingibjorg takes the hero as her lover, has him abducted to the Otherworld, and eventually sends him back to Olaf blinded (as the Queen of Elfland in the ballad of *Tam Lin* wishes she had done to Tam).[66] The two Grims try to injure Olaf by offering him drink in two splendid horns sent by Gudmund as a Christmas gift, but are foiled by the bishop's blessing and vanish, killing three men. The motif of the destructive drink, used by Odd in the story of the Trolls' Assembly, is prominent here, but Gudmund and Ingibjorg are more complex figures than trolls; they have the perilous allure of denizens of Elfland, even if Olaf does curtly sum Gudmund up as 'a great magician' (*mjǫk fjǫlkunnigr*). The story has much in common with international medieval folklore.

Odd's story of the Troll's Assembly may possibly have supplied a model for the opening of the *Tale of Thorstein Skelk*,[67] the hero of which goes out alone at night to a privy, despite Olaf's explicit orders that his men were to stay indoors. There, a demon comes popping up through one of the seats and regales Thorstein with accounts of tortures suffered by ancient heroes in Hell. Thorstein induces him repeatedly to imitate the agonised howls of one of these heroes, in the hope of rousing Olaf by the din; the trick works, for Olaf wakes and has a bell rung, thus putting the demon to flight in the nick of time to save Thorstein's life or reason. The creature in the privy is variously called 'fiend', 'devil', 'living corpse' (*draugr*), 'imp' (*púki*, which is cognate with 'puck'), and *dolgr*, a rather vague term for any hostile being such as a ghost, devil or troll. This story, like the preceding, is very reminiscent of international folktales. Its macabre and grotesque humour recalls 'The Youth Who Wanted To Learn What Fear Is' (A. T. Type 326), a few Irish versions of which include an encounter with a goblin in a cellar.[68] Indeed, Thorstein boasts to Olaf that he has never known what fear is, though the loudest howl did very nearly make him shudder—hence his nickname, *skelk*, 'shudder'.[69]

It is obvious that in the course of time Olaf's spiritual powers to assist his men against superhuman foes had become a mere conventional device to give a brief hint of piety to a humorous or exciting story. It is used in this way in various sagas which were never included in the conflated *Olaf Saga* (e.g. in *The Tale of Gest Bardarson*, against a living corpse; in *The Tale of Thorstein Bæjarmagn*, against giants; in Faroese versions of *The Tale of Orm Storolfsson*, against a giant and his mother). Any serious awareness of hostility between Christians and pagans had long vanished by the time such tales were composed, just as Odd's mistrust of myths and hero-tales had given way to the cultivated enjoyment of them shown by Snorri and others in thirteenth-century Iceland.

Turning back to the work of Odd, which supplies so much of the basic material for the development of this whole group of sagas, we find, as has been noted already, that some of his stories concern supernatural beings who try to injure Olaf, and others human beings who fight him by both normal and magical means. Both types of tradition are old, as far as one can tell, and both contain details showing accurate knowledge of heathen beliefs and practices; their original purposes, however, were probably different. The tales about Odin, Thor, and the Trolls' Assembly all point specifically religious lessons—against the fascination of myths and hero-tales, against food and drink used in heathen rites, against reliance on the protection of the gods, against sexual temptations. They would make excellent *exempla* for preachers in a missionary situation, and it may very well have been in such a milieu that they first arose.

On the other hand, the stories about human adversaries, while not lacking religious motifs (e.g. the power of holy water and of churches), are most readily understandable as political propaganda. To establish his rule, Olaf had to struggle against the Earls of Hladir, against independent chieftains of remote areas, and, in the case of Eyvind kelda, against a rival in his own family. Like Harald Greycloak before him and St Olaf after him, he saw the imposition of Christianity and of his own authority as part and parcel of the same process. To him and his adherents, his opponents would easily seem embodiments of pagan obstinacy, and it might well appear expedient to try to discredit them by accusations of forms of magic (e.g. *seiðr* or storm-raising) which were probably already considered disgraceful or pernicious in heathen society.[70] Such accusations would be remembered and understood even when time had blurred the details of the political picture. Interestingly, it seems to have been only comparatively minor opponents who were branded in this way; Earl Hakon is not in the early texts accused of magic (the sacrifice of his son for victory is not a magic act but a religious one), and among the alliance of foreign kings and domestic enemies who eventually brought about Olaf's death, not one is alleged to have used magic. Their political motives were obvious, and well remembered; no further imputations were needed, either then or later.

It must, however, be stressed that the group of tales studied here show only the most minimal signs of any actual identification between heathen worship and sorcery, and these only in the account of Earl Hakon and Thorgerd in the late *Tale of Thorleif the Earl's Poet*. True, Odd and his successors regard both the powers of the old gods and the effects of magic as manifestations of the devil, and they readily believe that a man who is a heathen may also be a sorcerer, but the distinction between the two remains perfectly sharp. Sorcery is not performed as part of the worship of a god, nor are we even told (except in *The Tale of Thorleif*) that a god's assistance is required to perform it; conversely, to offer sacrifices to the gods is idolatry, but not a magic act. And when gods, giants or trolls appear as actors in a story, they keep all the vigorous individuality of their old selves; they do not conform to the stereotypes of medieval demonology.

The idea of a pact with the devil is absent, despite the many references to the 'devilish skills' of sorcerers; on this point clerical theories were at odds with Nordic tradition (which normally regarded the powers of seers, shape-changers and magicians as innate), and it is this tradition which predominates in all the stories except that of the demonic incarnation of Eyvind kinnrifa. When faced with a tradition about a shape-changer, Odd's solution to the theological problem it poses is not that the devil gave Thorir exceptional powers, but that he tricked the onlookers into seeing something which did not in fact occur. Nor is there the slightest trace of such ideas as familiars, sabbaths or night-flying. The magic and the accounts of supernatural beings both remain firmly rooted in traditional Scandinavian paganism; they cannot be said to foreshadow the characteristics of medieval witchcraft accusations, nor to support the theory that when medieval Christians spoke of 'witchcraft' they meant a survival of heathen religious cults.

Notes

1 The chief Old Icelandic words for magicians are: *fjǫlkunnigr maðr (kona)*, 'man (woman) with much knowledge'; *seiðmaðr (seiðkona)*, 'man (woman) practising *seiðr*', a particular form of magic discussed on p. 168; *spámaðr (spákona)*, 'man (woman) with second sight or prophetic powers'; *hamhleypa* 'shape-changer'; *vǫlva* 'seeress'. Only the first two occur in the texts

discussed here; I translate them as 'magician' and 'wizard' respectively. In discussion I use 'sorcery' to mean the use of magic to injure another, and I endeavour to avoid the ambiguous word 'witchcraft'.

2 *Saga Óláfs Tryggvasonar* (Oddr Snorrason), ed. Finnur Jónsson, Copenhagen, 1932. The longer version (A) is the better text, and is that quoted here unless otherwise indicated. Hereafter referred to as Odd, *S.O.T.*

3 It has been suggested by Finnur Jónsson in *Aarbøger for Nordisk Oldkyndighed*, 3rd series, 20 (1930), pp. 123–4, that *The Tale of Thorvald Tasaldi* (see above, p. 176) was his work; for an opposing view, see Bjarni Aðalbjarnarson, *Om de Norske Kongers sagaer*, p. 117.

4 *Heimskringla*, ed. Finnur Jónsson, Copenhagen, 1911, pp. 104–81. Hereafter referred to as Snorri, *S.O.T.*

5 *Óláfs saga Tryggvasonar en mesta*, ed. Óláfur Halldórsson, Copenhagen, 1958–61. See also Finnur Jónsson, 'Óláfs saga Tryggvasonar (hin meiri)', *Aarbøger for Nordisk Oldkyndighed*, 3rd series, 20 (1930), pp. 119–38. Hereafter referred to as *Greater S.O.T.*

6 *Flateyjarbók*, ed. G. Vigfússon and C. R. Unger, Copenhagen, 1860–8, I, pp. 39–561. See also Finnur Jónsson, 'Flateyjarbók', *Aarbøger for Nordisk Oldkyndighed*, 3rd series, 17, (1927), pp. 139–90. Hereafter referred to as *Flb. S.O.T.*

7 See N. F. Blake, *The Saga of the Jomsvikings*, 1962, Appendix III; N. K. Chadwick, 'Þorgerðr Hǫlgabrúðr and the Trollaþing', *Early Cultures of North-Western Europe*, ed. C. Fox and B. Dickins, Cambridge, 1950, pp. 395–417.

8 Odd, *S.O.T.* chapters 36 and 44 (A), ed. cit., pp. 114–16, 134–6.

9 See G. Turville-Petre, *The Origins of Icelandic Literature*, Oxford, 1953, p. 83.

10 Theodoricus the Monk, *Historia de Antiquitate Regum Norwagiensium*, c. 1180, ed. G. Storm, in *Monumenta Historica Norvegiæ*, 1880, pp. 2–68.

11 Dag Strömbäck, *Sejd*, Lund, 1935; H. R. Ellis Davidson, *Gods and Myths of Northern Europe*, London, 1964, pp. 117–22; see also Ellis Davidson's article in this volume, pp. 20–41.

12 Snorri, *S.O.T.* ch. 62, ed. cit., pp. 149–50.

13 *Ágrip af Norges Konunga Sǫgum*, ed. Finnur Jónsson, Copenhagen, 1929, ch. 3. Cf. Snorri, *Heimskringla*, ed. cit., p. 63.

14 The *Greater S.O.T.* and *Flb. S.O.T.* follow Snorri here; the S version of Odd *S.O.T.* seems also influenced by him, for it omits the church and merely says Eyvind and his men were blinded, without saying how, and also has them drowned (not beheaded)—ed. cit., pp. 134–5.

15 Cf. F. Ström, *On the Sacral Origins of the Germanic Death Penalties*, Lund, 1942, pp. 171–8, 242–5, 254.

16 J. Grimm, *Deutsche Mythologie*, 1852, p. 432.

17 Odd, *S.O.T.*, chapters 37 and 55 (A), ed. cit., pp. 117–19, 165–6.

18 Snorri, *S.O.T.*, chapters 78, 80, *Hkr.*, ed. cit., pp. 158–60; cf. Odd, *S.O.T.* ch. 56 (A), ed. cit., pp. 166–7.

19 Jón Steffensen, 'Aspects of life in Iceland in the heathen period', *Saga-Book of the Viking Society*, 17: 2–3, 1967–8, pp. 184–6.

20 Odd, *S.O.T.*, ch. 45 (A), ed. cit., pp. 139–40.

Olaf Tryggvason versus the Powers of Darkness

21 Borgarþing Law and Eidsivaþing Law, in R. Keyser, P. R. Munch and G. Storm, *Norges Gamle Love*, 1846–55. Cf. D. Strömbäck, op. cit. in n. 11.
22 Greater *S.O.T.*, ch. 204, ed. cit., II, pp. 118–19. Cf. *Flb. S.O.T.*, ch. 311, ed. cit., p. 385.
23 Many theologians denied that an incubus could beget a child except by the use of human sperm, or that demons could take on a real, rather than an illusory, human body.
24 Odd, *S.O.T.*, ch. 45 (A), ed. cit., p. 141.
25 Snorri, *S.O.T.*, ch. 78, *Hkr.* ed. cit., pp. 158–9.
26 *Hrólfs saga kraka*, ch. 33, ed. D. Slay, Copenhagen, 1960, pp. 116–18.
27 Cf. the two Icelanders who fought all night as bear and bull; next day, both were confined to bed by their wounds (*Landnamabók*, ed. Finnur Jónsson, Copenhagen, 1900, pp. 109, 220, 237). Cf. also the colourful episodes from the late sagas *Hjálmþérs saga ok Olvérs* and *Friðþjófs saga*, discussed by H. R. Ellis Davidson, above, pp. 29–30.
28 There is something slightly similar in the late *Sturlaugs saga starfsama*, where two magicians fight first as men, then as dogs, then as eagles, till one eagle drops dead and the other flies away, but no details are given of the physical characteristics of this eagle. (See Ellis Davidson, above, p. 30). In any case, this does not have the typical Nordic shape-changer's trance; it is simply an instance of the international motif of the Transformation Combat (D615.1).
29 Odd, *S.O.T.*, ch. 45 (A), ed. cit., pp. 142–3. The S text says: 'If such things are said ... we are not able to give a clear explanation to account for them. But everyone knows how many marvels and magical illusions (*sjónhverfingar*) the Devil has produced for his own men, and in such matters we can believe whatever we think best.'
30 Odd, *S.O.T.* chapters 19 and 45 (A), ed. cit., pp. 67–70, 141. Cf. the Danish historian Saxo Grammaticus, who says (Book X: 339) that Olaf was 'much given to auspicies, omens and divination' (ed. P. E. Muller, 1839, pp. 500–1).
31 Odd, *S.O.T.*, chapters 43–4 (A), ed. cit., pp. 131–4, 136.
32 Cf. Alcuin's letter to Bishop Hygebald of Lindisfarne in AD 797, on the choice of subject for refectory readings:
   It is seemly to hear a reader there, not a harper; to hear the sermons of the Fathers of the Church, not the lays of the heathen. For what has Hinieldus to do with Christ? The house is narrow, it cannot contain them both; the King of Heaven will have no part with so-called kings who are heathen and damned, for the One King reigns eternally in Heaven, while the other, the heathen, is damned and groans in Hell.
33 Odd, *S.O.T.*, ch. 59 (A), ed. cit., pp. 173–4.
34 E. O. G. Turville-Petre, *Myth and Religion of the North*, London, 1964, pp. 88–91.
35 Cf. the attitude of Grendel to the feast at Heorot, *Beowulf* ll. 86–90.
36 Odd, *S.O.T.*, ch. 60 (A), ed. cit., pp. 174–9. The S text (ch. 48, pp. 174–9) adds a few details, notably that the first troll escapes Olaf's grip by sinking into the ground, and that the two others were 'forced to take the lower road', which seems to mean the same thing. Sinking into the ground or

to the bottom of the sea is a common exit for evil beings of various types in sagas.
37 N. K. Chadwick suggests (op. cit. in n. 7) that because this troll was Hakon's friend he and his companions must be meant as parodies of the goddesses Thorgerd and Irpa. A more general allusion to Hakon's paganism seems likelier, since this particular troll behaves as a male throughout, while his 'female' companions are in no way linked with Hakon.
38 C. R. Unger, *Heilagra Manna Sǫgur*, Copenhagen, 1877, I, pp. 222–3. Cf. G. Turville-Petre, op. cit. in n. 9, pp. 135–7.
39 *Flb. S.O.T.*, ed. cit., p. 321. Odd's original Latin text being lost, one cannot tell what term he used which his translator rendered 'troll'.
40 H. R. Ellis Davidson, 'The smith and the goddess', *Frühmittelalterliche Studien*, 3, 1969, p. 222.
41 *Poetic Edda*, prose link-passage in the *Sigrdrífumál*.
42 H. R. Ellis Davidson, *Pagan Scandinavia*, London, 1967, p. 130 and pl. 63.
43 Snorri alludes to stories of trolls and evil spirits who tormented Olaf and his men, but says that he prefers to write of other matters (Snorri, *S.O.T.*, ch. 80, ed. cit., p. 160). He may mean Odd's stories of the apparition of Thor and of the Trolls' Assembly, both of which he omits, or he may mean the folk-traditions current in his own time.
44 See n. 3. *Greater S.O.T.*, ch. 201, ed. cit., II, pp. 93–102; = *Flb. S.O.T.*, chapters 308–10, ed. cit., pp. 378–83.
45 H. R. Ellis, *The Road to Hel*, 1943, pp. 132–4.
46 See Johannes Bolte, 'Über die 72 Namen Gottes', *Zeitschrift des Vereins für Volkskunde*, 13, pp. 444–50.
47 *Hallfreðar saga* ed. Einar O. Sveinsson, *Íslenzk fornrit*, 8, Reykjavík, 1939, ch. 6, p. 164. *Greater S.O.T.*, ch. 173, ed. cit., I, pp. 394–400; = *Flb. S.O.T.*, ch. 274, ed. cit., pp. 329–31. The text quoted is from the longer version of *Hallfreðar saga*; the shorter says Thorleif was sitting on a mound, but does not use the actual term 'sitting out'.
48 *Norges Gamle Love*, ed. R. Keyser, P. R. Munch and G. Storm, 1846–55, V: 1, p. 19. Cf. Dag Strömbäck, op. cit. in n. 11, pp. 127–9.
49 *Maríu saga* ed. C. R. Unger, 1871, pp. 147–8. This saga is thought to be written by a cleric, Kygri-Bjǫrn Hjaltason (d. 1237 or 1238). Similar ceremonies at crossroads are described in more modern Icelandic folklore, where it is sometimes elves, sometimes the dead who appear (Jón Árnason, *Þjóðsǫgur*, Reykjavík, 1862, I, pp. 125 and 436–7).
50 Axel Olrik, 'At sidde paa Hoj', *Danske Studier*, 1909, pp. 1–10; H. R. Ellis, op. cit. in n. 45, pp. 105–11; for stones on tumuli possibly connected with this practice, see H. R. Ellis Davidson, op. cit. in n. 42, pp. 104–5 and pl. 43.
51 Jón Steffensen, op. cit. in n. 19, pp. 186–9.
52 *Greater S.O.T.* chs 173–4, ed. cit., II, pp. 2–18; = *Flb. S.O.T.* chapters 275–8, ed. cit., pp. 332–9.
53 E. O. G. Turville-Petre, op. cit. in n. 34, pp. 169–70 and 247; H. R. Ellis Davidson, op. cit. in n. 11, 1964, pp. 93–6.
54 *Flb. S.O.T.*, chapters 168–74, ed. cit., pp. 207–15; trans. J. Simpson, 'The Scoffing Verses', *The Northmen Talk*, London, 1965, pp. 141–51.
55 Odd, *S.O.T.*, ch. 20 (A), ed. cit., p. 71; S reads: 'Thorleif the Icelander

composed a satirical poem against him, because he had burnt his ship.'
56 Bo Almqvist, 'Um Ákvæðaskáld', *Skirnir* 135, 1961, pp. 72–98. The medieval instances, including that of Thorleif, are fully discussed in the same author's *Norrön Niddiktning*, 1965; in his view, the traditions about Thorleif's *nið* go back at least as far as the twelfth century.
57 See V. Mercier, *The Irish Comic Tradition*, Oxford, 1962.
58 Jón Árnason, op. cit. in n. 49, I, pp. 317–54.
59 *Vǫluspá*, strophes 17–18, and Snorri, *Prose Edda, Gylfaginning* ch. 9; Snorri, *Prose Edda, Skáldskaparmál* ch. 24.
60 *Þorsteins þáttr uxafóts*, *Flb. S.O.T.* chapters 201–14, ed. cit., pp. 249–63; transl. J. Simpson, op. cit. in n. 54, pp. 212–31.
61 *Flb. S.O.T.* chapters 228–36, ed. cit., pp. 275–83.
62 It first appears in the tenth-century poem *Ragnarsdrápa*, and was known to Saxo and Snorri, who both attribute the nightly resuscitation to Hild's spells.
63 N. K. Chadwick, 'Norse ghosts', *Folklore*, 57, 1946, pp. 117–23. *Nornagests þáttr* is *Flb. S.O.T.* chapters 282–92, ed. cit., pp. 346–59.
64 *Agallamh na Seanóach*, ed. Nessa ní Shéaghdha, 1942–5; trans. S. H. O'Grady, *Silva Gadelica*, 1892, II.
65 *Flb. S.O.T.*, ch. 293, ed. cit., pp. 359–62; trans. J. Simpson, 'Helgi and the Women of the Otherworld', op. cit. in n. 54, pp. 175–80.
66 F. J. Child, *English and Scottish Ballads*, 1882–98, I, p. 339.
67 *Flb. S.O.T.*, ch. 333, ed. cit., pp. 416–18; trans. J. Simpson, 'The Howls of the Damned', op. cit. in n. 54, pp. 152–5.
68 R. T. Christiansen, *Studies in Irish and Scandinavian Folktales*, Copenhagen, 1959, pp. 186–7.
69 In Type 326 the hero often learns fear at last when his wife drops an eel or cold water down his back, making him shudder.
70 As almost all the extant texts bearing on magic date from Christian times, it is extremely risky to theorise on the attitude to magic in heathen society. However, it is broadly true that some practices (e.g. shape-shifting) may be attributed to both good and bad characters, while others are confined to the villains in sagas.

10

Cain's Kin

Beatrice White

Witches and warlocks of the common breed cut no great figures in the medieval English romances. Nor do they appear with startling force in English ballads—poetry in which magic roamed unchecked. 'Willy's Lady' suffered from the demonic attentions of his mother, 'that vile rank witch of vilest kind', until her witchcrafts were foiled, the nine witchlocks were loosened, the combs of care were removed and the master-kid was killed. Alison (a witch name with erotic echoes) Gross was 'the ugliest witch in the north country' and punished disdain with cruel enchantment, like the stepmother of the Laily Worm. But not all witches were evil enchanters. 'An auld witch wife' gave a cautious maiden very good advice about behaviour on the dangerous Broomfield Hill. In fact, though magic plays an integral part in the romances and ballads its principal contrivers bear, on the whole, little resemblance to village dabblers in the ways of darkness like the old woman dexterously enchanting her cow-sucking bag before an inquisitive bishop, or less distinguished but more sinister crones directing their attendant imps to malevolent attacks on neighbours.

Increase in the severity of persecution for witchcraft in the fourteenth century did not imply a boom in necromancy, but more probably a keener awareness of existing superstitions which in this country never reached terrifying dimensions of Scandinavian or Scottish magnitude, but were altogether tamer, drabber affairs. Here the Mome Helwises and the Dame Siriths were mumbling or meddling old sinners whose rightful place in literature was the folk tale rather than the romance or ballad. In one fourteenth-century romance of outstanding quality the folk tale witch makes a brief appearance heavily disguised in the trappings of nobility. But enough of her is visible to be recognisable as the vindictive old woman who should have been busy with wax and pins and imps in a corner of some smoky medieval cottage.

Arrived at Sir Bertilak's castle, Sir Gawain met two highly contrasted ladies, one glowing with the beauty of youth and the other hideous with the ugly ravages of age. What her wimple revealed of her face with its wrinkled, sagging cheeks was ill-tempered, while her body was short and thick, with broad buttocks —in fact she was a most unattractive old thing and it would be difficult to believe that she was the 'Goddess' Morgan, except that the poet tells us so and casts such a subtle spell with his verse that we hesitate to doubt him.[1] As we meet her here, Morgan La Faye has obvious connections with the 'Loathly Lady', Celtic in origin and herself a victim of enchantment as she appears in the 'Wife of Bath's Tale' and in Gower's story of 'Florent', and not only the Loathly Lady whom a kiss cures of the ugliness of age, but the portrait of Elde herself as it was painted on the wall of the beautiful garden that contained at its centre the Rose of the Lover's desire.

In the large majority of medieval English romances the principal malefactors and representatives of rampant evil were giants whose very size was a symbol of power. Boethius admitted the force of the symbol when he bestowed upon Philosophy the ability to increase her stature to an enormous, cosmic height. Dante gazing at the Archfiend supine in the very lowest depths of Inferno saw him as a giant:[2]

> con un gigante io mi convegno,
> Che i giganti non fan con le sue braccia.

Milton's Satan shared this characteristic of immense size as, 'huge in length', he 'lay floating many a rood', 'prone on the flood extended long and large', while his cohorts of fallen angels could reduce their height when convenient as easily as they could change their sex:[3]

> Thus incorporeal spirits to smallest forms
> Reduced their shapes immense.

Great size exerted its fascination not only in mythology from China to Scandinavia, but in hagiology and epic. St Christopher and Hygelac were both of prodigious height.[4] If the romancers wanted authority for the existence of giants they had no further to look than the sacred scriptures where there is plenty of evidence for their appearance on earth both before and after the Flood.[5] Chronicler and encyclopedist lend weight to the testimony. According to Geoffrey of Monmouth the original inhabitants of Albion, like those of Canaan, were giants, and he relates how the greatest of them, Goemagot,[6] twelve cubits tall, was routed by Corineus. Bartholomew Anglicus repeats the story with variations and in his time it seemed to be an accepted fact that invaders expected to confront indigenous inhabitants of gigantic size. The transition from Chronicle and Encyclopedia to Romance was an easy one, and merely implied the extension of a common area of fantasy.

Elemental creatures of huge size and chaotic force, the giants share certain marked features in the romances, features which, in the same works, distinguish the churls from the adventuring heroes. And at this one point, particularly, the romances allow the intrusion of reality into the realms of fantasy. We have only to study the canvases of Breughel, Grünewald and Bosch to grasp how effective fantasy can become if presented in a guise that may have been repulsive but was certainly familiar to observers of the medieval serf. As the average attitude towards 'bloody' peasants[7] was, in the Middle Ages, one of contempt, it is unlikely that they would often find sympathetic treatment in contemporary literature. Pious talk about Lady Poverty did not create any confidence in her attraction. Churls, surly oafs grotesquely brutalised by toil, were lumped together with the 'eotenas, ylfe, ond orcneas' of *Beowulf*, those monstrous descendants of the first murderer, and like Grendel were despised as 'Cain's kin'.[8] What more natural than to assume the transmittal of both features and disposition to churl and to monster from a common ancestor described in the Bible as 'a tiller of the soil'?

The prototype can be found in Chrétien de Troyes's *Yvain* (*c*. 1173) vv. 268 et seq. where Calogrenant describes the rustic he met in a clearing (*launde*) in a wood. This fellow was sitting on a stump with a great club in his hand, a lout, black, big and hideous, in fact so ugly that he defied description. His head was bigger than that of a horse, his hair stuck up in tufts and his forehead was more than two spans in width. His ears were like an elephant's, his eyebrows bushy and his face flat. He had eyes like an owl's, a nose like a cat's, jowls like a wolf's, and sharp, yellow teeth like a boar's. His beard was black and he was short-necked and hunch-backed. He stood leaning on his club, dressed in the recently flayed hides of two bulls and he was seventeen feet in height. All this is reproduced faithfully in the later English version which continues:

> To him i spak ful hardily
> And said, 'What ertow, belamy?'
> He said again, 'I am a man.'
> I said, 'Swilk saw i neuer nane.'
> 'What ertow?' alsone said he.
> I said, 'Swilk als þou here may se.'
> I said, 'What dose þow here allane?'
> He said, 'I kepe þir bestes ilkane.'

Aucassin, searching for his lost Nicolette, comes across just such a rustic in a forest clearing. Tall, ugly and hideous, he had a monstrous shock-head, black as coal and between his brows the width of a full palm-breadth. Flabby cheeks, a huge flat nose, wide nostrils, thick lips and ugly, yellow teeth further distinguished the peasant, who was leaning on a great club. In fact, Chrétien's description provided a pattern which was repeated *ad nauseam* from story to story—the huge, repulsive churl, the primal wild herdsman, guardian of beasts and of territory whose true ancestor is the giant Humbaba of the Babylonian epic *Gilgamesh*—a deadly, terrifying forest warden, breathing fire, whose jaws were death.[9]

In the medieval romances these churlish giants proliferate. All conforming to the same convention, impressive in size, repulsive in looks and manners, lurking in caves or inaccessible places, fighting as often as not with huge, iron-shod clubs, they are libidinous, predatory, cannibalistic, and, like Nabal, another 'churl', 'evil in their doings'. The only considerable body of medieval literature they do not invade is the Robin Hood ballads and in such a sensible yeoman atmosphere they would be out of place.

Many of the romances work up to a climax with the description of a fight, generally a single combat in which the hero faces an opponent of immense size and strength who, since narratives gain in appeal through contemporary touches, is not infrequently a Saracen with the prescribed churl/giant features and proportions. We may be certain that mere size and strength were no deterrent to the hero who invariably triumphs, as Horn does, taking on and destroying 'a geaunt suþe kene' 'iarmed fram paynyme', whose name is given in the French version as Marmorin, born, appropriately, in Canaan.[10]

Havelok, heir to the throne of Denmark, was himself of prodigious height and strength:

> Hauelok stod ouer hem als a mast.
> Als he was heie, als he was long,
> He was boþe stark and strong.

And he had the less difficulty in despatching the 'carls [churls] of Cain's kin' who attacked him (l.2045).

Horn and *Havelok* are early tales. The later fourteenth-century Arthurian romances and the lengthy verse narratives translated with varying ability from the French are happy hunting-grounds for the traditional giant. Saracens of gigantic proportions are liberally scattered through the romance of *Arthour and Merlin*. Arthur destroyed one named Caulaug, and Gawain killed a regal Saracen malefactor called Taurus. Chrétien's Yvain, with the aid of his faithful lion, was successful in killing a marauding and lustful giant referred to as Harpin of the Mountain, whose fall was compared to that of a giant oak tree. In the tamer English version we are told:[11]

> The geant was both large and lang,
> And bar a lever of yren ful strang...
> Al the armure he was in
> Was noght bot of a bul-skyn.

Sir Tristrem, after a terrible fight, finished off the lecherous Urgain who laid about him with a twelve-foot staff. Sir Triamour destroyed a family of giants, employed by the Emperor of Germany, who were active on the borders of Hungary—the champion, Marradas, his elder brother, Burlong, and two of lesser note. Sir Percival of Galles encountered the giant brother of the Sowdan Gollerotherame who wielded an iron club with a steel head weighing altogether twenty-three stone:

> Ful evyll myght any man smale
> Þat men telles nowe in tale,
> With siche a lome fighte.

But he could not prevail against Sir Percival who smote off his head, an action which provoked the narrator to a wry smile:

> He was ane unhende knaue
> A geaunt berde so to schafe,
> For sothe, als i say.

Sir Eglamour of Artoys met up with two very individual giants, Sir Maroke, over fifteen feet tall, a sort of game warden like Humbaba, and his brother, Sir Manas, who made a pet of a huge bear and after its death mourned with misdirected grief for his 'little spotted hoglin'.

The alliterative *Morte Arthure*, a splendid, sinewy poem, involved Arthur with the giant of St Michael's Mount, a fierce and horrifying cannibalistic creature already described by Geoffrey of Monmouth (Book X. cap. 3). This wretch was not only lustful but a bit of a gourmet, discreetly flavouring his gruesome meal with spices and devouring it to the accompaniment of choice wine:[12]

> He sowppes all þis seson wi*th* seuen knaue childre,
> Choppid in a chargeo*ur* of chalke-whytt sylu*er*
> Wi*th* pekill & powdre of p*re*cious spyces
> And pyment full plenteuous of Portyngale wynes.

In appearance the monster conformed to type—tangled hair, bushy brows, great black beard, rough skin, hooked nose, huge ears, burning eyes, flat face, thick lips, bull-neck, and brawny, thick thighs, 'schouell' feet, measuring from face to foot five fathoms. This 'carl', however deadly his club of iron, found it impossible to overcome the righteously furious Arthur. Sir Bertilak, the shape-shifter in *Sir Gawain and the Green Knight*, an 'aghlich mayster' and 'on the most on the molde on mesure hyghe', with bushy brows and beard, hardly resembled the churlish type in appearance, being well-proportioned, besides having red eyes (characteristic of some giants) and being green in colour. Yet 'he is a man methles [utterly reckless] and mercy non uses':

> For be hit chorle other chapleyn that by the chapel rydes,
> Hym thynk as queme hym to quelle as quyk go hymselven.

And the great Danish axe he wielded had a handle tipped with iron, perhaps for practical use as an alpenstock, or for ceremonial use as a refði. In either case the detail reinforces a traditional notion.

The stories concerned with Charlemagne and his paladins are thickly littered with huge Saracens, either more, or less, churlish according to their dispositions and circumstances. Vernagu, a general of the Sowdan of Babylon, was forty feet tall, fifteen feet broad, measured four feet across the face, and had a formidable nose:

> He looked lothliche,
> And was swart as pitch.

But his height could hardly have been so impressive in view of Charlemagne's reputed twenty feet. However, being a giant, Vernagu was typically obtuse, and failing to profit from Roland's lengthy exposition of the Trinity, he was deservedly vanquished.[13]

Sir Firumbras and *The Sowdone of Babylon* cover similar ground, and produce for elimination by Christian heroes the Ethiopian giant Algolofur who had made an ingenious network of chains to protect the bridge of Mantrible where he was slain.[14]

> This geaunte hade a body longe,
> And hede like an libarde.
> Thereto he was devely stronge;
> His skynne was blake and harde.
> Of Ethiope he was bore,
> Of the kinde of Ascopartes.

Bearded like the pard, he had tusks of regulation size and fought with an oaken club bound with steel. He was succeeded as antagonist by a female giant, Dame Barrok, wife to Astragot. After her death her twin sons, seven months old, were found to be fourteen feet long. They were at once adopted and christened 'Roland' and 'Oliver' by Charlemagne, but could not survive without their mother's milk.

Octavian introduces a warring Sowdan of Babylon who brought with him on his campaign:[15]

> '... a fowll geaunt
> Of Egypte; he hette Guymerraunt,
> Greet as an ok:
> No dosyper n'as so auenaunt
> To stonde hys strok.
>
> He was of lengthe twenty feet,
> And two elle yn brede with scholdrys greet:
> Ech day he wold et a neet
> And messes more:
> Twey tuxlys out of his mouth set,
> As of a bore.
>
> A greet fot was betwex his bryn,
> His browys as brystelys of a swyn;
> Betweene his fortop and his chyn

> Length of an elle:
> With blake yghen, as seyd the Latyn,
> He lokede felle.

Guy of Warwick, a redoubtable fighter, easily despatched the Amiraunt of Ethiopia, giant champion of the Sowdan. His most famous single combat was against the Danish giant, Colbrand:

> Well foul he was and loathlich,
> A grisly gome to fede.

Colbrand, appropriately for a Dane, fought with battle axes (cf. Sir Bertilak), a stroke from one of which caused his death.[16]

Bevis of Hampton, another popular hero, was a connoisseur of giants. The most typical in size and character was Ascopard (cf. Algolofur 'of the kinde of Ascopartes'), a mighty and powerful giant, thirty feet tall, 'bristled like a sow', with brows far apart, great slobbering lips, wide mouth, and hollow eyes:

> Lothly he was to look on than,
> And liker a devil than a man;
> His staff was a young oak,
> Hard and heavy was his stroke.

This unwieldy creature became page to Sir Bevis, but proved an unsuitable retainer who objected violently to being christened:

> For Ascopard was made a tun;
> And when he should therein be done,
> He lept out upon the brench,
> And said 'Churl! wilt thou me drench?
> The devil of hell mot fetche thee!
> I am too much christened to be!'—

disrespectful language which revealed his propensities for evil and prognosticated for him a bad end.

The giant Maugys, whom Sir Libeaus Desconus had to face, resembled in ugliness Guymerraunt of Egypt (*Octavian*):[17]

> He is as blacke as pyche,
> Nowher is none suche
> Of dedis sterne and stowte...
> He is thirty fote on leynthe
> And myche more of strenthe
> Than other knyghtis fyve...

Beatrice White

> He berreth on euery browe
> As it were brystillus of a sowe;
> His hede grete as an hyve,
> His armys the lenthe of an elle,
> His fystis arne full felle
> Dyntys with to dryve.

There is little variation anywhere from the original churlish type. Giants were generally lone wolves, but occasionally they had relations (as in *Sir Triamour*, *Sir Perceval*, and *Sir Eglamour*) and showed family feeling, or rather a united front in evil intent. We meet a formidable pair in *The Romans of Partenay*—Guedon and Grimold. Both had some individuality. Guedon told the hero, Geoffrey, to clear off ('Trusse hens') and was given to irony ('Off the in my hert renneth gret pite'), and Grimold, with his tongue in his cheek, offered a large ransom to prevent a fight. He was a 'fers Geant huge and comerous, Horrible, myghty, strong and orgulous'. Both met their doom at Geoffrey's hands.

Finally Chaucer's Sir Thopas rode off to 'the contree of Fairye' hell-bent on adventure but no one approached him:

> Til that ther cam a greet geaunt,
> His name was sire Olifaunt,
> A perilous man of dede.
> He seyde, 'Child, by Termagaunt!
> But if thou prike out of myn haunt,
> Anon I sle thy steede
>   With mace.
> Heere is the queene of Fayerye,
> With harpe and pipe and symphonye
> Dwellynge in this place.'

Sir Olifaunt was a giant armed, unusually in these contexts, with a 'fel staf-slynge' and as Sir Thopas prudently retired to don his armour his gigantic adversary cast stones at him:

> But faire escapeth child Thopas,
> And al it was thurgh Goddes gras
> And thurgh his fair berynge.

There is a direct link here between Sir Olifaunt, the warden of the fairy marches, and the primeval giant guardian of territory, Humbaba. It appears:

Cain's Kin

> For nedes moste he [Sir Thopas] fighte
> With a geaunt with hevedes three,

that Sir Olifaunt, like Geryon and Cacus, was three-headed. As he swore by Termagant, he probably had Saracen leanings, and obviously had an ear for music. But Chaucer is too wise to break the delicate web of his parody by over-emphasis and we can only guess at the size of his giant from his appropriate name. He unites in his person the most ancient Gilgamesh tradition and the common romance custom of bestowing pagan characteristics on the hero's adversary.

Later centuries continued the process of transferring brutalised features from peasants to fabulous giants, sometimes presenting fiction as fact. Bartholomew Anglicus had spoken of veritable giants in India. Mandeville characteristically assigned such beings to a still more distant land and emphasised their monstrosity: 'and thei ben hidouse for to loke upon, and thei han but on eye, and that is in the myddylle of the Front, and thei eten no thing but raw Flessche and raw Fyssche.' Some were forty-five or fifty feet tall and must have made an impressive sight as they lounged along taking alternate bites at handfuls of sailors grabbed from passing ships.[18]

Malory's Lancelot had several fights with giants one of whom was a 'foul churl' who lashed out with a massive club shod with iron (Book VI. cap. X). The fifth chapter of Book V of the *Morte Arthur* is devoted to an account of Arthur's great fight with the giant of St Michael's Mount who had appeared before in the *Historia Regum Britanniae* and the alliterative *Morte Arthure*. This hateful cannibal, true to giant tradition, attacked with an iron club.

Bunyan strewed his allegory with giants all conforming in appearance and behaviour to the old, familiar pattern of churlish bestiality. Some individual touches, however, served to enliven his narrative. The giant Maul was argumentative, and Dame Diffidence gave her husband, Giant Despair, advice in a cosy conjugal atmosphere suggesting rather a pleasant nook in Suburbia than a giant's lair.

There is a great gulf between Bunyan's conventional presentation of giants as the quintessence of evil and Swift's Brobdingnagian giants who were fully intelligent and responsible beings far superior in every way to men, seen in comparison as: 'the most pernicious race of little odious vermin that nature ever suffered to crawl upon the face of the earth'.

Terrors like those aroused by the revolt of 1381 when the oppressed peasants made an unsuccessful bid for freedom would be enough to account for the role assigned in the fourteenth-century romances to menacing giants with churlish features. They made conveniently huge targets for conquering heroes to aim at. Their size ensured that they could not be missed; their unprepossessing appearance and brutal churlish behaviour marked them out for punishment in an ideal world where transgression against clearly defined moral standards always brought condign punishment.

Terrors of a different order, proceeding not from the familiar but from the supernatural world were far more frightening. Sinister in their secrecy, the devil's disciples doing his work unobserved as they went to and fro in the earth, walking up and down seeking whom to devour, were as dangerous as the fifth column of an alien power. Once a belief in witches and warlocks was established, once the proportions of the delusion increased and persecution became extensive, the fear of malevolent presences unknown and unseen, would have been too threatening, too insidious, and too immediate to find a commanding place in verse which only incidentally reflected the changing patterns, moods and sorrows of its time.

The magic of the romances was primarily a magic of dreams and seldom of nightmares.

Notes

1 *Sir Gawain and the Green Knight*, ll. 947 et seq.; l. 2452.
2 *Inferno*, Canto 34, l. 30.
3 *Paradise Lost*, Book I, l. 777.
4 St Christopher 'was of the lineage of the *Canaanites*, and he was of a right great stature, and had a terrible and fearful cheer and countenance. And he was twelve cubits of length' (*Golden Legend*). Compare the account of Hygelac's tomb. (*Liber Monstrorum*, Part I, cap. 2, 'De Getarum rege Huiglauco mirae magnitudinis'.)
5 Genesis VI: 4; Numbers XIII: 32, 33; Deuteronomy II: 10, 11; III: 11; Samuel XVII: 4.
6 *Historia Regum Britanniae*, Book 1, ch. 16. Cf. *The Koran*, ch. 18. Gog and Magog (Goemagot) were kept at bay because Dhul Qarnain (Alexander the Great) built a wall for the purpose. English place-names preserve the Anglo-Saxon belief in giants (e.g. Thursford and Tusmore, from A.S. þyrs (giant).

Cain's Kin

7 See G. G. Coulton, *Medieval Village*, reprinted Harper, New York, 1960, p. 342. The Viguier of Béziers in the time of St Louis addressed recalcitrant peasants as 'rustici sanguinolenti'.
8 *Havelok*, l. 2045. *Beowulf*, l. 111. According to Rabbinical legend Cain, conceived after the disobedience and before the true repentance of Adam and Eve, was the ancestor of all monsters. Cf. the apocryphal *Book of Enoch* which equates giants and evil spirits.
9 *The Epic of Gilgamesh*, English version with introduction by N. K. Sandars, Penguin, 1960. Humbaba, a nature divinity, was killed by Gilgamesh and Enkidu. Cf. Cacus, giant offspring of Hephaestus and Medusa, who breathed fire and was destroyed by Hercules.
10 Numbers XIII: 32, 33; Deuteronomy II: 10, 11.
11 In 'The Lady of the Fountain' (*The Mabinogion*, trans. Lady Charlotte Guest, Everyman, 1937) the lion is given a more important part in the fight between Owain and the giant.
12 *Morte Arthure*, herausgegeben von Erik Björkman. Heidelberg, 1915.
13 Early English Text Society, extra series, 39, ed. S. J. Herrtage, 1882.
14 *Sultan of Babylon*, in *Middle English Metrical Romances*, ed. W. H. French and C. B. Hale, Prentice Hall, New York, 1930.
15 *Metrical Romances*, ed. H. Weber, Edinburgh, 1810.
16 An ancient motif. The antagonist can only be slain by his own weapon. Compare the fate of Grendel's mother in *Beowulf*.
17 Early English Text Society, 261, ed. M. Mills, 1969.
18 This invites comparison with the Cyclopes, whose association in classical mythology with metal working finds an echo in references to iron weapons used by giants in medieval romances.

11

The Witch as a Frightening and Threatening Figure

John Widdowson

Witchcraft and sorcery in various forms appear to have existed from the dawn of human history, and throughout the ages the witch has been regarded as a figure of fear. Indeed to some extent witches embody human fears, and the concepts we have of them emphasise their frightening and unpleasant characteristics.

Fear is a potent force at work in all levels of society. We may fear certain things which exist in the real world or are physically present to the senses. For instance, we may be afraid of certain people or animals; natural phenomena such as storms or earthquakes may also frighten us, as may accidents, physical injury, disease and death. On the other hand some fears centre on less tangible concepts which are often vague and unspecified. Typical of these is the fear of the unknown which most of us experience at some time in our lives. We speculate about life after death, for example, or about the inscrutable workings of chance, fate or destiny—whatever we may call the capricious forces which play a part in our lives for good or ill. On a more immediate level we also have nameless fears of many kinds. We may imagine, or even believe in the existence of certain supernatural entities, often shadowy and ill-defined, perhaps thought to be especially active and potent during the hours of darkness. Certainly the imagination of children is often filled with frightening concepts of this kind. In this way we may bring about the evolution of a host of figures which symbolise or personify many of our fears.

As fear seems to be a universal phenomenon and a constant aspect of human life it is not surprising that certain frightening

The Witch as a Frightening and Threatening Figure

concepts are embodied in broadly similar ways in many different parts of the world. People in all cultures are frightened by a wide range of concepts, many of which take the form of specifically named figures which are intrinsically frightening. These might include gods, demons, spirits and other supernatural or invented beings, and also living people, especially those thought to have supernatural or extranormal powers and characteristics. In addition, certain animals such as wolves, reptiles and rodents may be felt to be more fearsome than others and develop an unpleasant connotation in popular tradition.

Whether they are supernatural or invented, human or animal, such figures have a number of characteristics in common. They are all abnormal in some way and their abnormalities are central to the frightening aura which surrounds them. This wide-ranging group, which one might designate as 'frightening figures',[1] has attracted the attention of folklorists from time to time. Among studies of frightening figures from various cultures there are numerous references to witches, wizards and similar figures of popular belief. Although the term 'witch' is now generally restricted to women it could formerly be applied to both sexes. The *Standard Dictionary of Folklore, Mythology and Legend* defines a witch as: 'A person who practices sorcery; a sorcerer or sorceress; one having supernatural powers in the natural world, especially to work evil, and usually by association with evil spirits or the Devil.'[2] Without entering into the controversial problems of nomenclature and definition which surround such terms as 'witchcraft', 'wizardry' and 'sorcery' one might perhaps point out that witch-figures of various types, whatever their sex or function, share characteristics which mark them out as not only abnormal but also frightening. Although they may often be regarded as human beings with supernatural powers, some concepts of them, e.g. those common among children, may have a primarily supernatural connotation. This is fostered at least partly by folktales and legends depicting the witch in many guises, virtually all of them exaggeratedly extrahuman. In common with fairies and other figures of popular belief, witches are often thought to have such a degree of supernatural power, certainly as far as children are concerned, that their basically human identity is obscured.

Witches appear to be conceptualised in two ways: as extraordinary human beings, and as beings which are basically supernatural or invented rather than human. Katharine Briggs has highlighted the problems of definition and nomenclature as follows:[3]

> The witch sabbats and the witches' covens hardly belonged to more than literature in this country, but the folk witch beliefs have persisted to the present day. It would no doubt be a convenience if a single word could be found to distinguish the ritual witchcraft of the Inquisitors from the magical witchcraft of common tradition, but the word 'witch' is too old and too deeply rooted in common use for it to consent to work on half-pay for any Humpty Dumpty however learned or reasonable.

Dr Briggs is here discussing witchcraft in England as well as in its more general context and does much to untangle the complex web of definitions surrounding witches and witchcraft.

Although they have a wide variety of names, characteristics and functions, witch-figures and their counterparts are parallel in conception in different cultures. These concepts invariably emphasise the unpleasant and fearful aspects of each figure. In physical appearance and in their supposed supernatural powers they all have a great deal in common, whatever their nomenclature or however we may choose to define them. This is seen particularly in the many descriptions of the appearance and powers of witches both in real life and in folk belief and narrative.

The physical appearance of witch-figures is typically frightening and is often almost a caricature of all the most unpleasant human characteristics. Extreme ugliness, bodily deformity of all kinds, birthmarks, warts and similar features are typical of descriptions both of living women denounced as witches during the Inquisition and also those depicted in folk narrative. They are usually old, wrinkled, bent, crippled and reclusive. They often dress in dark, dirty, ragged clothes. They may mutter to themselves or display other signs of abnormal or antisocial behaviour. Commentators on the history of witchcraft frequently draw attention to such characteristics. At the time of the witch trials in England, for example, 'It was dangerous . . . to be ill-favoured, or foul-mouthed, or unfriendly by nature, and still more so to be deformed in body or eccentric in habit.'[4] Reports of witchcraft from various parts of England echo the typical descriptions and even though the belief has declined or died the memory lingers, as in this account, taken at random from a host of references, which briefly sketches the com-

The Witch as a Frightening and Threatening Figure

mon picture of local witches, this time from Herefordshire: 'A great many old women, thin, brown, wrinkled old crones bent nearly double and wearing long cloaks, went about by night carrying walking sticks. How they lived no one knew. They inhabited the old houses deserted by the forgemen....'[5]

Even the white witches and wise women who claimed to help people by curing them or offering advice were feared by the common people. Like their malevolent counterparts, they were also often ugly, reclusive and eccentric and, quite apart from any other reason, their supposed powers to cure, divine or even advise made them abnormal. This characteristic abnormality, this difference from 'ordinary' people, made them the obvious target for denunciation as witches.

Traditional concepts of the witch emphasise her malevolence, and this characteristic of *maleficium* distinguishes her from her less harmful sisters, the white witches, wise women and the like. Witches are commonly regarded as having malevolent powers through which they may cast spells, bewitch and use the evil eye, cause disease and plague, raise storms and harm cattle and crops, among other things. These supposed powers lay at the heart of the popular fear of the witches. Indeed it was this fear which brought about the denunciation of so many people as witches during times of persecution, as has been pointed out by Christina Hole, among others:[6]

> The strong popular hatred of witchcraft in every century and in all countries was founded upon the age-old belief in *maleficium*, that secret, malicious activity of sorcerers, backed by hidden power and knowledge, which constantly threatened the health, happiness, and prosperity of ordinary men. This belief was as old as magic itself, and was the shadow cast from time immemorial by the practice of magical arts.... Its strength sprang from the natural fears of simple folk who believed in magic but did not understand it.... Mediaeval stories of Satanic cults and blasphemous rites naturally added to the terrors of their hearers, but they did not create those terrors in the first place. It was the far older dread of *maleficium* that underlay the long-enduring hatred of the black witch, and lent popular support to every anti-witchcraft law and edict devised by the civil or ecclesiastical authorities.

The malevolent powers of the witches are also graphically described by Miss Hole:[7]

> Witches were suspected of murder by image-magic or by poison; of wasting goods by magically stealing their essence; of destroying crops and enchanting cattle; and of every sort of domestic malice, from the clouding of a man's reason down to the infestation of clean houses with lice, or the prevention of successful butter-making. They were blamed for storms, floods, outbreaks of fire, and plague epidemics; for droughts, murrain, bad harvests, and all the ills that can befall a farmer. They were accused of making women barren and men impotent, parting friends and lovers, causing accidents and nightmares, spoiling food and drink, blunting weapons in battle, and afflicting young and old with mysterious diseases. Their curses, directly uttered to the victim, or written down and buried, brought failure in enterprises, poverty, and the slow decline of families; and by various other means they could induce paralysis, fits, delusions and, occasionally, curious compulsive actions.

This admirably economical summary merits full quotation not least because it presents a formidable list of powers, each of which is more than enough to arouse deep-rooted dread of any person believed to be a witch. Virtually all basic human misfortune may be attributed to the witch, who becomes a scapegoat for almost every ill.

A similar dread may also play a part in the formulation of our concepts of fictional witches in folk narrative. It is sometimes difficult to differentiate between our fear of the supernatural elements in witchcraft and our fear of their supposed manifestation in a living person. Problems of definition again inevitably arise between the unfortunate individuals in real life who are denounced and condemned as witches, and their fictional counterparts depicted in folktales. Witch-figures appearing in legends, however, may share characteristics of both the human witch and her often conventionalised supernatural equivalent. In some legends a witch may be depicted as an extraordinary human being, whereas in others her characteristics may be more fantastic and supernatural. In folktales witches play predictably sinister and frightening roles and in European *Märchen* their appearance and behaviour are often conventionalised to the point of caricature. In Russian folktales, for example, Bába Yagá is sometimes described as filling a whole room in her revolving hut on chicken legs in the forest, her blue-veined nose reaching to the ceiling. Even so, the descriptions may be frightening to children and the fear they engender may persist

The Witch as a Frightening and Threatening Figure

despite the fact that in the *Märchen* the witch is usually outwitted and good is seen to triumph over evil:[8]

> Next evening she came to the mead where Bába Yagá's hut stood. The fence round the hut consisted of human bones, and on the stakes skeletons glared out of their empty eyes. And, instead of the doorways and the gate, there were feet, and in the stead of bolts there were hands, and instead of the lock there was a mouth with sharp teeth. And Vasilísa was stone-cold with fright.

After the horrors of the outside of Bába Yagá's hut, the reader or hearer still has the various descriptions of the old witch herself to savour in the tales:[9]

> 'Daughter mine, darling, heat the oven quickly; make it very hot.'
> So the maiden looked up and was frightened to death. For Bába Yagá with the wooden legs stood in front of her, and to the ceiling rose her nose. So the mother and daughter carried firewood in, logs of oak and maple; made the oven ready till the flames shot up merrily.
> Then the witch took her broad shovel and said in a friendly voice: 'Go and sit on my shovel, fair child.'
> So the maiden obeyed, and the Bába Yagá was going to shove her into the oven.

Here, as in many other *Märchen*, the witch, like the ogre, is pictured as a devourer. She is also an imprisoner of children as seen in such famous tales as that of Hansel and Gretel. She is associated with dark places such as the forest and has an aura of uncontrollable menace typical of many other frightening figures. It is characteristics such as these which link the figures together in such a way that their individual identities are blurred. The witch shares certain fearsome propensities with other figures of folk belief so that it is difficult, if not impossible, to differentiate between them at times. Runeberg notes that: 'There is no essential difference between the various kinds of witches, who all appear to be members of one large family. As regards other demoniacal beings, their close mutual relationship has also been obvious to many students.'[10] He adds that: 'Witches and other demoniacal beings have also ... many features in common, which become more obvious the farther back in time we go.'[11] Runeberg also points out the connections between witches and other demoniacal beings, spirits of the dead, dwarfs and subterranean spirits, wind and weather spirits, water-spirits, marshland

and moor spirits, wood spirits, death, nightmare spirits, elves and fairies, and house spirits.[12]

From such accounts as Runeberg's it is clear that in addition to the conventionalised witch of the folktale and the real-life manifestations of witches, a broad group of figures in European folklore has characteristics very similar to those of witches. In addition to their passive role as fearsome beings, these figures may be utilised to serve certain social functions. These include the threatening of children, either playfully or seriously, in order to encourage good behaviour or conformity with certain accepted familial or cultural norms. When employed to serve such ends, the various entities might be termed 'threatening figures' to distinguish them from their counterparts which, although intrinsically frightening, are not used in threats. The threatening function of such figures has received comparatively little attention and scarcely any references are made to their use in a system of verbal social control. Major works which comment in detail on frightening figures concentrate on enumerating the vast range of such beings but rarely mention that a proportion of them may be selected as part of a pattern of deliberate threatening.

As witches have so much in common with other threatening figures it is surprising that there are so few reports of them in this threatening role. Again, it seems that attention has been concentrated on other aspects, such as the relationship between witchcraft and religion or on the problems of differentiating witchcraft from sorcery. It is only in recent years that the social functions of witchcraft have received fuller investigation. As Runeberg's work amply demonstrates, witches share with such supernaturals as fairies and bogeymen many of the extrahuman powers which may be referred to in threats used against children. The occasional references to figures in this threatening capacity suggest that both the figures and the linguistic structure of the threats are similar in many cultures. The witchlike figures of the Germanic *Kornmutter* tradition, for instance, are used in threats of a practical nature to discourage children from spoiling the growing corn:[13]

> The most evident connection with the witches, however, is found in those corn-spirits which people use to frighten away the children from the fields. In Austria this spirit is an old witch who sits in the corn; she is naked and black and has glowing red iron-fingers, by which she stings out the children's eyes; she pecks at them till they

The Witch as a Frightening and Threatening Figure

are roasted. This spirit is close akin to the deadly 'old one' in the corn, a being who eats children, sucks blood out of them, forces them to drink deadly black milk, blood, or tar out of her long black iron breasts, or kills them in some other way. In Silesia people thus say, to keep their children from the field: 'The old one sits there; she will take you'. Here the rustle of the trees is spoken of as the whispering of the witches, and the people speak at the same time of 'the old witch' and 'the old one who sits in the corn'.

Such descriptions illustrate how figures may be selected from a range of choices to function in a complex system of control. More specifically, witches, like other threatening figures, are used in many different places to prevent or discourage children from acting in ways which incur disapproval or social censure.

In the British Isles, reports of witches as threatening figures are surprisingly rare. However, they are known elsewhere in the English-speaking world. Recent research in Newfoundland, for example, indicates that witches, along with a variety of other figures, occur quite frequently in both a frightening and a threatening capacity. This tradition is parallel to that found in Europe and elsewhere and suggests a widespread patterning of usage across cultures.

The Newfoundland witch-figures are of two main kinds: supernatural/imaginary witches; and witches identified with real people, living or dead. A general survey of traditional usage carried out by the Department of Folklore at the Memorial University of Newfoundland indicates that some sixty communities in the island are familiar with the use of witch-figures in the threatening of children. This survey, which forms part of a comprehensive collecting programme of Newfoundland folklore, is a continuing project directed by Professor H. Halpert. Material from numerous surveys and individual contributions is correlated in the University's Archive of Folklore and Language. It is from this that the data for the ensuing discussion has been drawn.[14]

An exploratory questionnaire completed by a large number of students at the University in 1966-7 revealed that the witch is used widely in Newfoundland as a threatening figure in much the same way as similar figures are employed in the European references. The majority of the Newfoundland reports refer to witches of the *Märchen* type, i.e. those which are primarily supernatural in connotation. Like other threatening figures they are conceived of as vague, monstrous creatures who have power to 'get' children, especially at night. They inhabit attics, old buildings, rock walls or woods, and take children to their abode as servants or food. In common with most other threatening figures they are pictured as abductors and devourers of the children on whom they are threatened.

Although the witch in Newfoundland may be described in the conventional terms appropriate to the traditional witch-figures of folktale, when used as a threatening figure her most terrifying aspects are strongly emphasised. Typical descriptions from the Archive collection reflect traditional concepts of fairy-tale witches.[15] An informant from Middle Brook, Gambo, on the east coast of the island, describes the witch as

> 'a creature with long, straight hair, a very sharp nose, and long slender fingers. She has a big mouth with pointed teeth. She dresses in black. Her dress is black and she wears a pointed black felt hat on her head. A witch usually sails through the air on a long broom and is always accompanied by a fierce-looking cat.'

From Burnt Woods, on the south coast, comes the description:

> 'Witches are thought of as evil old ladies with long sharp crackling laughter, a green whiskery face, bony hands with six-inch long fingernails, a long crooked sharp nose with a whisker at the tip, long straight black hair, a tall, sharp, black hat, a long black gown with big-heeled shoes.'

From St John's an informant pictures a witch as

> 'a creature with long feet, bandy legs, bent, humpy back, long arms... long straggly wisps of hair, floppy ears, pointed chin, tusky teeth, beaky nose, sunken eyes, wrinkly forehead, a raspy, scratchy voice, dressed in black symbolising darkness, death, despair; riding on a broom, spreading her cloud of doom far and wide.'

And from nearby Bell Island she is depicted as

> 'an old hag, very ugly, and wearing black cloak and hat, and carrying a broom.'

The witches are thought to live not only in the woods but also in caves, old dilapidated houses or simply somewhere in the darkness:

> 'the witches are thought of as living in the woods. But... like the devil, are more frequently thought of as forever roaming the fields, gardens, and roads at night.' (Burnt Woods)[16]

The Witch as a Frightening and Threatening Figure

'The witch lived in a deserted house with other witches and ghosts.' (Bloomfield)

'The witch was supposed to live in a cave waiting for unsuspecting children who wandered into the woods.' (Terra Nova)

'The fairies and witches live in the woods or forest.' (Newman's Cove)

'the witches [live] in big caves or castles.' (Gull Island)

Sometimes the location was more specific—a nearby island, headland or hill:

'Others were said to live on Shag Island.' (Bloomfield)

'The witches were "up on the point".' (Winterton)

'On Southside Hill there were supposed to be witches.' (St John's)

Like the boogie-man[17] the witches '... live in the dark.' (Windsor)

'the witches live in an old house in the woods.' (Terrenceville)

or again:

'According to children, their habitations are also located in woods behind the town or in some haunted, dilapidated building.' (Buchans)

Many of the physical characteristics of witches are also found to typify the appearance of various local women who, in Newfoundland as in many other parts of the world, are regarded by children—and sometimes even by adults—as frightening, and who may occasionally be used in threats. These women are usually old and often reclusive; they live alone, or speak, dress or act oddly in some way. These are traits shared by many other human threatening figures, and they emphasise various types of abnormality or deviation from accepted cultural norms of behaviour and appearance:

'When I was small the[re] was an old lady who we thought was a witch.... We were very frightened of her and would hide and call her names when she passed in the street. She would walk several feet out into the street and never on the sidewalk.... I used to use this rhyme when the old lady ... passed on the street:

> Old mother witch
> Couldn't sew a stitch,
> Picked up a penny
> And thought she was rich.' (St John's)

'The ... witch might be an old woman who lived in a house all by herself. She would probably wear a black shawl, black clothing and walk as if some part of her body gave her pain.' (St John's)

'Sometimes old women, usually Old Maids, were said to be witches and people would use these as a means of scaring the children.' (Deer Lake)

'I remember... one old lady.... She was usually dressed in a long black dress and coat, stockings and shoes. A few times a year she would come over.... Many of the older people said she was a witch and whenever I saw her I would run home. Most of the other children were the same. She had all the features of a witch we saw in our reader.[18] She was even bent over and wore a large black hat. Most of the older people respected her and let her get served first in the store even if it wasn't her turn.' (community in Bonavista Bay)

'My mother remembers a particularly frightening old woman who was used by all the parents in that part of the town as a means of making children behave. She was supposed to be the proverbial witch feared by all.' (St John's)

'A very old woman may be thought of as a witch. As an example, I have visited a community where all the children were terrified by an old woman.... This fear was because of her appearance as she was dressed poorly and had a limp.' (St John's)

The dividing line between reality and fantasy is by no means always clearly drawn in the descriptions, as is seen in the following report from the capital city of St John's:

'The granny witch:[19] An old woman who lived several streets away from us. She spent all her afternoons sweeping her front stoop,[20] and it was believed that if you walked on it she would grab you and turn you into an animal, and to avoid this you always crossed the street when you passed her house. About ten years later I found out she was a bootlegger and didn't want children [near her house]. She had a number of china dogs and cats in her window which we thought were children she had changed.'

Other accounts also illustrate the similarity between real people and the traditional witch of fiction:

'When I was small I lived in a new area which was right behind a large field. In that field there was an old beat-up house. The old woman who lived there was... dressed very ragged like. All the young children were sure that she was a witch and no-one would ever be caught near that field after dark or alone.' (St John's)

'One old lady was believed to have been a witch because she kept over a dozen cats and resembled an old witch in a picture book.

The Witch as a Frightening and Threatening Figure

Some children were afraid to enter her house and would walk slowly by it and then run.' (community on the Southern Shore)

'Every settlement has its witch and she was usually called "Aunt."[21] Mothers would usually say, "Aunt so-and-so is coming" and children would go to bed.' (Corner Brook)

'there was one old lady who was believed to have powers of witchcraft. If she asked a favour of anyone they always tried to fulfil her wishes because they were scared she would put some spell on them. The children would keep off her property because they believed she would put a spell on them; they were told to keep away from her property because "Aunt —— would get them".' (community in Green Bay)

'Children were usually frightened of local people (usually women) because the theory grew up that they were witches. One spinster with a black dog and very overgrown garden—I think she had a pimple on her nose, and of course she was old—she very rarely came out except to chase us out of her back garden.... Kids used to believe that there were traps in her back garden, and that she could cast a spell on you if you went through [it]. I think some parents might have said this to keep us out.' (St John's)

'A town "witch" was known and feared by grown-ups as well as children. They were afraid of evil spells that she might cast. Very often, too, people blamed illnesses on the "spells" of the witch. The remedy for this was to draw a picture of her, then shoot at the effigy. It was supposed to cure the ailment.' (community in Bonavista Bay)

'When I was growing up there was a very old lady who always dressed in long black clothes, and she was called a "witch". We ran from her whenever we could, but unfortunately she frequently visited our home and we would just have to sit quietly, terrified, until she had her tea, and left. She talked very little, but she claimed she could remove warts by charming them away. Oddly enough, she offered to "charm" mine away, and they did disappear completely, but I suspect they might have gone anyway.' (community in Labrador)

Some of the accounts of local women thought to be witches refer to a single characteristic which was sufficient to arouse suspicion:

'One of the local old ladies ... was thought to be a witch because she had a split finger-nail.' (community in Placentia Bay)

It is the vivid memories which people have of their childhood days, however, which often produce the fullest and most graphic accounts:

> 'Now when I was small... there was a witch figure.... I was really scared of her, an' I would run past her house.... It was a children's thing.... I don't think my parents ever said anything, you know, but the kids all thought she was a witch. I was in... Grade 1 [at school] there, and everybody was afraid of her. I remember we went on a class picnic by her house and in groups we'd hide until she went in. She'd come out chopping wood, and we were scared of the axe, mainly. And we would hide until she went back in and then we'd run past her house—this kind of thing. But it was just the children. My brother, see, was older than I was; he was about ten. Now he remembered the woman, but he didn't remember any kind of witch idea with her, but he knew that she muttered to herself.... She was just an old woman and she's alone a lot.' (community in Fortune Bay —tape-recorded source)

Even the conventionalised witch-figures appearing among the mummers at Halloween and Christmas in Newfoundland may be frightening to children, especially the very young. However conventional their disguises may be they are an integral part of the elaborate network of frightening manifestations which may be used to scare children:

> 'If mummers and janneys[22] are distinguished as witches or some other creature which reminds the child of someone with whom he has been threatened, then the child becomes scared and thinks that he will be harmed.' (Buchans)

The reasons why witches are threatened on children in Newfoundland are similar to those commonly found in other parts of the world. They fall into four main categories: General threats to discourage misbehaviour and encourage obedience; specific threats to get children indoors before dark and discourage them from going out at night; specific threats to keep children away from dangerous or forbidden places; miscellaneous threats involving other specific prohibitions. In the final section of this discussion, each of these categories will be commented on briefly, and illustrative examples will be cited from the Newfoundland Archive material. It is interesting to note that virtually all these citations refer to the more supernatural, fairy-tale concepts of the witch.

Like other threatening figures such as the 'boogie-man', witches

The Witch as a Frightening and Threatening Figure

are threatened in a general way to discourage misbehaviour of various kinds and encourage obedience within the family unit and also within the surrounding culture. Examples of threats used in this general system show that the witch is only one of several figures which may be employed in this threatening role:

'The threats that I have heard for getting children to behave are the Black Man,[23] the witches, the boogie-man.' (Dunville)

'The witches are used when the children are naughty. Parents warn them that they will give the children to the witches if they aren't good.' (Heart's Delight)

'The children are threatened by various figures [such] as boo-man, fairies, witches, mouse and rat.' (St Phillips)

'The children are threatened by, "The boo-man will get you," "Witches will come and take you," or "The Devil will get you."' (Avondale)

'Witches: grotesque old ladies with long stringy white hair, warts on their faces, no teeth and long crooked noses, who wear high pointed hats, black dresses and went around on brooms with black cats on them. These witches were supposed to be waiting to catch naughty children and turn them into animals. *Usage*: "I'll tell the witches".' (Northwest Brook)

'In situations where the children were naughty the terms "Black Man," "boo-man," and "witches" were used to frighten them into being good.' (Freshwater, Placentia Bay)

'Witches are usually thought of as old men and women who can bring a true wish upon you. If children are bad they are sometimes told that the witches will come and something will happen to them. Sometimes people tell them they are going to tell the witches to do something to them.' (Blue Cove)

'The witches were used to scare kids as well though he [the informant] knew of no specific ones. They seemed to be the Halloween type—black dresses, flying around.' (St John's)

At times the threats are playful in tone:

'The witches are going to change you into gingerbread.' (Lawn)

But the general theme of disobedience persists:

'I have often heard parents threaten their children when they are disobedient by saying that the boogie-man or the witches would come and take them away if they did not behave.' (St John's)

'These threats succeeded in the majority of cases because the children were really terrified at the mention of these frightening creatures. They would hurry off to bed even though they would shiver under the clothes as they pictured the witches and fairies that would carry them off for being naughty or disobeying.' (Topsail)

The witches are usually nocturnal, and have power to transform children into unpleasant creatures:

'The witches were supposed to come and take children on their journeys at night, if the children were naughty that day.' (Mount Pearl)

'The witches ... would come and take the children and either cast a spell on them and turn them into frogs, snakes or some other horrible creature or they would cook and eat them.' (Grand Falls)

This motif of devouring is common elsewhere in the island:

'the witches would come and eat them if they weren't good.' (Curling)

The connection of witches with mummers, stories and children's games is also revealed in the questionnaire responses which refer to general threats used to encourage good behaviour:

'The witches are also connected with Halloween. [They] are ... used to frighten children and also to make them behave. The stories told to children often contain witches and other strange characters.' (Gull Island)

'Witches were commonly used to frighten kids. There were even games about witches. For example, one child would be the witch in the well, another the mother and the rest of the children were the mother's kids. The children would go in and ask for a slice of bread and jam; then the mother would say, 'Go wash your dirty hands.' The children would go to the well to find a witch who would frighten them away by much shouting and booing. The children would return to their mother who would tell them they were imagining things, and to go back and wash their hands or there would be no more bread and jam. So again they would go to the well. The same things happen three times; finally the mother goes to find the kids are telling the truth. The witch chases all of them and the first one she catches is the witch [in the next game].' (St John's)

The Witch as a Frightening and Threatening Figure

General disobedience in the house sometimes involves a threat in which the witch is pictured as being somewhere indoors:

'If a child was tormenting in the house the parents would sometimes warn [him] to be quiet or they would put him in the dark closet under the stairs with the witch.' (Western Bay)

Sometimes the witch is named, although this seems not to alter the conventional concepts of her:

'One frightening figure used . . . is "Granny Wicks." She is pictured by the children as an old witch with very unpleasant features who collects "bad children" in a bag and takes them to her hut as either servants or food.' (Harbour Deep)

Witches are threatened to get children in before dark and discourage them from venturing outdoors at night. Again this type of threat emphasises the nocturnal activities of the witch, although, as the citations show, other figures may also be used for the same purpose:

' "The Witches" was used if a child refused to come in during the night.' (Dunville)

'If you don't come in before dark, the witches will have you.' (Mount Pearl)

'witches lived in woods and caves and came out after dark.' (Campbellton)

'Around Halloween time we were sometimes threatened with seeing witches if we weren't in by dark.' (Freshwater, Carbonear)

'If you stayed out late the witches would get you.' (St John's)

'Don't stay out too late or the witches will have you.' (Burin)

'The witches were used to get the children in before dark.' (Terra Nova)

'Come in before the witches get ya!' (Mount Pearl)

'To get them in before dark: "The witch comes out when it gets dark".' (St John's)

'Both the boogie-man and witches are used to get children in before dark.' (Stephenville)

'Get in before dark or the witches'll get you.' (Gander)

'Don't go outdoors tonight or the witches will take you.' (Terrenceville)

'You can't go outside in the dark now 'cause the witches and bears are out of the woods.' (Burnt Woods)

The above citations also illustrate the variety of linguistic forms which such threats may take.

Some questionnaire responses draw attention to the reasons which lie behind the use of threats and also give valuable insights into the success or failure of the threats in controlling children:

'When children stay out too late after dark, parents become worried. To induce children to return home earlier, parents often tell them that if they don't return home at a certain hour, a witch will swoop down and carry them away on a magic broom.' (Middle Brook, Gambo)

' "The Old Witch flies across the moon on Halloween night." This used to be a popular belief among children ... about eight to ten years ago. Often it was said that she would fly across on her broom at midnight only, but other times any late hour was mentioned. This seems to have been a way to get the younger children in at an early hour by telling them that if they stayed out late they would see the wicked old witch. But among the older children this ruse sometimes backfired; they might still believe it, but they would stay out late on purpose to see if the witch really flew across the moon late on Halloween night, and also what she looked like.' (Grand Bank)

Witches were also used to keep children away from dangerous or forbidden places just as European children are threatened with the *Kornmutter* and similar figures:

'In order to prevent them from going to dangerous places they are threatened by, "The witches live in there".' (St John's)

'To prevent them from going to dangerous places—"The old witch will bake you in her oven".' (St John's)

'if there was a certain place parents did not want their children to visit, they were told the witches, fairies, bears [or] boo-baggers lived there.' (Campbellton)

'My parents often used such threats as boogie-man, the witches and the bear to keep us from going to dangerous places.' (Mount Pearl)

The Witch as a Frightening and Threatening Figure

'Parents told their children that certain [places] were inhabited by witches. In this way children [be]came afraid to go to these so-called haunted areas. These usually included old deserted houses, and forests.' (Torbay)

'The old witch is usually used as a threat to keep children out of dangerous places, such as woods and ponds. When [the witch is] used as a threat the story of Hansel and Gretel is usually brought to the attention of the child.' (Stephenville)

'My aunt threatens her son when he wants to go up into the attic: "The witch lives up there and if you ever see her you'll never forget it".' (Gander)

'Witches I think were the most horrible of all these people as frightening figures. They were said to live in all the old, deserted, run-down houses around the community. Children were told that if they went near these places they might be caught by a witch and stewed. Threat: "Stay away from there or the witch'll come after ya".' (St John's)

'When I was about nine I went to visit my grandparents in St Lawrence and in the hill behind the town there was a pond. It wasn't really dangerous but it could be messy because it was surrounded by mud. I was told there was a big rock near the pond and a witch lived there. The rock was sharp and jagged but it looked to our eager imaginations like a little house. We used to look at it and notice tiny holes filled with water in which, we were told, she did her washing. There was a split in the middle which extended [to] one quarter of the rock, then down the central and side sections. We were told, and believed devoutly, that if you went near the pond the witch came out of her house and dragged you into her house through the crack, which she could enlarge as we open a door, and then you were trapped for ever.' (St Lawrence)

Not only is the witch thought to live in wells in some children's games; she is also said to live there in some of the threats:

'Most of these threats were made to keep us from going to dangerous places. Sometimes we were told that a witch lived in the well. I don't think we believed it, but it kind of discouraged us from playing there.' (Freshwater, Carbonear)

'I would never go near any deep wells, for I had often been told that a[n] evil witch dwelled there just waiting for little girls to come along so she could boil them in her pot.' (Blaketown)

In addition to the more common reasons for threatening children as described above, there are a few reports in the Newfoundland Archive of other specific threats against various types of misbehaviour. For instance, there are reports of witches being used instead of the sandman and similar sleep-figures to encourage children to go to bed and to sleep:

> 'I have heard people saying, "Go to bed else the witches will certainly get you".' (St Joseph's, Placentia Bay)

> 'They [i.e. children] may go to sleep when they are threatened by such figures as fairies, witches, Jack the Ripper and the Black Man.' (Gull Island)

> 'Some parents in Bonavista sometimes used the word[s], "Sally Cushion will get you" in order to get their children to bed or to keep them quiet. Sally Cushion was supposed to be a witch who lived under a wall of rocks in one section of Bonavista.' (Bonavista)

Some degree of control over the activities of mummers at Halloween appears to be behind the threat that

> 'Witches are watching you on Halloween night if you play a trick on an old woman.' (Heart's Delight)

And making fun of other people is also actively discouraged by means of such threats as

> 'If you make fun at other people, the witches will get you.' (Bloomfield)

Finally, it is interesting to note the occasional reports of older children threatening younger ones in much the same way as adults threaten them:

> 'Older children threatened the informant with boogie-man ... and witches if he tagged along with them.' (St Vincent's)

From even such a cursory sampling of recently collected material from a single English-speaking area it is clear that the witch may appear frequently not only as an intrinsically frightening figure but also as a threatening figure along with various other entities with similar fearful connotations. It is reasonable to suppose that more detailed investigation will reveal similar interaction between figures of popular belief in the verbal systems of social control through threats which are used by adults to direct the behaviour of children

The Witch as a Frightening and Threatening Figure

in many different parts of the world. Such investigation would probably also reveal that witch-figures form part of a complex network of frightening entities which may be employed for such specific social functions as the disciplining of children by means of deliberately structured threat-patterns.

Notes

1. There is no equivalent term in English for the German *Kinderschreck* which in any case does not always distinguish between figures which are simply frightening and those which are used for threatening children.
2. M. Leach (ed.), *Standard Dictionary of Folklore, Mythology and Legend*, New York, 1950.
3. K. M. Briggs, *Pale Hecate's Team*, London, 1962, p. 3.
4. C. Hole, *A Mirror of Witchcraft*, London, 1957, p. 140.
5. Mrs Murray-Aynsley, 'Scraps of English folklore, XVI. Herefordshire', *Folklore*, vol. 39, no. 4, December 1928, p. 383.
6. C. Hole, op. cit., p. 88.
7. Ibid., p. 89.
8. L. A. Magnus (ed. and trans.), *Russian Folk-tales*, New York, 1916, p. 112.
9. Ibid., p. 67.
10. A. Runeberg, *Witches, Demons and Fertility Magic*, Helsinki, 1947, p. 109.
11. Ibid., p. 110.
12. Ibid., pp. 106-48.
13. Ibid., pp. 135-6.
14. I am greatly indebted to Professor Halpert for permission to use material from the Archive as the basis of the latter section of the present account. I should also like to express my gratitude to all the students from Memorial University who collected the bulk of the data and to the many people in all parts of the island who contributed information on this subject.
15. Archive material is quoted verbatim from questionnaire responses, with minimal alterations of spelling and punctuation where this is necessary for clarity of presentation. All the quoted material is filed in the Memorial University Folklore and Language Archive in St John's, Newfoundland.
16. Names in parenthesis after quotations from the Archive sources indicate the community from which the information was recorded.
17. Pronounced ['bwgi mæn] this is the Newfoundland version of 'bogeyman' and is the most common threatening figure.
18. School reading-books are mentioned in a number of questionnaire responses in the Archive as being the source of pictorial representation of such figures as witches and the Devil. This example also illustrates the close connection in children's imagination between the fictional witch and any woman in real life who displays similar characteristics.
19. The term 'granny witch' usually designates an entirely fictional creature in the archive references, but this citation clearly relates it to a real person.
20. Raised wooden platform in front of house.

21 'Aunt' is a common term of respectful address for an older woman in Newfoundland, just as an older man may be addressed as 'uncle'.
22 'Janney' is an alternative name for Christmas mummers in parts of the island. *Vide* J. D. A. Widdowson, 'Mummering and janneying: some explanatory notes', *Christmas Mumming in Newfoundland*, ed. H. Halpert and G. M. Story, Toronto, 1969, pp. 216–21.
23 Euphemistic for the Devil.

Publications by Katharine M. Briggs

Books on folklore

The Personnel of Fairyland (Oxford, 1953).
The Anatomy of Puck (London, 1959).
Pale Hecate's Team (London, 1962).
The Fairies in Tradition and Literature (London, 1967).
Englische Volksmärchen (Düsseldorf, 1970).
A Dictionary of British Folk-tales in the English Language (London, 1970–1).
The Last of the Astrologers (London, 1973).
With Ruth Tongue *The Folktales of England* (London, 1965).
Editor: *County Folklore—Somerset* by Ruth Tongue (London, 1965).

Articles on folklore

'Some seventeenth-century books of magic', *Folklore*, vol. 64 (London, 1953).
'The English fairies', *Folklore*, vol. 68 (London, 1957).
'The fairy economy as it may be deduced from a group of folk tales', *Folklore*, vol. 70 (London, 1959).
'Some late accounts of the fairies', *Folklore*, vol. 72 (London, 1961).
'Making a dictionary of folk-tales', *Folklore*, vol. 72 (London, 1961).
'English fairy tales', *Internationaler Kongress der Volkserzählungsforscher* (Berlin, 1961).
'A tentative essay', *Folklore*, vol. 73 (London, 1962).
'Historical traditions in English folk-tales', *Folklore*, vol. 75 (London, 1964).
'The three bears', *IV International Congress for Folk-Narrative Research* (Athens, 1965).
'Historical traditions in English folklore', *Actas do Congresso Internacional de Etnografia* (Lisbon, 1965).

Publications by Katharine M. Briggs

'A dictionary of British folktales in the English language', *Journal of the Folklore Institute*, vol. 2, part 3 (Bloomington, 1965).
'The transmission of folk-tales in Britain', *Folklore*, vol. 79 (London, 1968).
'Heywood's Hierarchie of the Blessed Angells', *Folklore*, vol. 80 (London, 1969).
'The fairies and the realms of the dead', *Folklore*, vol. 81 (London, 1970).
'The folklore of Charles Dickens', *Journal of the Folklore Institute*, vol. 7, part 1 (Bloomington, 1970).
'New developments in the Folklore Society', *Journal of the Folklore Institute*, vol. 7, parts 2–3 (Bloomington, 1970).

Contributions to collections

'The influence of the brothers Grimm in England', *Brüder Grimm Gedenken 1963* (Marburg, 1963).
'The folds of folklore', (Shakespeare Survey 17), *Shakespeare and His Own Age*, ed. Allardyce Nicoll (Cambridge, 1964).
'Charlotte Yonge's ethics', *A Chaplet for Charlotte Yonge*, ed. G. Battiscombe and M. Laski (London, 1965).

Pamphlets

Henry Briggs & Company: A History of Seventy Five Years, 1860–1935 (Oxford, 1936).
With R. C. Douglas, *Some Traditional Singing Games of Scotland and the Border* (London, 1936).

Fiction

The Lisles of Ellingham (Oxford, 1935).
The Castilians (Oxford, 1949).
Hobberdy Dick (London, 1955).
Kate Crackernuts (Oxford, 1963).

Poetry

Lost Country (Dunkeld, 1938).
The Half-Cut Wood (Burford, 1959).

Publications by Katharine M. Briggs

Plays

The Garrulous Lady (London, 1935).
The Peacemaker (Dunkeld, 1936).
Lady in the Dark (Dunkeld, 1937).
The Fugitive (Dunkeld, 1938).

The Contributors

Carmen Blacker M.A., Ph.D.
Lecturer in Japanese, University of Cambridge. Publications include *The Japanese Enlightenment: A Study of the Writings of Fukuzawa Yukichi*.

H. R. Ellis Davidson M.A., Ph.D., F.S.A.
Calouste Gulbenkian Research Fellow, Lucy Cavendish College, University of Cambridge, President, The Folklore Society. Publications include *The Road to Hel, The Golden Age of Northumbria, The Sword in Anglo-Saxon England, Gods and Myths of Northern Europe, Pagan Scandinavia, The Chariot of the Sun, Scandinavian Mythology*.

Margaret Dean-Smith B.A., F.S.A.
Sometime Librarian, The English Folk Dance and Song Society. Publications include *Guide to English Folk Song Collection 1822–1952, Playford's English Dancing Master*.

L. V. Grinsell O.B.E., F.S.A.
Sometime Curator, Archaeology and Anthropology, The City Museum, Bristol. Publications include *The Ancient Burial Mounds of England, Egyptian Pyramids, Archaeology of Wessex, Dorset Barrows, Brief Numismatic History of Bristol, Archaeology of Exmoor*.

Christina Hole
Hon. Editor of *Folklore*. Publications include *Folktales of Many Nations, English Folklore, Haunted England, English Custom and Usage, Witchcraft in England, English Folk Heroes, English Sports and Pastimes, English Shrines and Sanctuaries, Saints in Folklore, Encyclopaedia of Superstitions*.

Ruth Michaelis-Jena
Sometime Secretary of P.E.N. Publications include *Grimms' Other Tales, New Tales from Grimm, The Brothers Grimm*.

The Contributors

Venetia Newall M.A., F.R.G.S., F.R.S.A.
Hon. Research Fellow in Folklore, University College, University of London; Lecturer in Folklore, Department of Extra Mural Studies, University of London; Hon. Secretary, The Folklore Society. General Editor of Series on County and Regional Folklore of the British Isles. Publications include *An Egg at Easter*, *The Folklore of Birds and Beasts*.

Geoffrey Parrinder M.A., D.D.
Professor of the Comparative Study of Religions, King's College, University of London. Publications include *Worship in the World's Religions*, *Upanishads, Gita and Bible*, *Witchcraft: European and African*, *African Mythology*, *Religion in Africa*, *The World's Living Religions*, *Avator and Incarnation*, *Man and his Gods*.

Anne Ross M.A., Ph.D.
Sometime Research Fellow in Custom and Belief, School of Scottish Studies, University of Edinburgh. Publications include *Pagan Celtic Britain*, *Everyday Life of the Pagan Celts*.

Jacqueline Simpson M.A.
Publications include *Penguin English Dictionary*, *The Olaf Sagas*, *The Northmen Talk*, *Everyday Life in the Viking Age*, *Beowulf and its Analogues*, *Icelandic Folktales and Legends*, *The Folklore of Sussex*.

Beatrice White M.A., D.Lit., F.R.S.L. F.R.Hist.S., F.S.A.
Sometime Professor of Medieval English, Westfield College, University of London. Publications include *The Vulgaria of John Stanbridge and the Vulgaria of R. Whittinton*, *Royal Nonesuch: A Tudor Tapestry*, *Mary Tudor*, *Cast of Ravens: The Strange Case of Sir Thomas Overbury*, *Philobiblon*.

John Widdowson M.A., Ph.D.
Lecturer in English Language, University of Sheffield, Hon. Editor of *Lore and Language*.

Index

Aarne, Antti, 97; *see also* Tale Types
Abduction, 48–9, 53, 56, 65, 111–13, 205, 208, 211, 214, 215, 216, 217
Abel, 104
Aberdeen, 45, 129
Addy, S. O., 90
Africa, 16, 125, 126, 130–7; *see also individual countries*
Ailesworth, 83
Albertus Magnus, 107
Albion, *see* Britain
Alexander the Great, 70
Algiers, 116
Almqvist, B., 29, 33–4
America, 31, 42, 98, 100, 112, 119, 207–19; *see also* Eskimos; Greenland; Labrador; Newfoundland; U.S.A.; West Indies
Ammianus Marcellinus, 141
Amulets, 108, 109
Anglo-Saxon Chronicle, 111
Anglo-Saxons, 83
Antichrist, 107, 125, 170
Antioch, 108
Anti-semitism, 95–119
Aomori, 2
Aphrodisiac, 114
Apparition and invisibility, 10, 21–4, 29–30, 37, 65, 169, 179
Apple, 91–2
Arabic, Arabs, 97, 100, 117, 118–19; *see also individual Arab countries*
Ardee, 82
Armagh, county, 152, 156
Armenia, 98–9
Arnold, Matthew, 49
Arrow, magic, 31
Arthur, King, Arthurian romances, 55, 56, 192–3, 197
Asia, 34, 97; *see also individual countries*
Atinga movement (Nigeria), 133–4
Aubrey, John, 106
Aucassin and Nicolette, 191
Audley, 91–2
Augustine, St, 97, 114, 131
Auldearne, 82
Austria, 104, 109, 117, 118, 206–7; *see also* Tyrol; Vienna
Avondale, 213
Azande of Sudan and Zaïre, 132, 135

Bába Yagá, 204–5
Babylon, 191, 193–5
Baëta, C. G., 133
Baltic, 23; *see also* Denmark; Finland; Latvia; Lithuania; Poland; Sweden
Bamberg, 130
Bamucapi movement (east and central Africa), 133
Baptism, 106, 127, 134, 168, 170, 180; *see also* Unbaptised baby
Baptists, 113–14, 134
Bartholomew Anglicus, 190

Index

Baskervilles, black dog of the, 17
Bat, 131
Bath, 151, 153, 154–5, 189
Bathwick, 151
Bear, 30, 32, 53, 172, 193, 216, 221
Beattie, J., 132
Beauvais, 99
Becket, Thomas, 126
Bed, overturning of, 109
Bedford, Bedfordshire, 74, 76
Bedford, Duchess of, 87–8
Belgian Congo, 134; *see also* Zaïre
Belgium, *see* Brabant; Brussels; Liège
Bell Island, 208
Benedictine order, 166
Beowulf, 189, 190
Berkshire, 76
Berlin, 112, 118–19
Bernard of Clairvaux, St, 108
Berserks, 26
Bertilak, Sir, 189, 193, 195
Bessarabia, 113
Biarmaland, Biarmians, 23, 27, 28, 38
Bible, 103, 104, 114, 146, 190
Bingo, 2
Bird, birds, 16, 17, 103, 140, 143–4, 150, 157, 162
Birka, 175
Birmingham Museum, 76
Black Death, 115, 116, 118, 203
Black Magic, *see* Magic spells
Black Mass, 82, 86
Black Mountains (Germany), 102
Blackwater, river, 155
Blaketown, 217
Blasphemy, *see* Black Mass; Heresy
Blindness, supernatural, 23, 114, 144, 147, 157, 161, 167, 172, 173, 181
Blood, 27, 30, 32, 35, 112–15, 144, 147, 158, 160, 161, 167, 207; *see also* Vampire
Bloomfield, 209, 218
Blue Cove, 213
Boece (Boëthius), Hector, 83, 189
Bogeyman, 110–11, 204–19
Boguet, Henri, 115
Bohemia, 112, 118; *see also* Prague
Boleyn, Anne, 126

Bonavista, Bonavista Bay, 210, 211, 218
Bone, magic, 11, 33, 52, 76, 78, 179, 205
Book of Days, 111
Bordeaux, 99
Border Minstrelsy, 45
Bosch, Hieronymous, 190
Boudicca, 141, 158
Boy, radiant, 16
Boyne, river, 155, 156
Brabant, 77
Brackley, Viscount, 61
Brand, John, 99–100
Brett, 112
Breughel, Pieter, 190
Bridgewater (John Egerton), Earl of, 42, 61, 67, 69
Briggs, Katharine M., ix–xiii, 72, 73, 201–2, 221–3
Brigid, St, 158, 162
Brignall, 93
Britain, British Isles, 72, 80–93, 96, 100, 117, 125, 129, 141, 147, 155, 158, 190, 207; *see also* Channel Isles; England; Ireland; Isle of Man; Scotland; Wales; and individual counties and places
Brittany, 73, 102, 161; *see also* Finistère
Bronze Age, 73, 74, 75, 78
Broom, witch's, 208, 213, 216
Brothers Karamazov, The, 105
Brown, Anna Gordon, 45–6
Browne, Sir Thomas, 98–9, 105
Browning, Robert, 55, 59
Brussels, 100
Buchans, 209, 212
Buckinghamshire, 91
Buddhism, 3, 4, 6
Bulgaria, 113
Bulgars of the Volga, 38
Bull, 29; *see also* Cow
Bungo, 9
Bunyan, John, 74, 197
Bunyoro of Uganda, 132
Burd Ellen, 44, 54–61
Burin, 215

Index

Burning or baking, death by, 8, 77, 90, 127, 128-9, 132, 204, 216
Burnt Woods, 208, 216
Burton-on-Trent, 88
Buryats of Transbaikalia, 28
Buxton, J., 132
Byron, Lord, 100
Byzantium, 28, 108

Cain, 103-4, 190
Cain's Hunt, 103
Cain's Mark, 104
Calf, see Cow
Cambridge, 87
Campbelltown, 215, 216
Canaan, 190, 191
Canada, see Labrador; Newfoundland
Candle, 87, 90-1, 180
Cannibalism, 111, 127, 130, 131, 191, 197, 205, 208, 214, 215, 217
Canterbury Tales, 108, 111, 189, 196-7
Capitalism, 96, 116, 118-19
Carbonear, 215 217
Carlisle, 55, 56, 58
Carrawbrough, 145
Cartimandua, 141
Cat, 4, 29, 109, 129, 190, 208, 210, 213
Caterpillar, 11, 12
Cauldron, magic, 142
Cavan, county, 147
Celtic, Celts, 126, 139-62, 177, 179, 189; see also Britain; Brittany; Cornwall; Gaul; Ireland; Isle of Man; Scotland; Wales
Centipede, 11, 12
Cewa of Zambia, 136
Chair, enchanted, 66, 67
Chambers, William, 111
Ch'ang-chou, 12-13
Channel Isles, 77
Charlemagne, 193-4
Charles I, 126
Charles V (Charles of Spain), Emperor, 116
Charles the Bold, 117
Chastity, 65
Chaucer, Geoffrey, 108, 111, 189, 196-7

Chaumont, 108
Chester, 87
Chicken, 57, 77, 134, 135, 136, 204
Child, F. J., 54-5, 111-12
Child Aller, 49, 50
Child corpses, 110, 111-13
Child Roland, 44, 46, 47, 48, 49-52, 53, 54-61, 63, 69
Child sacrifice or murder, 77, 82, 142, 182; see also Murder
China, 1, 11-14, 111, 189
Chrétien de Troyes, 190, 192
Christ, Christianity, 23, 36, 42, 50, 56, 58, 59, 62, 67, 68, 97-8, 99, 103-6, 107, 108, 109, 111, 112, 113, 114-15, 116, 125, 126, 128, 134, 144, 148-9, 156, 158-9, 162, 165, 167-71, 173-5, 176, 177-8, 180, 181, 182-3, 190, 193, 194, 195, 212
Christians and Jews, 98
Christmas, 108, 173, 181, 212
Christopher, St, 189
Chronicon Norvegiae, 31
Chrysostom, St John, 108, 109
Chūgoku, 2
Chukchis of the Bering Sea and Arctic, 22
Churchyard, 92
Cicero, Marcus Tullius (Tully), 146
Circe, 43, 64
Circumcision, 106, 114-15
Clay image, 81, 82-3
Cock, see Chicken
Combs of care, 188
Communism, 96, 116; see also Soviet Union
Comus, 42-70
Congo, 134; see also Zaïre
Conn, King, 146
Connacht, 142
Consecrated host, 115
Corfu, 112
Cork, county, 159
Corner Brook, 211
Cornwall, 78, 110-11, 161, 193
Corp Creadh, 81-3
Côtes-du-Nord, 77
Coven, 38, 77, 125, 202

229

Index

Coventina, 145
Coventry, 83-5, 91-2
Cow, 57, 92, 110, 144, 154, 156-7, 180, 191, 203
Crabbe, George, 100
Crete, 108
Cross, crucifixion, 91, 99, 102, 105, 111
Crow, 51, 140, 150, 158; *see also* Raven
Crusades, 100
Curbar, 90
Curling, 214
Curse, *see* Magic spell
Czaplicka, M. A., 30
Czechoslovakia, *see* Bohemia; Libenice; Prague

Daghestan, 113
Dagini rite (Japan), 5-6, 17
Dan, tribe of, 107
Dante Alighieri, 189
Darmstadt, 115
Dartmoor, 75, 76
Dead man's hand, 53
Decapitation, *see* Head
Deer, 140, 161, 171-2; *see also* Fawn; Reindeer
Deer Lake, 210
Deity, benevolent, 15, 16, 17, 24
Denmark, 24, 29, 44, 45, 46-52, 60, 75, 78, 102, 151, 192, 193, 195
Derby, Countess of, 67
Derby, Lord, 88-9
Derbyshire, 73, 90
Devil, 82, 108, 109, 115, 119, 125, 127, 128, 129, 130, 131, 165, 169, 172, 173, 174-5, 177-8, 181, 183, 189, 195, 198, 201, 208, 213
Devil's spot (numb area), 128, 129
Dianic rite, 125-6, 130
Dice, 76
Dickens, Charles, 222
Didcot, 76
Dio Cassius, 141
Diodorus of Sicily, 140-1
Dionysius, 141
Divination, 36, 86, 133, 172-3, 177, 203

Divine King in England, The, 126
Dnieper, river, 118
Doctor-sorcerer, 117-18; *see also* Witch-doctor
Dog, 2, 6, 7, 8-9, 13, 14, 16, 17, 30, 35, 129, 140, 151, 157, 160, 171, 172, 173, 210, 211; *see also* Hounds
Doré, Gustave, 101
Dorset, 73, 74
Dorson, Professor Richard M., ix, xii
Dostoyevsky, Fyodor, 105
Doulting, 73
Dragon's blood, 91, 115
Drayton, 73
Drayton, Michael, 67
Dreams, dream-interpretation, 31-2, 109
Druids, 139, 144
Drum, shamanistic or magic, 31, 37, 38, 133
Dublin, 156
Ducks, 89-90
Duff, King, 83
Duhallow, 159
Dunstable, 74
Dunville, 213, 215
Dvina, river, 23
Dyce, Alexander, 52-3

Eagle, 30, 151
Earthquake, 115; *see also* Eruption
East Indies, 99
Easter, Easter period, 88, 99, 106, 107, 111, 112, 114, 129
Edda, Poetic, 28, 33
Edda, Prose, 24
Edward I, 104
Edward II, 84
Edward IV, 87-8
Eggs, eggshells, 107, 109
Egils Saga, 25, 33
Egypt, 194-5
Elfland, 44, 47, 54-61, 63-4, 181
Elfshot, 31
Elgin, 58
Elizabeth I, 54, 129
Elworthy, F. T., 75
England, 16, 42-70, 78, 83-93, 95,

230

Index

96, 106, 110–11, 119, 125–6, 127, 128, 129, 149, 150, 151, 158, 161, 188–98, 202–3, 221–2
English Fairy Tales, 44, 55
Epidemics, 102
Epona, 152, 161
Erik Bloodaxe, 25, 34
Ériu, 139–40
Eruption, volcanic, 25, 26, 36; *see also* Earthquake
Eskimos, 37
Espeyran, 149
Essex, 72, 108
Ethiopia, 194, 195
Europe, 34, 95, 97, 98, 100, 103, 106, 107, 109, 112, 125, 126, 130–1, 132, 135, 137, 161, 165, 204–7, 216; *see also individual countries*
European Witch-Craze in the Sixteenth and Seventeenth Centuries, The, 107
Evans, Sir Arthur, 78
Evans-Pritchard, E. E., 132, 135
Evil eye, 25, 26, 115, 144, 203
Evil Eye, The, 75
Exeter, Bishop of, 73
Exorcism, 1, 4–5, 6, 9, 10, 11
Eye, *see* Blindness; Evil eye
Eye-next-Westminster, 85–6
Eyrbyggja Saga, 21, 35
Eyvind kelda, 167–9, 172, 182

Faerie Queene, The, 67, 69
Fairies, 60, 73, 74, 77, 201, 206, 214, 216, 218, 221–2
Faithful Shepherdess, The, 43, 69
Familiar, 3, 4, 109, 208, 210
Famine, 102
Faroes, 165, 181–2
Fawn, 154; *see also* Deer
Fertility magic, 114, 125–6, 140, 141, 148, 149, 150, 158, 167, 177–8, 204
Fifeshire, 75
Finistère, 73, 77
Finland, 110
Finnmark, 25, 109
Finno-Ugrians, 38
Fire, firebrand, 21, 22–3, 32, 53, 81, 82, 90–1, 102, 167, 204

Fire, ordeal by, 135
Firefly, 131
Fischer, Ruth, 96
Fish, 29, 36
Flame, *see* Fire
Flateyjarbók, 33, 166–83
Fletcher, John, *see The Faithful Shepherdess*
Fljotsdæla Saga, 21–2
Fly (insect), 31
Flying witch or wizard, 16, 38, 117, 130, 131, 161, 183, 208, 213, 216
Fog (mist), 23, 24, 169
Folklore, 76, 221–2
Folz, Hans, 107
Fornaldarsǫgur, 23, 28, 29–30, 38, 39
Fortune Bay, 212
Fortune-telling, 109, 133
Fóstbrœdra Saga, 22–3, 31, 35
Fourth Lateran Council, 104, 115
Fox, 1–11, 14–17
France, 72, 73, 76–7, 95–6, 98, 99, 100, 101–2, 105, 107, 108, 111, 114, 118, 119, 130, 149–50, 161, 191; *see also* Brittany; Gaul
Frankfurt-am-Main, 107, 115
Frankfurt-an-der-Oder, 108
Frazer, Sir James, 125–6
Friesland, 115
Frog, 12, 13, 90, 214

Gambo, 208, 216
Gander, 215, 217
Gardner, G. B., 76, 77
Garlic, 105
Gatherley Moor, 92
Gaul, Gallic, 140–1, 149–50, 152
Gawain, Sir, 189, 192, 193
Geoffrey of Monmouth, 170, 190, 193, 197; *see also Historia Regum Britanniae*
Geography of Witchcraft, The, 72
Germany, 72, 96, 99, 101, 102, 103, 104, 105, 107, 108, 109, 110, 112, 115, 116, 117–19, 128, 130, 150, 191, 206–7
Ghana, *see* Nana Tongo
Ghost, 2, 6, 15, 53–4, 66, 110, 111, 146, 179, 181, 205, 209

231

Index

Ghostly army, 103
Giant, giantess, 24, 27, 28, 29, 32, 49–51, 60, 142, 143, 173, 174–5, 179, 180, 181, 189–98
Gilgamesh, 191, 197
Gísla Saga, 35
Glamorgan, 100–1
Glass, magic, 53, 54, 64, 66
Gloucester, Duke and Duchess of, 85–7
Gloucestershire, 73
Goat, goatskin, 21, 23, 24, 25, 38, 57
God, 96, 98, 104, 172, 176
God of the Witches, The, 125
Gold, 36, 51, 54, 58, 64, 116, 146, 150, 156
Golden Bough, The, 125–6
Goldi of the Amur river, 28
Golem, 109–10
Gollancz, Israel, 44
Goose, 33
Gotland, 175
Grafton, 87
Grand Bank, 216
Grand Falls, 214
Greater Saga of Olaf Tryggvason, The, 166–83
Greece, Greek, 107, 112, 117, 177; *see also* Corfu; Crete
Green Bay, 211
Greenland, 22–3, 165; *see also* Eskimos
Gregory of Nyssa, St, 108
Gregory the Great, Pope, 175
Grendel, 190
Grettis Saga, 32
Grey, Lady Jane, 126
Grierson, H. J. C., 62
Grimm, Jacob and Wilhelm, xi, 103, 110, 222
Grünewald, Mathias, 190
Guernsey, 77
Gull, *see* Seagull
Gull Island, 209, 214, 218
Gull-Thóris Saga, 21, 26, 29
Gunnlaugs Saga, 26, 167, 176

Hair, human, 75

Hakon, Earl (*Jarl*) of Hladir, 33–4, 167, 174, 178–9, 182–3
Halévy, Jacques, 101
Hallfreðar saga, 176–7
Halliwell (Halliwell-Phillips), James Orchard, 55
Halloween, 212, 213, 214, 215, 216, 218
Hallucination, 21–4, 29–30, 65
Halogaland, 169–72
Halpert, Professor H., 207
Hamburg, 99
Hampshire, 75, 150
Hanging, 128, 129
Hansel and Gretel, 205, 217
Harald Fairhair, King, 167, 168
Harald Greycloak, King, 182
Harðar Saga, 21, 23, 29
Harris, Isle of, 149
Haute-Savoie, 150
Havarðar Saga, 31–2
Havelok, 192
Hayami Yasutaka, 10
Head, binding of, 109
Head, severed, 57, 140, 144, 149–50, 158, 168, 192
Healing magic, 36–7, 80, 88, 111, 172, 203, 211
Heart's Delight, 213, 218
Heaven, 62
Hebrew, 109, 117
Hebrides, 81, 149
Heidelberg, 115
Heiðarvíga Saga, 27
Heimskringla, 29, 166–83
Hell, 58, 59, 62, 181
Hellwald, Friedrich von, 97
Hen, *see* Chicken
Henderson, William, 91
Henry VI, 85–7
Henry, Prince of Wales (1610), 67
Herb, magic, 66, 117
Hereford, Herefordshire, 87, 89, 203
Heresy, 107, 111, 127, 171, 203
Herzog von Burgund, 107
Hirose, 8
Hiroshima, 2
Historia Regum Britanniae, 197

Index

History of the Kings of Norway, 168
Hitler, Adolf, 96, 104, 116, 117, 118–19
Hole, Christina, 203–4
Holtved, E., 37
Holy Ark, 113
Hood, witch's, 23, 24, 37, 38
Hopkins, Matthew, 128
Horace, 106
Horn, 54, 108, 174, 175, 180, 181
Horn, 192
Horned god, goddess, 131, 153, 161, 165
Horned hat, 104–5, 108
Hornsey, 86
Horse, horseman, 32, 34, 35, 36, 38, 57, 76, 78, 117, 140, 142, 146, 152, 157, 161, 162, 179, 190, 196
Horse's hoof print, 103
Hounds of death, 103; *see also* Baskervilles; Dog
Howard, Katherine, 126
Howth, 156
Hrólfs Saga, 24
Hugh of Lincoln, 111
Hultkrantz, A., 31
Hungary, 103, 104, 105, 112, 191
Hunt, Leigh, 106
Huntingdonshire, 72, 149
Hygelac, King, 189

Iberian peninsular, 64, 72; *see also* Portugal; Spain
Iceland, 20–39, 44, 50, 51, 165–83
Ilkley, 154
Ille-et-Vilaine, 77
Illustrations of Northern Antiquities, 44, 45, 46, 47
Image-magic, 80–93, 204, 211
Immigrants, 119
Impotence, sterility, 33, 34, 80, 170–1, 178, 204
Inari, 5, 15
Incest, 50, 51
India, 18, 197
Infanticide, 142, 158, 167, 207; *see also* Murder
Inferno, The, 189

Inquisition, 125, 127–8, 129, 130, 202
Insanity, 35, 54, 80
Invisibility, *see* Apparition
Ipswich, 90
Ireland, Irish, 36, 81–2, 127, 139, 142–4, 146–9, 150, 151, 152–4, 155–8, 159–61, 175, 180, 181
Iron Age, 75
Isaac, Professor Jules, 98
Ishizuka, Professor, 8, 11, 15
Israel, 98, 103, 118–9; *see also* Jews
Italy, 72, 100, 102; *see also* Romans; Sicily
Itch, 33, 174, 178
Ivan the Terrible, Tsar, 117
Iwate, 2
Izumo, 2, 8, 10–11
Izuna, Izuna rite (Japan), 2, 5–6, 17

Jack the Giant-killer, 60
Jack the Ripper, 218
Jacob, 102
Jacobs, Joseph, 44, 48, 55, 59–61, 69, 70
James I (VI), King, 45, 67, 129
James, Henry, 69–70
Jamieson, Robert, 43–4, 45, 55–60, 69
Japan, 1–17
Japan Sea, 2, 6, 15
Jerusalem, 97–8, 100
Jesus, *see* Christ
Jew and Human Sacrifice, The, 112
Jew badge, 104–5, 115
Jew of Malta, 118
Jews, 95–119, 175
Joan of Arc, 126
Jomsviking Saga, 167
Journey Prayers, 144–6
Judaism, 97
Jüdel, 110
Judenhut, 104–5, 108
Judenstein, 102
Judgment, day of, 102
Juif errant, Le, 101
Julius, Johannes, 130
Juvenal, 106

Index

Kaempe Viser, 44, 45, 46–52, 53, 59, 60, 69
Kansai, 2
Kantō, 2
Keats, John, 162
Kent, 138
Kenya, 133
Kerry, county, 159
Key, 107
Kidnapping, *see* Abduction
Kildal, Jens, 30
Kilkenny, 127
King Lear, 44, 45, 47, 53, 54, 59, 60
Kirk, Robert, 74–5
Kissing a witch, 27, 28
Klingsor, 70
Kochi, 8
Kolin, 112
Kormáks Saga, 27, 29, 33
Kornmutter, 206, 216
Krappe, A. H., 100
Krausz, Ernest, 106
Ku magic (China), 11–15
Kyoto, 1
Kyteler, Dame Alice, 127
Kyūshū, 2, 8

Labrador, 211
Lancashire, 72, 103
Lancaster, 129
Lancastrians, 87
Landnámabók, 24, 28, 30, 35, 36
Landslide, 36
Lapps, 20, 23, 29, 30, 31, 34, 37, 38, 109, 110, 168, 170–1, 172; *see also* Finnmark
Lasker, Bruno, 97
Latvia, *see* Biarmaland; Dvina (Daugava); Riga
Lavey, 147
Lawes, Henry, 42, 61–2, 63–9
Lawn, 213
Laxdæla Saga, 25, 34, 35, 175
Lea, H. C., 128
Leaden image, tablet, 87–8, 92
Leicester, 83
Lele of Zaïre, 134
Lepers, 118

Levin, Bernard, 96
Lévi-Strauss, Claude, 15
Liathmor, 148
Libenice, 158
Lice, infestation by, 204
Liège, 77
Lincoln, 111
Linwood, 150
Liss, 75
Lithuania, 102, 113, 117
Little Moreton, 76
Living corpse, 174, 179, 181
Lizard, 11
Ljósvetninga Saga, 27
Locmariaquer, 77
Locrine, King, 67
Loew, Rabbi, 109–10
Loewenstein, Rudolph M., 98
Loire, 141
London, 45, 87, 90, 92, 106; *see also* Eye; Hornsey; London Bridge
London Bridge, 83, 87
Long Compton, 78
Louth, county, 82
Louvre, the, 108
Ludlow, 42, 48, 60, 63
Luther, Martin, 117–18
Luton, 76
Lynx, 78

Macbeth, 75
Macclesfield, 45
Maclagan, R. C., 81
Magic spells, formulas, 22, 24, 25, 26, 32–3, 34–5, 37, 38, 55, 57, 66, 67, 81, 89, 91–3, 108, 131, 141, 154–5, 156, 157, 160, 167, 168, 170, 178–9, 180, 203, 204, 211, 221
Mahler, Gustav, 118
Malawi, *see* Bamucapi
Malory, Sir Thomas, 197
Man in the Moon, 102–3
Man, Isle of, 77, 87
Manche, La, 77
Mandari of the Sudan, 132
Mandeville, Sir John, 197
Marco Polo, 70
Mare, *see* Horse

Index

Mariu saga, 177
Marlowe, Christopher, 118
Marseilles, 149
Martial, 106
Marwick, M. G., 136
Materials Toward a History of Witchcraft, 128
Matsue, 9
Megalithic period, 73, 76–7, 159
Meged, Aharon, 118
Meiji, Emperor, 5
Mein Kampf, 116
Mendip Hills, 73
Merlin, 53, 55, 56, 57, 58, 170, 192
Merman (Rosmer Harmand or Hafmand), 44, 45, 47, 48–52, 53, 59, 60, 69
Messiah, 98
Methuselah, 102
Mezuzah, 109
Milton, John, 42–70, 189
Moldavia, *see* Bessarabia
Mongolia, *see* Buryats
Monster, 29, 64, 65, 66, 102, 143, 158, 160, 179, 191
Moon, 22, 51, 76, 102–3, 216
Morbihan, 77
Mosaic law, 115
Moslems, 113
Motif Index of Folk Literature, 103, 105, 106, 108, 111, 118
Mount Pearl, 214, 215, 216
Mozambique, *see* Shona
Mtsensk, 113–14
Mumming, 212, 214, 218
Murder (ritual), charges of, 110, 111–14, 117, 127, 129, 204
Murray, Dr Margaret, 76, 125–6
Museum of Witchcraft (Boscastle), 78
Museum of Witchcraft (Castledown), 77
Mystère de la Passion, Le, 108

Nadel, S. F., 137
Nagano, 2
Nail-parings, 91
Nana Tongo movement (Ghana, Nigeria), 133–4
Naples, 100
Napoleon, 111
Navan, 155
Navan Fort (Emain Macha, co. Armagh), 152, 156, 157, 158
Nazism, 95–6, 98, 101, 113, 115, 118–19, 120
Ndembu of Zambia, 132
Negroes, 119
Neolithic period, 76, 78, 125
Netherbury, 73, 74
New Statesman, 96, 113–14
New York, 101
Newfoundland, 207–19
Newman's Cove, 209
Nigeria, *see* Atinga; Nana Tongo
Niurenius, O. P., 31
Njals Saga, 23, 32, 33
Nord, 77
Northamptonshire, 83, 87–8
Northumberland, 145
Northwest Brook, 213
Norway, 31, 33, 34, 36, 109, 110, 165–83
Norwich, 91, 111
Nottingham (John de Notingham), 83–5
NSDAP (National Socialist German Workers' Party), 120; *see also* Nazism
Nyakyusa of Tanzania, 132

Odin, 26, 27, 167, 171, 173, 175, 180, 182
Oita, 8
Oki island, 8
Olaf, St, 182
Oldenburg, 103
Old Wives' Tale, The, 43, 45, 48, 52–4, 59, 60, 69
Omens, *see* Prediction
Opie, Peter and Iona, xiii, 106
Oracle, 15, 135
Orgies, 126, 131
Orkneys, 165
Ottomans, 107
Owl, 131, 151, 190
Ox, *see* Cow

Index

Oxford, Oxfordshire, 69, 78, 87, 149
Oyster shell, 91

Paradise Lost, 42, 189
Parkes, Rev. James, 119
Passover, 96, 106, 109, 112, 114
Patrick, St, 144, 180
Peele, George, 43, 44, 45, 52–4; *see also Old Wives' Tale*
Percy, Bishop Thomas, 100
Perth, 74
Picardy, 102
Pig, 21, 26, 29, 57, 115, 132, 147, 190, 195; *see also* Pork
Pillory, 129
Pins, pin-cushion, 81–4, 90–2
Placentia Bay, 211, 213, 218
Plague, *see* Black Death
Platform, 34, 35, 37, 38
Ploss, E., 28
Poison, ordeal by, 134–5, 137
Poland, 113, 116
Poly-Olbion, 67
Popular Antiquities, Observations on, 99–100
Popular Ballads and Songs, 46–8
Pork, 106, 110
Porpoise, 29
Portugal, 101, 102, 193; *see also* Iberian peninsular
Posidonius, 141
Possession, 2, 3, 4–5, 7–8, 9, 13
Postbridge, 75
Prague, 109–10, 116
Prediction, 11, 20, 37, 108–9, 141, 143, 158, 168, 170, 172, 177
Protestantism, 98, 106–7; *see also* Puritans
Protocols of the Elders of Zion, 114, 116–17
Psychoanalysis, 117
Purgation, 127, 133
Puritans, 111

Rain-making, 109
Rais, Gilles de, 126
Raven, 146, 147, 150, 151, 152–3
Regensburg, 109

Reindeer, 22, 30, 31
Reinheim, 150
Reliques of Ancient English Poetry, Percy's, 100
Resurrection, magical, 67, 143, 179, 180
Reykdæla Saga, 23, 27
Rhodesia, *see* Bamucapi; Shona
Richard III, 88
Richmond (Richemondshire), 92
Riga, 46, 47
Ritual slaughter, 114
Robin Hood, 191
Rod, stick or wand, magic, 24, 31, 34, 38, 64, 66, 77, 78
Roman Catholicism 98, 106–7, 111, 113
Romans, 97–8, 106, 111, 127, 141, 149, 150, 158, 177
Romans of Partenay, The, 196
Rosmer Hafmand, *see Kaempe Viser*; Merman
Ross, A. S. C., 38, 39
Roussas, 161
Rumania, *see* Moldavia
Runeberg, A., 205–7
Runes, 32–3, 34, 37
Rupert of the Rhine, Prince, 111
Russia, 9, 38, 39, 96, 105, 110, 112, 113–14, 117, 118, 119, 204–5; *see also* Soviet Union
Ryūgū, 15

Saarland, 150
Sabbath (sabbat), witches', 76, 77, 115, 117, 130, 183, 202
Sabbath breaking, 102–3
Sabbath observance, 106
Sacrifice, 33, 90, 125–6, 131, 141, 142, 158, 167, 170, 177, 182
Sæmund the Learned, *see History of the Kings of Norway*
Saga of Harald Fairhair, 168
Saga of Olaf Tryggvason (Gunnlaug Leifsson), 166–83
Saga of Olaf Tryggvason, The (Odd Snorrason), 166–83
Saint-Briac, 102

Index

St Ives, 149
St John's, 208, 209, 210, 211, 213, 214, 215, 216, 217
St Lawrence, 217
St Michael's Mount, 193, 197
St Vincent's, 218
Salamanca, 100
Salisbury, Bishop of, 17
Salzburg, Bishop of, 109
Samoyed of Siberia and Arctic Russia, 30
Sanuki, 7–8, 14
Saracens, 191, 192, 193, 197
Sarrebourg, 150
Satan, 90, 104, 108, 189, 203; *see also* Devil
Saxo Grammaticus, 23, 24, 28, 34
Saxony, 128
Scandinavia, 20, 31, 34, 38, 165, 178, 183, 188, 189; *see also* Denmark; Finland; Lapland (Lapps); Norway; Sweden
Schermerhorn, R. A., 107
Science of Folklore, The, 100
Scot, Reginald, 130
Scotland, 43–4, 45, 46, 54–61, 73, 74–5, 81–3, 111, 125, 128, 129, 143, 144–6, 149, 155, 158, 160–1, 165, 188, 222
Scotorum Historia, 83
Scott, Professor Robert, 45
Scott, Sir Walter, 45, 60
Seagull, 158
Seal, sealskin, 21, 38
Secret Commonwealth of Elves, Fauns and Fairies, 74–5
Seelisberg, 98
Seven Hours of Dread, 76
Seven League Boots, 101
Seven Whistlers, 103–4
Sevenfold vengeance, 104
Severn, river, 64, 67, 69
Sexual relations, sexuality, 34, 38, 60, 61, 140, 141–2, 143, 146, 147, 148, 149, 156, 160, 162, 170, 174–5, 178, 181, 182, 191, 192, 193; *see also* Aphrodisiac; Chastity; Fertility; Impotence; Incest; Kissing; Orgies
Shag Island, 209
Shakespeare, William, xii, 44, 45, 47, 52, 54, 59, 60, 62, 72, 75, 111
Sheelagh-na-gig, 147–9, 162
Sheep, 57, 90
Shelley, Percy Bysshe, 100
Shepton Mallet, 73
Shikoku, 2, 7–8
Shimane, 8
Shirt, witch's, 28
Shizuoka, 2
Shona of Mozambique and Rhodesia, 135
Shylock, 111
Siberia, 20, 22, 28; *see also* Samoyed
Sicily, 140–1
Silesia, 207
Silver, 51, 58, 151
Sir Firumbras, 194
Sir Gawain and the Green Knight, 189, 192, 193
Six Day War, 118–19
Skeleton, 205
Skull, 76
Slave trade, slavery, 133, 167
Slieve Gullion, 156
Smell, 105–6, 108, 119, 129
Smith (blacksmith), 144
Snake, 2, 3, 6, 7–8, 11, 12, 14, 15, 17, 78, 108, 146, 153, 170, 214
Snow, 22, 23, 35, 91, 102, 159, 177
Somerset, 73, 153
Soul, separable, 131, 136, 171–2
Southern Shore, 211
Southey, Robert, 100
Southside Hill, 209
Soviet Union, 96; *see also* Armenia; Bessarabia; Bulgars of the Volga; Buryat; Chukchis; Daghestan; Goldi; Latvia; Lithuania; Russia; Samoyed; Siberia; Ukraine; Yakut
Sowdone of Babylon, The, 193–5
Spain, 72, 100, 101, 102, 107, 108, 114, 115, 116, 128; *see also* Iberian peninsular
Spee, Friedrich, 130
Spenser, Edmund, 43, 62, 67; *see also The Faerie Queene*
Spirit, benign or protective, 29, 30, 31, 37, 38, 172

Index

Spirit, evil or hostile, 35, 103, 109, 117, 170, 172, 174–5, 201
Springhead, 158
Staff, *see* Rod
Stag, *see* Deer
Stalin, Josef, 117
Standard Dictionary of Folklore, Mythology and Legend, 201
Stephenville, 215, 217
Stoke Bruern, 87–8
Storm, storm-spirit, 35–6, 37, 102, 115–16, 169–70, 182, 203, 204
Stow, John, 88–9
Strabo, 141
Strack, Professor Hermann, 112, 115
Strangling, death by, 129
Strasbourg, 99, 114
Streatley, 76
Strömbäck, Professor Dag, 20, 37, 38
Sturluson, Snorri, *see Heimskringla*
Sudan, 132; *see also* Azande; Mandari
Suffolk, 89–90
Suicide, 8–9, 113
Summers, Montague, 72
Sun, 51
Sussex, 73
Suwa, 4–5, 6
Swallow, 25
Swan, swanmaiden, 26, 172
Sweden, 35, 102, 110, 175, 177; *see also* Gotland
Swift, Jonathan, 197–8
Switzerland, 98, 101, 102, 118
Sword, magic, or magic concerning, 26, 30, 54, 55, 57, 58, 66, 204
Sympathetic magic, 26, 80, 88

Tacitus, 106
Tale of Thorlief the Earl's Poet, 33, 167, 178–9, 183
Tale Types, International, 97, 111, 181
Tam Lin, 48, 181
Tansy, 106
Tanzania, *see* Nyakyusa
Tatars, 38
Terra Nova, 209, 215
Terrenceville, 209, 216

Tethy's Festival, 67–8
Theodoricus, 168
Thomas Aquinas, 107
Thomas the Rhymer, 48, 59
Thompson, Professor Stith, 97, 103; *see also Motif Index of Folk Literature*; Tale Types
Thor, 24, 171, 173–4, 182
Tibet, 18
Tipperary, county, 148
Titus, Emperor, 97
Toad, 4, 11
Tōhoku, 2
Tokugawa perod, 5, 10, 14
Toland, John, 42
Topsail, 214
Torbay (Newfoundland), 217
Torture, 111, 127–8, 129–30, 134, 181
Totalitarianism, 128; *see also* Communism; Nazism
Tottori (Taikyūji), 9–10, 16
Trachtenberg, Joshua, 110
Trance, 20, 24, 29–30, 31–2, 37, 58, 134, 168, 171
Transformation, 21–2, 23, 24, 29–31, 35, 37, 52, 53, 65, 67, 109, 115, 140, 153, 154–5, 156, 157, 159, 171–2, 173, 179, 183, 189, 210, 213, 214
Tree, magic, 32, 78, 145, 159
Trevor-Roper, Professor H. R., 107, 131
Trolls Assembly, 174–6, 181, 182
Tryggvason, Olaf, 23, 165–83
Tudors, 69
Tula, 113
Turkey, 112; *see also* Antioch; Ottomans; Saracens
Turn of the Screw, The, 69–70
Turner, V. W., 132
Typhus, 116
Tyrol, 102

Uganda, *see* Bunyoro
Ukraine, 113, 118
Ulster, 142, 143–4, 156
Unbaptised babies, 103
United States, *see* America, New York
Urgel, 107

Index

Valkyries, 27, 28, 29, 167, 175, 180
Vampires, 130, 207; *see also* Blood
Vatnsdæla Saga, 24 25, 26, 29, 34, 36, 38
Vaumort (Yonne), 77
Vence, 149-50
Venice, 100
Venus, 149
Verbeia, 154
Veronese, 108
Vichy, 98
Vienna, 109, 117
Vienna Council (1267), 108
Víglunder Saga, 35
Virgin Mary, 158
Vitry, Jacques de, 108
Volga, river, 38
Vulture, 30

Wales, 42, 45, 60, 67, 69, 100-1, 142, 146, 151, 152, 155
Wallonie, 77
Walrus, 29-30
Wand, *see* Rod
Wandering Jew, 97, 98-104
War-goddess, 140, 143-4, 146, 147, 148, 149-50, 152-3, 157, 162
Warbeck, Perkin, 126
Warsaw, 116
Wart charming, 211
Warton, Thomas, 42, 43, 44, 48
Warwick, Earl of, 87
Warwick, Warwickshire, 64, 91-2, 195
Water, holy, 169, 170, 174, 182
Water, ordeal by, 127
Water serpent, 146
Waxen image, 83, 84-5, 86, 88-9
Weasel, 78
Weather magic, 23, 35-6, 37; *see also* Snow; Storm
Well, bewitched, 214, 217
Well, poison, 118
Well, sacred, 145, 159
Wells, Evelyn Kendrick, 52
Werewolf, wolf, 32, 172, 190, 201
Western Bay, 215
West Indies, *see* Immigrants
Weyer, Johann, 130

Whale, 29, 31
Wheaten image, 81-2
Wherstead, 89-90
Widdershins (widershins, wrang-gaites), 35, 36, 48, 57
Wild hunt, wild huntsman, 103-4
Will-o'-the-wisp, 110
William II (Rufus), 126
William of Norwich, 111
Williamson, Hugh Ross, 126
Wilson, Monica, 132
Wiltshire, 73, 152
Wimpstone, 91-2
Winchester, Earl of, 84
Windsor (Newfoundland), 209
Winterton, 209
Witch Cult in Western Europe, The, 125
Witch-doctor, witch-finder, 78, 133-4; *see also* Doctor-sorcerer
Witchball, 31
Witchcraft Today, 77
Witches' synagogue, 115, 130
Witchlock, 188
Wolf, *see* Werewolf
Woman, power of, 140-62
Wootton, Sir Henry, 42
Worcester, Synod of (1240), 108-9
Wordsworth, William, 100
Wrang-gaites, *see* Widdershins
Würzburg, 130

Yakut, 28, 30
Yamanashi, 2
Yanagita Kunio, 2, 7, 11, 14
Ynglinga Saga, 26
Yonge, Charlotte, xiii, 222
Yonne, 77
York, Yorkshire, 25, 73, 87, 90, 92, 149, 154; *see also* Erik Bloodaxe
Yvain, 190

Zaïre, *see* Azande; Bamucapi; Lele
Zambia, *see* Bamucapi; Cewa; Ndembu
Zante, 107
Zedekiah, 117
Zermatt, 102
Zombie, *see* Living corpse